Introducing Morphology

Morphology is the study of how words are put together. A lively introduction to the subject, this textbook is intended for undergraduates with relatively little background in linguistics. Providing data from a wide variety of languages, it includes hands-on activities such as "Challenge Boxes," designed to encourage students to gather their own data and analyze them, work with data on websites, perform simple experiments, and discuss topics with each other. There is also an extensive introduction to the terms and concepts necessary for analyzing words. Topics such as the mental lexicon, derivation, compounding, inflection, morphological typology, productivity, and the interface of morphology with syntax and phonology expose students to the whole scope of the field. Unlike other textbooks it anticipates the question "Is it a real word?" and tackles it head-on by looking at the distinction between dictionaries and the mental lexicon.

ROCHELLE LIEBER is Professor of Linguistics in the English Department at the University of New Hampshire. Her recent publications include *The Oxford Handbook of Compounding* (2009), *Morphology and Lexical Semantics* (Cambridge, 2004), and *The Handbook of Word Formation* (2005).

Cambridge Introductions to Language and Linguistics

This new textbook series provides students and their teachers with accessible introductions to the major subjects encountered within the study of language and linguistics. Assuming no prior knowledge of the subject, each book is written and designed for ease of use in the classroom or seminar, and is ideal for adoption on a modular course as the core recommended textbook. Each book offers the ideal introductory material for each subject, presenting students with an overview of the main topics encountered in their course, and features a glossary of useful terms, chapter previews and summaries, suggestions for further reading, and helpful exercises. Each book is accompanied by a supporting website.

Books published in the series
Introducing Phonology David Odden
Introducing Speech and Language Processing John Coleman
Introducing Phonetic Science John Maidment and Michael Ashby
Introducing Second Language Acquisition Muriel Saville-Troike
Introducing English Linguistics Charles F. Meyer

Forthcoming:
Introducing Semantics Nick Riemer
Introducing Psycholinguistics Paul Warren

Introducing Morphology

ROCHELLE LIEBER
English Department
University of New Hampshire

CAMBRIDGE UNIVERSITY PRESS
Cambridge, New York, Melbourne, Madrid, Cape Town, Singapore, São Paulo, Delhi, Dubai, Tokyo

Cambridge University Press
The Edinburgh Building, Cambridge CB2 8RU, UK

Published in the United States of America by Cambridge University Press, New York

www.cambridge.org
Information on this title: www.cambridge.org/9780521719797

First published 2010

Printed in the United Kingdom at the University Press, Cambridge

A catalogue record for this publication is available from the British Library

ISBN 978-0-521-89549-1 Hardback
ISBN 978-0-521-71979-7 Paperback

Additional resources for this publication at www.cambridge.org/lieber

Contents

Preface

One of the things that drew me to linguistics several decades ago was a sense of wonder at both the superficial diversity and the underlying commonality of languages. My wonder arose in the process of working through my first few problem sets in linguistics, not surprisingly, problem sets that involved morphological analysis. What I learned first was not theory – indeed at that moment in linguistic history morphology was not perceived as a separate theoretical area in the US – but what languages were like, how to analyze data, and what to call things. I love morphological theory, but for drawing beginning students into the field of linguistics, I believe that there is no substitute for hands-on learning, and that is where this book starts.

This book is intended for undergraduate students who may have had no more than an introductory course in linguistics. It assumes that students know the International Phonetic Alphabet, and have a general idea of what linguistic rules are, but it presupposes little else in the way of sophistication or technical knowledge. It obviously assumes that students are English-speakers, and therefore the first few chapters concentrate on English, and to some extent on languages that are likely to be familiar to linguistics students from language study in high school and university. As the book progresses, I introduce data from many languages that will be "exotic" to students, so that by the end of the book, they will have some sense of linguistic diversity, at least with respect to types of morphology.

There are some aspects of the content of this text that might seem unusual to instructors. The first is the attention to dictionaries in chapter 2. Generally, texts on linguistic morphology do not mention dictionaries, but I find that beginning students of morphology retain a reverence for dictionaries that sometimes gets in the way of thinking about the nature of the mental lexicon and how word formation works. Instructors can skip all or part of this chapter, but my experience is that it sets students on a good footing from the start, and largely eliminates their squeamishness about considering whether *incent*, or *bovineness* or *organizationalize* or the like are 'real' words, even if we can't find them in the dictionary.

Another section that might seem odd is the part of chapter 7 devoted to snapshot descriptions of five different languages. These also might be skipped over, but they serve two important purposes. One purpose is simply to expose students to what the morphology of a language looks like overall; much of what they're exposed to in the rest of the book (and in most other morphology texts that I know of) are bits and pieces of the morphology of languages – a reduplication rule here, an inflectional paradigm there – but never the big picture. More importantly, having looked at the 'morphological toolkits' of several languages, students will be better prepared to understand both the traditional categories used in morphological typology and more recent means of classification.

The final thing that might strike instructors as unusual is that I largely hold off on introducing morphological theory until the last chapter. Clearly, no text is theory-neutral, and this text is no exception. It fits squarely in the tradition of generative morphology in the sense that I present morphology as an attempt to characterize and model the mental lexicon. I presuppose that there is much that is universal in spite of apparent diversity. And I believe that the ultimate aim of teaching students about morphology (indeed about any area of linguistics) is to expose them to what is at stake in trying to characterize the nature of the human language capacity. Nevertheless I start by presenting morphological rules in as neutral a way as possible, and hold off on raising theoretical disputes until students have enough experience to understand how morphological data might support or refute theoretical hypotheses. In a sense I believe that students will gain a better understanding of theory if they already have the ability to find data and analyze it themselves. Therefore the bulk of the morphological theory will be found in the last chapter, where I have tried to pick a few theoretical debates and show how one might argue for or against particular analyses. Having read this chapter, students will be able to go on and tackle some of the texts that are intended for advanced undergraduates or graduate students.

Since one of my main goals in this text is to teach students to do morphology, there are a number of pedagogical features that set this book apart from other morphology texts. First, each chapter has one or more 'Challenge' boxes. These occur at points in the text where students might take a breather from reading or class lecture and try something out for themselves. Challenge exercises are ideal for small teams of students – either outside of class, or as an in-class activity – to work on together. Some involve discussion, some analysis, some doing some work on-line or at the library. But all of them involve hands-on learning. Instructors can use them or skip them or assign them as homework instead of, or in addition to, the exercises at the ends of chapters. I have tried most of them myself as in-class activities, and have found that they get students excited, stimulate discussion, and generally give students the feeling of really 'doing morphology' rather than just hearing about it.

A second pedagogical feature that sets this book apart are the "How to" sections in chapters 3, 4, 6, and 9. These are meant to give students tips on finding or working with data. Some students don't need such tips; they have the intuitive ability to look at data and figure out what to do with it. But I've found over years of teaching that there are some students who don't have this knack, and who benefit enormously from being walked through a problem or technique systematically. The "How to" sections do this.

Instructors and students will also find what they would expect to find in any good text. First, there are several aids to navigating the text – chapter outlines and lists of key terms at the beginnings of chapters and brief summaries at the end, as well as a glossary of the terms that are highlighted in the text. A copy of the International Phonetic Alphabet is included at the beginning for easy reference. And each chapter has a number of exercises that allow students to practice what they've been exposed to.

A general point about examples in this text. Where I have cited data from different books, grammars, dictionaries, and scholarly articles, I have chosen to keep the glosses provided in the original source even if this results in some inconsistency in the use of abbreviations. In other words, slightly different abbreviations may occur in different examples (for instance, N or Neut for 'neuter'). Although students may be confused by this practice at first, it does give them a taste of the linguistic "real world." Any student going on and doing further work in morphology is bound to find exactly this sort of variation in the use of abbreviations in sources.

My goal in this text is to bring students to the point where they are not only ready to confront morphological theory but also have the skills to begin to think independently about it, and perhaps to contribute to it.

This text has benefitted from the help of many people. I am grateful to John McCarthy and Donca Steriade for suggesting examples, to Charlotte Brewer for supplying me with statistics about citations in the OED, to Marianne Mithun for suggesting Nishnaabemwin as a polysynthetic language to profile, and to several classes of students at UNH both for serving as guinea pigs on early drafts and for supplying me with wonderful examples from their Word Logs. Thanks go as well to the College of Liberal Arts at the University of New Hampshire for the funds to hire a graduate student assistant at a critical moment, and to Chris Paris for supplying assistance. I am especially grateful to several anonymous reviewers who made excellent suggestions on the penultimate draft of the text. Finally, thanks are due as well to Andrew Winnard at Cambridge University Press for inviting me to write this text and for his patience in waiting for it.

The International Phonetic Alphabet

(revised to 2005)

CONSONANTS (PULMONIC)

	Bilabial	Labiodental	Dental	Alveolar	Postalveolar	Retroflex	Palatal	Velar	Uvular	Pharyngeal	Glottal
Plosive	p b			t d		ʈ ɖ	c ɟ	k ɡ	q ɢ		ʔ
Nasal	m	ɱ		n		ɳ	ɲ	ŋ	ɴ		
Trill	ʙ			r					ʀ		
Tap or Flap		ⱱ		ɾ		ɽ					
Fricative	ɸ β	f v	θ ð	s z	ʃ ʒ	ʂ ʐ	ç ʝ	x ɣ	χ ʁ	ħ ʕ	h ɦ
Lateral fricative				ɬ ɮ							
Approximant		ʋ		ɹ		ɻ	j	ɰ			
Lateral approximant				l		ɭ	ʎ	ʟ			

Where symbols appear in pairs, the one to the right represents a voiced consonant. Shaded areas denote articulations judged impossible.

CONSONANTS (NON-PULMONIC)

Clicks		Voiced implosives		Ejectives	
ʘ	Bilabial	ɓ	Bilabial	ʼ	Examples:
ǀ	Dental	ɗ	Dental/alveolar	pʼ	Bilabial
ǃ	(Post)alveolar	ʄ	Palatal	tʼ	Dental/alveolar
ǂ	Palatoalveolar	ɠ	Velar	kʼ	Velar
ǁ	Alveolar lateral	ʛ	Uvular	sʼ	Alveolar fricative

VOWELS

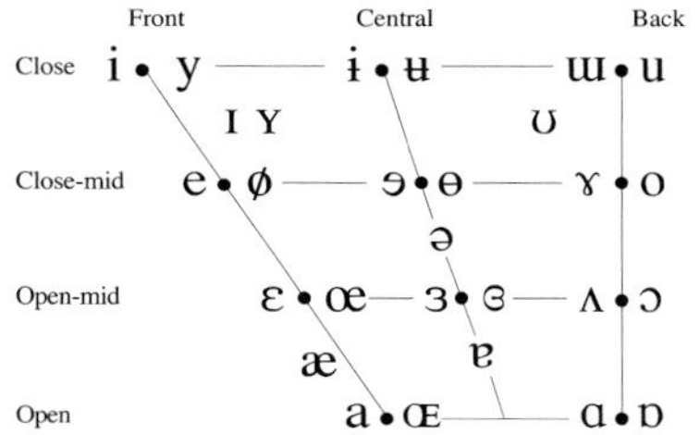

Front — Central — Back

Close: i • y — ɨ • ʉ — ɯ • u

ɪ ʏ — ʊ

Close-mid: e • ø — ɘ • ɵ — ɤ • o

ə

Open-mid: ɛ • œ — ɜ • ɞ — ʌ • ɔ

æ — ɐ

Open: a • ɶ — ɑ • ɒ

Where symbols appear in pairs, the one to the right represents a rounded vowel.

OTHER SYMBOLS

ʍ Voiceless labial-velar fricative

w Voiced labial-velar approximant

ɥ Voiced labial-palatal approximant

ʜ Voiceless epiglottal fricative

ʢ Voiced epiglottal fricative

ʡ Epiglottal plosive

ɕ ʑ Alveolo-palatal fricatives

ɺ Voiced alveolar lateral flap

ɧ Simultaneous ʃ and x

Affricates and double articulations can be represented by two symbols joined by a tie bar if necessary. k͡p t͜s

SUPRASEGMENTALS

ˈ Primary stress

ˌ Secondary stress ˌfoʊnəˈtɪʃən

ː Long eː

ˑ Half-long eˑ

˘ Extra-short ĕ

| Minor (foot) group

‖ Major (intonation) group

. Syllable break ɹi.ækt

‿ Linking (absence of a break)

DIACRITICS Diacritics may be placed above a symbol with a descender, e.g. ŋ̊

̥ Voiceless	n̥ d̥	̤ Breathy voiced	b̤ a̤	̪ Dental	t̪ d̪
̬ Voiced	s̬ t̬	̰ Creaky voiced	b̰ a̰	̺ Apical	t̺ d̺
ʰ Aspirated	tʰ dʰ	̼ Linguolabial	t̼ d̼	̻ Laminal	t̻ d̻
̹ More rounded	ɔ̹	ʷ Labialized	tʷ dʷ	̃ Nasalized	ẽ
̜ Less rounded	ɔ̜	ʲ Palatalized	tʲ dʲ	ⁿ Nasal release	dⁿ
̟ Advanced	u̟	ˠ Velarized	tˠ dˠ	ˡ Lateral release	dˡ
̠ Retracted	e̠	ˤ Pharyngealized	tˤ dˤ	̚ No audible release	d̚
̈ Centralized	ë	̴ Velarized or pharyngealized	ɫ		
̽ Mid-centralized	e̽	̝ Raised	e̝ (ɹ̝ = voiced alveolar fricative)		
̩ Syllabic	n̩	̞ Lowered	e̞ (β̞ = voiced bilabial approximant)		
̯ Non-syllabic	e̯	̘ Advanced Tongue Root	e̘		
˞ Rhoticity	ɚ a˞	̙ Retracted Tongue Root	e̙		

TONES AND WORD ACCENTS

LEVEL		CONTOUR	
e̋ or ˥	Extra high	ě or ˩˥	Rising
é ˦	High	ê ˥˩	Falling
ē ˧	Mid	e᷄ ˧˥	High rising
è ˨	Low	e᷅ ˩˧	Low rising
ȅ ˩	Extra low	e᷈ ˧˦˧	Rising-falling
↓	Downstep	↗	Global rise
↑	Upstep	↘	Global fall

Point and manner of articulation of English consonants and vowels

Consonants

	Labial	Labio-dental	Interdental	Alveolar	Alveo-palatal	Palatal	Velar	Glottal
Stop	p,**b**			t,**d**			k,**g**	ʔ
Fricative		f,**v**	θ,**ð**	s,**z**	ʃ,**ʒ**			h
Affricate					tʃ,**dʒ**			
Nasal	**m**			**n**			**ŋ**	
Liquid				**ɹ**,**l**				
Glide	(**w**)					**j**	(**w**)	

Characters in boldface are voiced.
[w] is labio-velar in articulation.

Vowels

	Front	Central	Back
High	i ɪ		u ʊ
Mid	e ɛ	ʌ,ə	o ɔ
Low	æ		ɑ

Tense vowels: i, e, u, o, ɑ
Lax vowels: ɪ, ɛ, æ, ʊ, ɔ, ʌ
Reduced vowel: ə

CHAPTER

1 What is morphology?

CHAPTER OUTLINE

KEY TERMS

morpheme
simplex
complex
type
token
lexeme
word form
inflection
derivation

In this chapter you will learn what morphology is, namely the study of word formation.

- We will look at the distinction between words and morphemes, between types, tokens, and lexemes and between inflection and derivation.
- We will also consider the reasons why languages have morphology.

1.1 Introduction

The short answer to the question with which we begin this text is that **morphology** is the study of word formation, including the ways new words are coined in the languages of the world, and the way forms of words are varied depending on how they're used in sentences. As a native speaker of your language you have intuitive knowledge of how to form new words, and every day you recognize and understand new words that you've never heard before.

Stop and think a minute:

- Suppose that *splinch* is a verb that means 'step on broken glass'; what is its past tense?
- Speakers of English use the suffixes *-ize* (*crystallize*) and *-ify* (*codify*) to form verbs from nouns. If you had to form a verb that means 'do something the way ex-Prime Minister Tony Blair does it', which suffix would you use? How about a verb meaning 'do something the way ex-President Bill Clinton does it'?
- It's possible to *rewash* or *reheat* something. Is it possible to *relove, reexplode,* or *rewiggle* something?

Chances are that you answered the first question with the past tense *splinched* (pronounced [splɪntʃt])[1], the second with the verbs *Blairify* and *Clintonize,* and that you're pretty sure that *relove, reexplode,* and *rewiggle* are weird, if not downright impossible. Your ability to make up these new words, and to make judgments about words that you think could never exist, suggests that you have intuitive knowledge of the principles of word formation in your language, even if you can't articulate what they are. Native speakers of other languages have similar knowledge of their languages. This book is about that knowledge, and about how we as linguists can find out what it is. Throughout this book, you will be looking into how you form and understand new words, and how speakers of other languages do the same. Many of our examples will come from English – since you're reading this book, I assume we have that language in common – but we'll also look beyond English to how words are formed in languages with which you might be familiar, and languages which you might never have encountered before. You'll learn not only the nuts and bolts of word formation – how things are put together in various languages and what to call those nuts and bolts – but also what this knowledge says about how the human mind is organized.

The beauty of studying morphology is that even as a beginning student you can look around you and bring new facts to bear on our study. At this point, you should start keeping track of interesting cases of new words

1. In this text I presuppose that you have already learned at least that part of the International Phonetic Alphabet (IPA) that is commonly used for transcribing English. You'll find an IPA chart at the beginning of this book, if you need to refresh your memory.

that you encounter in your life outside this class. Look at the first Challenge box.

Challenge: your word log

Keep track of every word you hear or see (or produce yourself) that you think you've never heard before. You might encounter words while listening to the radio, watching TV, or reading, or someone you're talking to might slip one in. Write those new words down, take note of where and when you heard/read/produced them, and jot down what you think they mean. What you write down may or may not be absolutely fresh new words – they just have to be new to you. We'll be coming back to these as the course progresses and putting them under the microscope.

Of course, if the answer to our initial question were as simple as the task in the box, you might expect this book to end right here. But there is of course much more to say about what makes up the study of morphology. Simple answers frequently lead to further questions, and here's one that we need to settle before we go on.

1.2 What's a word?

Ask anyone what a word is and ... they'll look puzzled. In some sense, we all know what words are – we can list words of various sorts at the drop of a hat. But ask us to define explicitly what a word is, and we're flummoxed. Someone might say that a word is a stretch of letters that occurs between blank spaces. But someone else is bound to point out that words don't have to be written for us to know that they're words. And in spoken (or signed) language, there are no spaces or pauses to delineate words. Yet we know what they are. Still another person might at this point try an answer like this: "A word is something small that means something," to which a devil's advocate might respond, "But what do you mean by 'something small'?" This is the point at which it becomes necessary to define a few specialized linguistic terms.

Linguists define a **morpheme** as the smallest unit of language that has its own meaning. Simple words like *giraffe*, *wiggle*, or *yellow* are morphemes, but so are prefixes like *re-* and *pre-* and suffixes like *-ize* and *-er*.[2] There's far more to be said about morphemes – as you'll see in later chapters of this book – but for now we can use the term **morpheme** to help us come up with a more precise and coherent definition of **word**. Let us now define a **word** as one or more morphemes that can stand alone in a language. Words that consist of only one morpheme, like the words in (1), can be

2. In chapter 2 we will give a more formal definition of **prefix** and **suffix**. For now it is enough to know that they are morphemes that cannot stand on their own, and that prefixes come before, and suffixes after, the root or main part of the word.

termed **simple** or **simplex** words. Words that are made up of more than one morpheme, like the ones in (2), are called **complex**:

(1) *Simplex words*
giraffe
fraud
murmur
oops
just
pistachio

(2) *Complex words*
opposition
intellectual
crystallize
prewash
repressive
blackboard

We now have a first pass at a definition of what a word is, but as we'll see, we can be far more precise.

1.3 Words and lexemes, types and tokens

How many words occur in the following sentence?

My friend and I walk to class together, because our classes are in the same building and we dislike walking alone.

You might have thought of at least two ways of answering this question, and maybe more. On the one hand, you might have counted every item individually, in which case your answer would have been 21. On the other hand, you might have thought about whether you should count the two instances of *and* in the sentence as a single word and not as separate words. You might even have thought about whether to count *walk* and *walking* or *class* and *classes* as different words: after all, if you were not a native speaker of English and you needed to look up what they meant in the dictionary, you'd just find one entry for each pair of words. So when you count words, you may count them in a number of ways.

Again, it's useful to have some special terms for how we count words. Let's say that if we are counting every instance in which a word occurs in a sentence, regardless of whether that word has occurred before or not, we are counting **word tokens**. If we count word tokens in the sentence above, we count 21. If, however, we are counting a word once, no matter how many times it occurs in a sentence, we are counting **word types**.

Counting this way, we count 20 types in the sentence above: the two tokens of the word *and* count as one type. A still different way of counting words would be to count what are called **lexemes**. **Lexemes** can be thought of as families of words that differ only in their grammatical endings or grammatical forms; singular and plural forms of a noun (*class, classes*), present, past, and participle forms of verbs (*walk, walks, walked, walking*), different forms of a pronoun (*I, me, my, mine*) each represent a single lexeme. One way of thinking about lexemes is that they are the basis of dictionary entries; dictionaries typically have a single entry for each lexeme. So if we are counting lexemes in the sentence above, we would count *class* and *classes*, *walk* and *walking*, *I* and *my*, and *our* and *we* as single lexemes; the sentence then has 16 lexemes.

1.4 But is it *really* a word?

In some sense we now know what words are – or at least what word types, word tokens, and lexemes are. But there's another way we can ask the question "What's a word?" Consider the sort of question you might ask when playing Scrabble: "Is *aalii* a word?" Or when you encounter an unfamiliar word: "Is *bouncebackability* a word?" What you're asking when you answer questions like these, is really the question "Is *xyz* a REAL word?" Our first impulse in answering those questions is to run for our favorite dictionary; if it's a real word it ought to be in the dictionary.

But think about this answer for just a bit, and you'll begin to wonder if it makes sense. Who determines what goes in the dictionary in the first place? What if dictionaries differ in whether they list a particular word? For example, the *Official Scrabble Player's Dictionary* lists *aalii* but not *bouncebackability*. The *Oxford English Dictionary On-Line* doesn't list *aalii*, but it does list *bouncebackability*. So which one is right? Further, what about words like *cot potato* or *freshmore* that don't occur in any published dictionary yet, but can be encountered in the media? The former, according to Word Spy (www.wordspy.com) means a baby who spends too much time watching television (Americans might use the term *crib potato* instead of *cot potato*), and the latter is a second-year high school student in the US who has to repeat a lot of first-year classes. And what about the word *cot potatodom*, which I just made up? Once you know what a *cot potato* is, you have no trouble understanding my new word. If it consists of morphemes, has a meaning, and can stand alone, doesn't it qualify as a word according to our definition even if it doesn't appear in the dictionary?

What all these questions suggest is that we each have a **mental lexicon**, a sort of internalized dictionary that contains an enormous number of words that we can produce, or at least understand when we hear them. But we also have a set of **word formation rules** which allows us to create new words and understand new words when we encounter them. In the chapters to follow, we will explore the nature of our mental lexicon in detail, and think further about the "Is it really a word?" question. In answering this question we'll be led to a detailed exploration of the nature of our mental lexicon and our word formation rules.

1.5 Why do languages have morphology?

As native speakers of a language we use morphology for different reasons. We will go into both the functions of morphology and means of forming new words in great depth in the following chapters, but here, we'll just give you a taste of what's to come.

One reason for having morphology is to form new lexemes from old ones. We will refer to this as **lexeme formation**. (Many linguists use the term **word formation** in this specific sense, but this usage can be confusing, as all of morphology is sometimes referred to in a larger sense as 'word formation'.) Lexeme formation can do one of three things. It can change the part of speech (or **category**) of a word, for example, turning verbs into nouns or adjectives, or nouns into adjectives, as you can see in the examples in (3):

(3) *Category-changing lexeme formation*[3]
V→ N: amuse → amusement
V → A: impress → impressive
N → A: monster → monstrous

Some rules of lexeme formation do not change category, but they do add substantial new meaning:

(4) *Meaning-changing lexeme formation*

A → A 'negative A'	happy → unhappy
N → N 'place where N lives'	orphan → orphanage
V → V 'repeat action'	wash → rewash

And some rules of lexeme formation both change category and add substantial new meaning:

(5) *Both category and meaning-changing lexeme formation*

V → A 'able to be Ved'	wash → washable
N → V 'remove N from'	louse → delouse

Why have rules of lexeme formation? Imagine what it would be like to have to invent a wholly new word to express every single new concept. For example, if you wanted to talk about the process or result of amusing someone, you couldn't use *amusement*, but would have to have a term like *zorch* instead. And if you wanted to talk about the process or result of resenting someone, you couldn't use *resentment*, but would have to have something like *plitz* instead. And so on. As you can see, rules of lexeme formation allow for a measure of economy in our mental lexicons: we can recycle parts, as it were, to come up with new words. It is probably safe to say that all languages have some ways of forming new lexemes, although,

3. The notation V → N means 'changes a verb to a noun.'

as we'll see as this book progresses, those ways might be quite different from the means we use in English.

On the other hand, we sometimes use morphology even when we don't need new lexemes. For example, we saw that each lexeme can have a number of **word forms**. The lexeme WALK has forms like *walk, walks, walked, walking* that can be used in different grammatical contexts. When we change the form of a word so that it fits in a particular grammatical context, we are concerned with what linguists call **inflection**. Inflectional word formation is word formation that expresses grammatical distinctions like number (singular *vs.* plural); tense (present *vs.* past); person (first, second, or third); and case (subject, object, possessive), among others. It does not result in the creation of new lexemes, but merely changes the grammatical form of lexemes to fit into different grammatical contexts.

Interestingly, languages have wildly differing amounts of inflection. English has relatively little inflection. We create different forms of nouns according to number (*wombat, wombats*); we mark the possessive form of a noun with *-'s* or *-s'* (*the wombat's eyes*). We have different forms of verbs for present and past and for present and past participles (*sing, sang, singing, sung*), and we use a suffix *-s* to mark the third person singular of a verb (*she sings*).

However, if you've studied Latin, Russian, ancient Greek, or even Old English, you'll know that these languages have quite a bit more inflectional morphology than English does. Even languages like French and Spanish have more inflectional forms of verbs than English does.

But some languages have much less inflection than English does. Mandarin Chinese, for example, has almost none. Rather than marking plurals by suffixes as English does, or by prefixes as the Bantu language Swahili does, Chinese does not mark plurals or past tenses with morphology at all. This is not to say that a speaker of Mandarin cannot express whether it is one giraffe, two giraffes, or many giraffes that are under discussion, or whether the sighting was yesterday or today. It simply means that to do so, a speaker of Mandarin must use a separate word like *one, two* or *many* or a separate word for *past* to make the distinction.

(6) Wo jian guo yi zhi chang jing lu.
    I see past one CLASSIFIER giraffe[4]

(7) Wo jian guo liang zhi chang jing lu
    I see past two CLASSIFIER giraffe

The word *chang jing lu* 'giraffe' has the same form regardless of how many long-necked beasts are of interest. And the verb 'to see' does not change its form for the past tense; instead, the separate word *guo* is added to express this concept. In other words, some concepts that are expressed via inflection in some languages are expressed by other means (word order, separate words) in other languages.

4. We will explain in chapter 6 what we mean by **classifier**. For now it is enough to know that classifiers are words that must be used together with numbers in Mandarin.

1.6 The organization of this book

In what follows, we'll return to all the questions we've raised here. In chapter 2, we'll revisit the question of what a word is, by further probing the differences between our mental lexicon and the dictionary, and look further into questions of what constitutes a "real" word. We'll look at the ways in which word formation goes on around us all the time, and consider how children (and adults) acquire words, and how our mental lexicons are organized so that we can access the words we know and make up new ones. In chapter 3, we'll get down to the work of looking at some of the most common ways that new lexemes are formed: by adding prefixes and suffixes, by making up compound words, and by changing the category of words without changing the words themselves. In this chapter we'll concentrate on how words are structured in terms of both their forms and their meanings. Many of our examples will be taken from English, but we'll also look at how these kinds of word formation work in other languages. Chapter 4 takes up a related topic, productivity: some processes of word formation allow us to form many new words freely, but others are more restricted. In this chapter we'll look at some of the determinants of productivity, and how productivity can be measured. Chapter 5 will also be concerned with lexeme formation, but with kinds of lexeme formation that are less familiar to speakers of English. We'll look at forms of affixation that English does not have (infixation, circumfixation), processes like reduplication, and templatic morphology. Our focus will be on learning to analyze data that might on the surface seem to be quite unfamiliar. In chapter 6 we will turn to inflection, looking not only at the sorts of inflection we find in English and other familiar languages, but also at inflectional systems based on different grammatical distinctions than we find in English, and systems that are far more complex and intricate. Chapter 7 will be devoted to the subject of typology, different ways in which the morphological systems of the languages of the world can be classified and compared to one another. We'll look at some traditional systems of classification, as well as some that have been proposed more recently, and assess their pros and cons. Chapters 8 and 9 will explore the relationship between the field of morphology and the fields of syntax on the one hand and phonology on the other. Our final chapter will introduce you to some of the interesting theoretical debates that have arisen in the field of morphology over the last two decades and prepare you to do more advanced work in morphology.

Summary

Morphology is the study of words and word formation. In this chapter we have considered what a word is and looked at the distinction between word tokens, word types, and lexemes. We have divided word formation into derivation – the formation of new lexemes – and inflection, the different grammatical word forms that make up lexemes.

Exercises

1. Are the following words simple or complex?

a. members	f. grammar
b. prioritize	g. writer
c. handsome	h. rewind
d. fizzy	i. reject
e. dizzy	j. alligator

   If you have difficulty deciding whether particular words are simple or complex, explain why you find them problematic.

2. Do the words in the following pairs belong to the same lexeme or to different lexemes?

a. revolve	revolution
b. revolution	revolutions
c. revolve	dissolve
d. go	went
e. wash	rewash

3. In the following sentences, count word tokens, types, and lexemes:

   a. I say now, just as I said yesterday, that the price of a wombat is high but the price of a platypus is higher.

      tokens ____________
      types ____________
      lexemes ____________

   b. I've just replaced my printer with a new one that prints much faster.

      tokens ____________
      types ____________
      lexemes ____________

4. In sentence (3b), what sorts of problems does the word *I've* pose for our definition of 'word'?
5. What words belong to the same word family or lexeme as *sing*?

CHAPTER

2 Words, dictionaries, and the mental lexicon

CHAPTER OUTLINE

KEY TERMS

word
mental lexicon
lexicography
the Gavagai problem
fast mapping
aphasia

In this chapter you will learn why we make a basic distinction between the dictionary and the mental lexicon.

- We will look at how linguists study the mental lexicon and how children acquire words.
- We will consider whether complex words are stored in the mental lexicon, or derived by rules, or both.
- And we will look further at how dictionaries have evolved and how they differ from one another and from the mental lexicon.

2.1 Introduction

In the last chapter, we raised the question "what's a word?" And we saw in section 1.2 that this question actually subsumes two more specific questions. In this chapter we will look more closely at those questions.

On the one hand, when we ask "what's a word?," we may be asking about the fundamental nature of wordhood – as we saw, a far thornier philosophical question than it would seem at first blush. Native speakers of a language seem to know intuitively what a 'word' is in their language, even if they have trouble coming up with a definition of 'word'. Interestingly, the *Oxford American Dictionary* seems to bank on this intuitive knowledge when it defines a word as "a single distinct meaningful element of speech or writing, used with others (or sometimes alone) to form a sentence and typically shown with a space on either side when written or printed." We've already debunked part of the OAD definition: languages need not be written, but they still have words, and words don't have blank space between them in spoken language. Nevertheless, the OAD's definition works for most people: most dictionary users probably do not know the word **morpheme**, which we used in our definition of **word** in the last chapter, but the OAD relies on the likelihood that they will not first think of something like the prefix *re-* as a single meaningful element, or something like *irniarualiunga* which means 'I am making a doll' in Central Alaskan Yup'ik (Mithun 1999: 203), and constitutes not only a word, but also a whole sentence. In other words, the OAD's definition works because dictionary users already have an intuitive idea of what a word is!

Morphologists, however, have the luxury of being more precise: we can define a **word** as a sequence of one or more morphemes that can stand alone in a language. But in doing so, we have not exhausted what's interesting about our question.

Indeed, in chapter 1 we saw that there is a second way of interpreting it, one that seems far more concrete at first: we can interpret our question as meaning "Is *xyz* a word?" where *xyz* is a specific morpheme or sequence of morphemes. Taken this way, our question asks what it means to say that *xyz* is a word of English, or Central Alaskan Yup'ik, or some other language. On the one hand, we are always making up new words, and when we say them, others understand what we mean. In the last chapter, I mentioned the words *freshmore* and *cot potatodom*, neither of which is in a (conventional) dictionary, at least as of the writing of this chapter, but both of which have been used (at least by me!). Does this qualify them as words? And two paragraphs up, I used the word *wordhood*, which you may or may not like, but which you certainly understood. This is the version of the "what's a word" question that we'll concentrate on in this chapter. In doing so we'll begin to explore the nature of dictionaries, and more importantly of our native speaker knowledge of words, which we might term our **mental lexicon**.

2.2 Why not check the dictionary?

When the question "Is *xyz* really a word?" comes up – whether in casual conversation, in reading an article in the newspaper, or in playing Scrabble – people will often look to the dictionary for an answer. Which dictionary, of course, depends on what's lying around the house or the office, or these days, what's available on-line. But is this the right way to answer our question? As morphologists, we need to think about how dictionaries come to be, and how much we credit them with the authority to decide what's a word.

There's a lot to be said about how dictionaries have evolved and how they are produced today. For a short history of English dictionaries, you can read section 2.4 of this chapter. But for our immediate purposes, we can identify a number of reasons why we wouldn't always want to base the answer to our question on what we find (or don't) in a dictionary. Here are a few such reasons.

2.2.1 Which dictionary?

Dictionaries come in all shapes and sizes, for all sorts of intended audiences. Size and audience are determined by individual publishers, and indeed the finished product is shaped by all sorts of market forces. And makers of dictionaries – **lexicographers** – are of course human; what gets into dictionaries has historically been subject to the individual foibles of lexicographers, not to mention the mores of society. If you grew up when I did, it was typical for dictionaries not to have taboo words like *fuck*, much less its derivatives *fucking, fuck up, fuckable, fuck all,* and *fucker*, all of which can be found today in the *Concise Oxford English Dictonary*; but until the 1970s, dictionaries avoided words that might offend. It is perhaps safe to say that individual or societal foibles play less of a role in dictionary-making today, but it's still a good idea to keep in mind that neither lexicographers nor the dictionaries they create are infallible.

Our first problem with giving final authority for wordhood to the dictionary, then, follows from the very concrete and temporal nature of dictionaries: if you look up a word in a pocket dictionary, or even a standard college desk dictionary, and it isn't listed, you might still have the nagging suspicion that a bigger dictionary or a more specialized dictionary might list the word. But even if you check the largest available dictionary – say, for English the *Oxford English Dictionary On-line* – or the most complete technical dictionary in a particular field, can you be sure that a word that's not listed isn't a word? Maybe it's too new a word to have gotten into the dictionary yet.

2.2.2 Nonces, mistakes, and mountweazels

Further, sometimes we find items in dictionaries that we might hesitate to call words – even if they do occur in the dictionary. Among these items are words that are labeled as 'nonce', meaning that they've been found just once, often in the writing of someone important, but that nevertheless don't seem to occur anywhere else. The OED On-line, for example, lists as a nonce the word *agreemony*, which they define as 'agreeableness', and illustrate with a single quotation from the seventeenth-century writer Aphra Behn. Was this ever really a word? Indeed, the OED even lists some words that occur only once, and further, in contexts which don't illuminate their meaning; for example, we can find the word *umbershoot* used by James Joyce in *Ulysses*, about which the OED maddeningly says only "meaning obscure"! Words or not?

Very extensive dictionaries like the OED sometimes also contain words that they identify as mistakes. For example, we can find an entry for the word *ambassady*, which occurs in a single quotation from 1693 and is, according to the OED, perhaps a mistake, where the author might have meant the word *ambassade* "the mission or function of an ambassador." It occurs in the dictionary, but is it really a word?

And finally, there are what have come to be called 'mountweazels'. A mountweazel is a phony word that is inserted into a dictionary so that its makers can identify lexicographic piracy. You can find a fuller explanation of this tradition in section 2.4, but the short version is this: lexicographers sometimes make up an entry and include it so that they can tell if another lexicographer is using their dictionary as a source without attribution (which is plagiarism, of course). Surely we wouldn't want to count such impostors as real words, but they're in the dictionary!

2.2.3 And the problem of complex words

We will learn much more about this in the chapters to come, but perhaps the worst problem for us with the idea of giving the dictionary the authority to determine whether *xyz* is a word is that dictionaries don't need to include every word. Every language has ways of forming new words that are so active and transparent that putting all the words formed that way into the dictionary would be a waste of space. For example, speakers of English know that any verb at all can have a present progressive form made with the suffix *-ing*. As soon as I make up a new verb, say *zax*, we know that the present progressive verb form is *zaxing*. So although a dictionary might eventually have to include the verb *zax*, it might never list *zaxing* as a word. But of course *zaxing* should be considered a word. Similarly, just about any adjective in English can be made into a noun by adding the suffix *-ness*. For example, the *Concise Oxford English Dictionary* contains the adjective *bovine*, but not the noun *bovineness*. Nevertheless, I'd have no problem if I saw the word *bovineness* written somewhere, and would never think to look it up in the dictionary. The dictionary doesn't have the word precisely because we'd never need to look it up.

The conclusion that we are inexorably led to is that we cannot rely on dictionaries to answer the question "Is *xyz* a word?" On the one hand, dictionaries don't list all the words of any language. They can't list all derivatives with living prefixes and suffixes, or all technical, scientific, regional, or slang words. And on the other hand, they sometimes include words used only once whose meanings are completely unknown. They occasionally even include purposely made-up words to guard their own copyrights. For the most part, dictionaries do not fix or codify the words of a language, but rather reflect the words that native speakers use. Those words are encoded in what we will call the **mental lexicon**, the sum total of word knowledge that native speakers carry around in their heads. So to answer our question, we must look more closely at what is in that mental lexicon.

2.3 The mental lexicon

By the **mental lexicon** I mean the sum total of everything an individual speaker knows about the words of her language. This knowledge includes information about pronunciation, category (part of speech), and meaning, of course, but also information about syntactic properties (for example, whether a verb is transitive or intransitive), level of formality, and what lexicographers call 'range of application', that is, the specific conditions under which we might use the word. For example, I know that the word *verandah* is a noun, pronounced (in my American English) [və**ɹæn**də],[1] that it refers to a type of porch, and that I'd only use it in reference to the sort of porch one finds in the southern part of the US or perhaps in some exotic tropical country. Unless I was being ironic, I probably would not call my own back porch 'the verandah'. I also know that *barf* is a verb that's pronounced [bɑɹf], that it means 'vomit', that it is intransitive (unless used with a particle like *up*) and that it is used only colloquially (I wouldn't use it if I were describing the symptoms of a stomach flu to the doctor).

It is quite likely that in our mental lexicons we have entries that are only partial. We may know the pronunciation of a word, but not its meaning (e.g., I know how to pronounce *amortize*, but I'm not sure what it means). Or the opposite: for example, I know what the word *hegemony* means, but I don't know if it's pronounced with the stress on the first or second syllable. We may also have only partial knowledge of the meaning of a word. I know, for example, that a *distributor* is part of a car and that if you have to replace it, it's a relatively expensive job, but I don't know what a distributor looks like or what it does.

Each person's mental lexicon is sure to contain things that are different from other people's mental lexicons. One person may know lots of words for types of birds or flowers, another might know all the specialized vocabulary of sailing, and so on. Auto mechanics surely know more details of the meaning of the word *distributor* than I do. But our individual mental lexicons overlap enough that we speak the same language. In this section we will look in more detail at the contents of our mental lexicons, both what is stored and what is created by rules of word formation, and how our mental lexicons are organized.

1. Stressed syllables are marked by bold type.

2.3.1 How many words?

Psycholinguists estimate that the average English-speaking six-year-old knows 10,000 words, and the average high-school graduate around 60,000 words. Paul Bloom describes how this estimate can be made (2000: 5):

> Words are taken from a large unabridged dictionary, including only those words whose meanings cannot be guessed using principles of morphology or analogy. . . . Since it would take too long to test people on hundreds of thousands of words, a random sample is taken. The proportion of the sample that people know is used to generate an estimate of their overall vocabulary size, under the assumption that the size of the dictionary is a reasonable estimate of the size of the language as a whole. For example, if you use a dictionary with 500,000 words, and test people on a 500-word sample, you would determine the number of English words they know by taking the number that they got correct from this sample and multiplying by 1,000.

Children generally begin to produce their first words around the age of one. Bloom calculates that between the ages of one and 18 we would have to learn approximately ten words every day to have a vocabulary of 60,000 words. It's worth pointing out, I think, that this figure just takes into account the words that we have stored (fully or partially) in our mental lexicon, and not the words – perhaps an infinite number of them – that we can create by using rules of word formation. We will return shortly to our knowledge of word formation rules and its relation to our mental lexicon. First, however, we will look more closely at how we acquire our mental lexicon.

2.3.2 The acquisition of lexical knowledge

Psycholinguists have devised experiments to try to learn how children and adults are able to acquire words so easily. You might think that the learning of new words is a simple matter of association: someone points at something and says "flurge" and you learn that that something is called a *flurge*. This may be the way that we learn some words, but surely not the way we learn the majority of words in our mental lexicons. For one thing, not everything for which we have a word can be pointed at.

And even if someone points and says a word, it is often not clear from the context what exactly is being pointed out. Psycholinguists sometimes call this **the Gavagai problem**, following a scenario first discussed by the philosopher W.O. Quine. To summarize:

> Picture yourself on a safari with a guide who does not speak English. All of a sudden, a large brown rabbit runs across a field some distance from you. The guide points and says "gavagai!" What does he mean?
>
> One possibility is, of course, that he's giving you his word for 'rabbit'. But why couldn't he be saying something like "There goes a rabbit running across the field"? or perhaps "a brown one," or "Watch out!," or even "Those are really tasty!"? How do you know?
>
> In other words, there may be so much going on in our immediate environment that an act of pointing while saying a word, phrase, or sentence will not determine clearly what the speaker intends his utterance to refer to.

Besides, we are rarely in a situation in which someone is actively instructing us about the meanings of words; although parents may point to things in a picture book and name them for a child, or school children may be asked to memorize a list of vocabulary words, we learn most words without explicit instruction and seemingly with very little exposure. Although we do not know nearly enough about this subject, there are several things that we do know about how word learning occurs.

First, it is believed that both children and adults are able to do what the psycholinguist Susan Carey has called **fast mapping** (Carey 1978). Fast mapping is the ability to pick up new words on the basis of a few random exposures to them. In one experiment, Carey showed that children who were casually exposed to a new color name *chromium* during an unrelated activity (following instructions to pick up trays of various colors) were able to absorb the word and recall it even six weeks later. Experiments have shown that adults exhibit this fast mapping ability as well; while the ability to learn linguistic rules (say, of syntax or phonology) is thought to decline after puberty, the ability to learn new words remains robust.

Challenge

Here's an experiment you can try. Collect five or six objects. All but one of your objects should be familiar items (a bunch of keys, a mug, a pencil, etc.). One object, however, should be something odd and not familiar to many people. Put all your objects on a tray, and ask your subject (anyone outside your class will do) to point out the *zorch*. Observe what you subject does. Now take away the unfamiliar object, leaving only the familiar objects, and ask a different subject to point out the *plitz*. Again, observe closely what the subject does.

Psycholinguists have proposed a number of other strategies that both children and adults seem to use in learning new words.[2] One might be called the **Lexical Contrast Principle**. For example, in an experiment similar to yours, children were asked to point to the *zorch* (or some other made-up word), and what they invariably did was to point out the unfamiliar object. According to the Lexical Contrast Principle, the language learner will always assume that a new word refers to something that does not already have a name.

A second word learning strategy might be called the **Whole Object Principle**. In the experimental condition described above, when subjects are presented with the word *zorch* and an unnamed object, they will assume the whole unnamed object to be a *zorch*. They will not assume that *zorch* refers to a part of the object, to its color or shape, or to a superordinate category of objects to which it might belong.

2. See Bloom (2000) for an extensive discussion of this subject.

A related strategy might be dubbed the **Mutual Exclusivity Principle**. In the second experiment above, there are only familiar objects for which subjects already have names. When asked to point out the *plitz*, experimental subjects typically do one of two things: they might first look around the room for something else that might be called a *plitz*, or they might assume that the word *plitz* refers to a part of one of the familiar objects or a special type of one of them. Subjects, in other words, will assume that if an object already has a word for it, the word *plitz* cannot be synonymous with those words.

These experiments are of course not just hypothetical. Paul Bloom, Susan Carey, and many other psycholinguists have conducted them both with children of various ages and with adults, and have obtained the results described above. What is perhaps most astonishing about their results is that their experimental subjects often remember the words they've been exposed to when they are retested weeks after the original experiment. But maybe we should not be surprised by this: how otherwise could we have learned 60,000 words by the time we're 18?

Children not only learn individual words, but – as we'll see in the chapters to come – they learn the rules that allow us to create and understand new words. Indeed, there is evidence that English-speaking children as young as 18- to 24-months old are able to create new compound words (that is, words like *wind mill* or *dog bed*) and to turn nouns into verbs, a process which is called conversion (see chapter 3). Not too long after this, children will begin to use prefixes and suffixes, both for inflection and lexeme formation. We know that they have learned the rules when they produce words that are novel and therefore that they could not have learned from the language spoken around them.

2.3.3 The organization of the mental lexicon: storage *versus* rules

Although linguists like to describe our knowledge of words as a mental lexicon, we know that the mental lexicon is not organized alphabetically like a dictionary. Rather, it is a complex web composed of stored items (morphemes, words, idiomatic phrases) that may be related to each other by the sounds that form them and by their meanings. Along with these stored items we also have rules that allow us to combine morphemes in different ways. Our evidence for this organization comes from experiments using both normal subjects and subjects with some sort of genetic disorder or trauma to the brain.

There is a great deal of evidence to support the idea that speakers do not merely learn and store complex words (although they may store some complex words which are used frequently), but rather construct complex words using rules of word formation. We will go into great detail in the chapters to come on exactly what these rules of word formation look like, but let us start with a simple example, and use that example to explore what linguist Steven Pinker calls the "words and rules" theory of the mental lexicon (Pinker 1999).

We will take as our example the rule for forming past tenses of verbs in English. At this point, if I asked you how to form the past tense of a verb in English, you would probably say that you usually add an *-ed*. And then you might point out that there are a number of verbs that have irregular past tenses like *sing~sang, tell~told, win~won, fly~flew,* and the like. We will look first at the regular past tense rule.

While it is true that in writing we add an *-ed* to form the past tense of a verb, in terms of spoken speech, the situation is a bit more complicated. Consider the next Challenge:

Challenge

Consider how you *pronounce* the past tenses of these verbs:

1. rap, tack, laugh, sheath, pass, lurch
2. pat, prod
3. rob, rove, bathe, buzz, rouge, judge, warm, warn, bang, roar, rule, tango

Transcribe the past tenses of these words in the International Phonetic Alphabet and observe how they differ.

You pronounce the past tenses of the first set of words in the Challenge box with a [t] sound, in the second with a sound like [əd], and the third with a [d] sound.

We do not choose the pronunciation of the past tense at random. Rather, the choice of which of the three endings to use depends on the final sound of the verb. Those words that are pronounced with final [t] or [d] sounds – those in the second list – get the [əd] pronunciation. The words that end in voiceless (with the exception of [t]) sounds get the [t] pronunciation. And all the rest get the [d] pronunciation. As for irregular forms like *sang* and *flew*, we must assume that English speakers simply learn them as exceptions.

We know that speakers of English have an unconscious knowledge of the past tense rule because we can automatically create the past tense of novel verbs. For example, if I coin a verb *blick*, you know that the past tense morpheme is pronounced [t]. Similarly, the novel verb *flurd* will have the past tense [əd], and the verb *zove* will be made past tense with [d]. We can even form the past tense of verbs that contain final sounds that do not occur at all in English, and when we do, we still follow the rule. For example, if we imagine that there are many composers imitating the style of Johann Sebastian Bach, and we coin the verb *to bach* to denote the action of imitating Bach, we will automatically form the past tense with the past tense variant pronounced [t], because the final sound of Bach is [x], a voiceless velar fricative. The important point here is that when we hear this sound at the end of a verb we know (unconsciously) that it's voiceless, and apply the past tense rule to it in the usual way.

Now that we know something about the English past tense rule, we can return to the question of how the mental lexicon is organized. It might be plausible to assume that speakers of English use the past tense rule when they are creating the past tenses of novel verbs, but simply store the past tense forms of words they have already heard. In other words, we might assume that once a past tense has been formed, it is entered whole in our mental lexicon, and we retrieve it whole just as we would the present tense form. This hypothesis, however, may not be correct.

2.3.4 Evidence from aphasia

Studies of aphasics – people whose language faculty has been impaired due to stroke or other brain trauma – show that there must be a past tense rule that speakers use for regular forms – even very frequent ones – and that irregular forms are stored whole, probably in a different part of the brain. Badecker and Caramazza (1999) describe how we can know this.

Some aphasics display **agrammatism**; this means that they have difficulty in producing or processing function words in sentences, but can still produce and understand content words. Interestingly, agrammatic aphasics have difficulty producing or processing both regularly inflected forms (like the English past tenses), and also productively derived words (those with suffixes that we use frequently in making up new words – for example, *-less* as in *shoeless* or *-ly* as in *darkly*), whereas they have far less trouble with irregular forms like *sang* and *flew*.

Other aphasics display **jargon aphasia**; these aphasics produce fluent sentences using function words, but have trouble producing and understanding content words. Instead, they have a tendency to produce nonsense words. Interestingly, jargon aphasics will use regular inflections appropriately on their nonsense words, but they have difficulty processing and producing irregular forms.

We can explain the differential behavior of agrammatical and jargon aphasics if we postulate that we have rules for producing regularly inflected and productively derived forms, and only store irregular forms, and that rules and stored items are located in different parts of the brain. For agrammatic aphasics, the rule is unavailable, presumably because the part of the brain has been damaged that apparently allows us to apply morphological rules, but the irregular forms are still accessible from an undamaged part of the brain. For jargon aphasics, the irregular forms have been lost because the part of the brain that apparently allows access to stored forms has been damaged, but the regular rule is still intact.

2.3.5 Evidence from imaging studies

Imaging studies of normal subjects, such as those done with **PET (positron emission tomography) scans** seem to show the same thing. PET scans measure the level of blood flow to different parts of the brain, which in turn shows us areas of activation in those parts. Jaeger *et al.* (1996) have reported that there are parts of the brain that are activated when subjects are asked to read regularly inflected past tenses that are distinct from those activated in reading or producing irregular past tenses.

2.3.6 Evidence from genetic disorders

Similar conclusions follow from studies of two different genetic disorders – **Specific Language Impairment (SLI)** and **Williams Syndrome** – that affect language in different ways. Individuals with SLI are generally of normal intelligence and have no hearing impairment. But they are slow to produce and understand language, and their speech is characterized by the omission of various inflectional morphemes. Individuals with Williams Syndrome have a genetic disorder linked to various heart problems, elevated levels of calcium in their blood, and a characteristic appearance (short stature, an upturned nose, a long neck, among other things). Their language and social skills are in the normal range, but in other respects such as motor control and spatial perception they display mild or moderate developmental delay.

What is significant for our purposes is that these disorders provide more evidence for the organization of our mental lexicon. Individuals with SLI find it difficult to create the past tenses of novel verbs, and often fail to inflect unfamiliar regular verbs correctly; they have less difficulty with irregular verbs, though. In spontaneous speech, they may leave the regular past tense off verbs (Redmond and Rice 2001). In contrast, individuals with Williams Syndrome speak fluently and produce sentences with correct regular past tenses, but have more trouble with irregular ones; indeed they seem to use regular past tense marking even where control subjects or individuals with SLI would not, for example, overgeneralizing the regular *-ed* ending on irregular verbs (for example, *falled*) (Clahsen, Ring, and Temple 2004). Assuming that the genetic anomalies associated with these disorders affect different parts of the brain, we can explain this pattern of behavior.

2.3.7 Reprise: is it really a word?

We have spent some time in this chapter contrasting the dictionary with the mental lexicon in order to understand the question "Is *xyz* really a word?" We are now in a position to understand this question better, at least from the point of view of morphologists. Most morphologists would say that *xyz* is a word if it can be formed by the rules of word formation in a particular language. So words like *wordhood* or *re-reprise* that you might never have seen before you read this chapter really are words, even though you won't find them in any dictionary. They are words because they follow the rules of English word formation. It is the rules of word formation that we know that most distinguish our mental lexicon from the dictionary. The dictionary does not need to list all the words that we know or that we could create, because once we know word formation rules we can produce and understand potentially infinite numbers of new words from the morphemes available to us. The remainder of this book will be an attempt to work out in some detail what those rules are.

2.4 More about dictionaries

In section 2.2 we considered all the reasons why morphologists don't look upon dictionaries as the ultimate arbiters of 'wordhood' in English, or indeed in any language. You may not need more convincing of this issue, but for those of you who have a fondness for dictionaries (most morphologists do!), it's worth knowing something about how dictionaries have developed. I'll again concentrate on English here, as our common language, but the history of dictionary-making for other languages can be equally fascinating.

Let's start with a thought experiment. Look at the next Challenge.

Challenge

Suppose that a great catastrophe has occurred and every single written or on-line dictionary has disappeared from the face of the earth. You and your classmates have survived the catastrophe (perhaps in a hidden concrete tunnel beneath the building in which you are now sitting), and have been delegated the task by other survivors of creating the first post-catastrophe dictionary of your language.

How would you start?

Your first instinct would probably be to make a list of words that you would need to define. Assuming that there were no surviving books to use as dictionary-fodder, a good way to begin would be by thinking of categories, and listing everything you could in each one. After you've listed all the animals, plants, and types of furniture you could think of, you'd come up with a list of hairstyles (*crewcut, bob, beehive, bun, buzz cut, duck's ass, cornrows, mullet, . . .*) and condiments (*ketchup, soy sauce, mustard, horseradish, wasabi, sambal oelek, . . .*), and so on, and eventually you'd come to articles (*a, the, this, that, . . .*), prepositions (*in, on, above, during, for, . . .*) and the other small words that form the grammatical glue that holds sentences together.

But along the way, you'd discover a number of problems. First, you'd have a suspicion that you'd be forgetting things (what, for example, was the name for that women's hairstyle that was the rage in the seventies?). Second, you and your classmates would get into constant arguments over this word or that: is it worth putting the word *mullet* in the dictionary as the name of a hairstyle? Wasn't that slang? Does slang go in the dictionary? What IS slang, anyway? Is it too vulgar to put *duck's ass* in the dictionary as a name of a 1950s hairstyle? What about really raunchy words? Is *sambal oelek* a word for a condiment in English, or is it just something we've borrowed from another language (what other language, though?)?

What this thought experiment does is to put you in the shoes of a lexicographer. In reality, it's been centuries since lexicographers have had to start from scratch in creating a dictionary – and perhaps they've never really done so. As the lexicographer Sidney Landau has said about the tradition of dictionary-making in English (2001: 43), "The history of English lexicography usually consists of a recital of successive and often successful acts of piracy." For years and years, each succeeding dictionary-maker has consulted already existing dictionaries to come up with a base list of words, often adding new ones and sometimes deleting words for various reasons. But at least at first, lexicographers did have to decide one by one on each of the English words to include. Of course, there were manuscripts and books available to suggest words that needed to be included, and in fact, the earliest English lexicographers did rely on the words they found in books as the material from which they built their dictionaries.

2.4.1 Early dictionaries

It was not until the early seventeenth century that anything we would recognize as a monolingual dictionary could be found for the English language. Dictionaries or glossaries for translating Latin to English date from a century or so earlier, and in the sixteenth century lists of so-called hard words could be found for English, explaining words which largely had been adapted from Latin. The first real dictionary of English is generally acknowledged to be Robert Cawdrey's (1604) *A Table Alphabeticall of Hard Words*. The tradition of lexicographical piracy goes at least as far back as Cawdrey, who is said to have used an available Latin–English dictionary of his day to help come up with the words to define. The first dictionaries going beyond the tradition of defining only 'hard' words to include ordinary, everyday words began to appear in the early eighteenth century; Landau (2001: 52) cites John Kersey's (1702) *A New English Dictionary* as the earliest of these, followed by Nathaniel Bailey's (1721) *An Universal Etymological English Dictionary*.

2.4.2 Johnson's dictionary

A more significant milestone in the history of English lexicography for our purposes was Samuel Johnson's *Dictionary of the English Language*, published in 1755. It contains more than 42,000 entries – even then, only a small fraction of English vocabulary – and took seven years to write, an astonishing feat for a single individual. Johnson's dictionary was not only the most comprehensive English dictionary of his time, but it was also among the first dictionaries to include illustrative quotations on a large scale.

What is most interesting for our purposes, though, are the idiosyncrasies of Johnson's dictionary: what he included, what he left out, and how he defined various words in odd ways. Henry Hitchings (2005: 110) notes that:

> . . . dictionaries are fraught with submerged ideas, narratives and histories. Johnson's is no exception. It offers no overarching system of knowledge, but it is a literary anthology, a compendium of quotable nuggets, and a mine of information – some trivial, some considerable – on subjects as diverse as heraldry and hunting, rhetoric and pharmacy, oracles and literary style, the zodiac and magic, law and mathematics, ignorance and politics, the art of conversation and the benefits of reading.

Johnson's dictionary, in other words, contains a lot about Johnson himself – both his interests and his prejudices. It was quite a comprehensive

Some Johnsonian definitions:

urim: *Urim and thummim were something in Aaron's breastplate; but what, criticks and commentators are by no means agreed.*

trolmydames: *[Of this word, I know not the meaning.]*

worm (v.): *To deprive a dog of something, nobody knows what, under his tongue, which is said to prevent him, nobody knows why, from running mad.*

network: *Anything reticulated or decussated, at equal distances, with interstices between the intersections.*

pastern: *The knee of an horse.*

dictionary in its time. But Hitchings notes that Johnson still left out entries for such words as *ultimatum, irritable, zinc, engineering, athlete,* and *annulment*, even though he actually used some of those words in his definitions. On the other hand, he included such words as *ariolation, clancular, deuteroscopy,* and *incompossiblity*, which even the nineteenth-century American lexicographer Noah Webster considered dubious. And it has often been pointed out that some of Johnson's definitions were odd, unhelpful, and occasionally downright wrong.

For example, the word *urim* is used by Milton, and therefore Johnson judged it important enough to be included even though he was unable to discern the meaning of the word from its literary context. Similarly, *trolmydames* is used in Shakespeare, and therefore it merited inclusion for Johnson – although, again, he had no idea what it meant. And what can we say about the definitions for *network* and *worm*? If you don't already know what they mean, you won't be enlightened by Johnson's definitions!

As Hitchings implies in the passage quoted above, we can learn a lot about Johnson's interests from his dictionary. For example, we can tell from Johnson's entry for *pastern* that he had no particular knowledge of or interest in horses: he defines the *pastern* as the knee of a horse. People who are interested in horses know that a *pastern* is part of a horse's foot. Similarly, as Hitchings points out, Johnson apparently had no interest in music. His definitions for a number of stringed instruments (*viola, lute, guitar*) are precisely the same: "a stringed instrument." Furthermore, the definition of *violin* suffers from the cardinal lexicographical sin of circularity: the entry for *violin* sends one to the entry for *fiddle*, which in turn sends one back to *violin*.

These examples are not intended to imply that Johnson's dictionary was incompetent – far from it, it was an amazing achievement for one man working alone for seven years. Much of it still holds up to twenty-first century scrutiny. For every entry that is obscure, weird, or unhelpful, there are a hundred that are brilliant and insightful. I devote this much attention to its deficiencies merely to point out that dictionaries are fallible, and often reflect the foibles of their makers.

2.4.3 Webster's dictionary

Johnson's dictionary was followed in 1828 by Noah Webster's dictionary – billed as the first American dictionary. Webster's agenda in writing his dictionary was at least partly political; through the dictionary he sought to establish American English as a national language. His dictionary included not only new words but also new meanings that had developed for old words in the context of American life, for example, words relevant to the newly minted form of democracy, such as *congress* and *senate*. Webster is also credited with promoting the spelling differences which even today distinguish American from British English – *color* instead of *colour*, *center* instead of *centre*, *tire* instead of *tyre*, and so on.

Webster was not particularly skilled at **etymology** (the study of where words come from); Baugh and Cable (1993: 361) suggest that his sense of nationalism caused him to ignore advances in historical and comparative linguistics that were taking place in Europe at that time. However, his definitions are excellent. Not surprisingly, though, some definitions in Webster's dictionary are pirated directly from Johnson. Note, however, that not all of Webster's contemporaries shared his desire to distinguish American English from British English. Joseph Worcester, for example, published his own *Comprehensive Pronouncing and Explanatory Dictionary* in 1830, in which he took a far more conservative approach to Americanisms and spelling.

2.4.4 The Oxford English Dictionary

By the mid-nineteenth century, members of the English Philological Society had come to feel that Johnson's dictionary was inadequate. As we saw above, Johnson had missed many words, and even if he had not, over the course of a century many new words are added to a language and many old words come to be used in new ways. After much deliberation and a number of false starts, the Philological Society chose James Murray, a Scottish schoolmaster, to edit the *New English Dictionary*. Oxford University Press contracted to publish it, and by 1895 it had come to be known as the *Oxford English Dictionary*. Murray began work on the dictionary in 1879, hoping to finish it within ten years. But it would be almost fifty years before the first edition of the dictionary was finished, during which time three more editors were added, and Murray himself died.

The OED took so long to compile because the goals of its originators were so ambitious. Murray and his colleagues sought to create a dictionary that would not only give current meanings of words, but also trace those words back as far into the history of English as they could, taking note of all the spelling variants and meaning changes along the way. Following Johnson's dictionary, all senses of words would be illustrated with quotations from literary works. Words that were already archaic or obsolete by the late nineteenth century would still be included, as long as they had not died out before 1250 CE. The dictionary was to be comprehensive in both breadth and depth, a task which turned out to be far more challenging than anyone in 1879 could have anticipated. The first edition of the OED ran to ten large volumes and contained almost a quarter of a million main entries. By the time the last volume was finished, the early volumes were already obsolete; one supplement was added in 1933, and a second one in 1972. A second edition of twenty volumes was issued in 1989, incorporating all of the supplements into the original volume. Today, work continues on the third edition, with segments issued on-line on a quarterly basis, as they are finished. Since the first edition, the OED has grown to include more than half a million entries; in its on-line form, size and space are no longer as much of a concern as they once were.

James Murray was well aware both of the weight his lexicographical decisions carried and of his potential fallibility in making those decisions – after all, most people do look to the dictionary to determine whether *xyz*

Of Obscure Meaning in the OED:

These entries for smazky *and* val-dunk *are among the 87 entries that the OED designates as "meaning obscure" or "of obscure meaning". Did they deserve to be in the OED? You decide!*

smazky, a. *Obs. (Meaning obscure.)* **1599** MIDDLETON Micro-cynicon A5, *Auant,..Ile anger thee inough, And fold thy firy-eyes in thy smazkie snufe.*

val-dunk *Obs. (Meaning obscure.)* **1631** R. BRATHWAIT Whimzies, Wine-soaker *102 By this time his cause is heard, and now this val-dunke growne rampant~drunke, would fight if hee knew how.*

really is a word. Perhaps Murray put it best when he noted in the Introduction to the first edition that:

> The Vocabulary of a widely-diffused and highly-cultivated living language is not a fixed quantity circumscribed by definite limits. That vast aggregate of words and phrases which constitutes the Vocabulary of English-speaking men presents, to the mind that endeavours to grasp it as a definite whole, the aspect of one of those nebulous masses familiar to the astronomer, in which a clear and unmistakable nucleus shades off on all sides, through zones of decreasing brightness to a dim marginal film that seems to end nowhere, but to lose itself imperceptibly in the surrounding darkness.

In other words, it's impossible to pin down the vocabulary of English (and we might add, any other language). Murray illustrates his point with a diagram (figure 2.1), reproduced from the Introduction to the first edition of the dictionary. His idea is that there is a core of words whose place in the dictionary nobody would dispute, encompassing what he called "common," "literary," and "colloquial" words. Common words are words that occur in all registers of English, like *mother, dog, walk, apologetic, wiggle, if, and, to, in, that,* and so on. Literary words are words that we might recognize when we read, but would not necessarily use in daily conversation, words, for example, like *omnipotent, notwithstanding, heretical, avatar,* and *ambulatory.* And also among the core words would be colloquial words, ones that we use frequently in spoken language, but far less frequently in written or formal language, for example, *grubby, pooch,* and *mad* (in the sense of 'angry'). But there is no clear dividing line between these words and words which are perhaps too technical or scientifically specialized (*circumfix, triptan*), not quite assimilated enough into English (*tchachka, sambal oelek*), too bound to a specific dialect (*frappé, black ice*), or too informal, impermanent, or bound too narrowly to a particular time or a particular segment of society (*groovy, homie*). Deciding which of these uncommon words merit inclusion in the dictionary is a judgment call, often based more on practical considerations – the size of the dictionary, its intended audience – than on strict

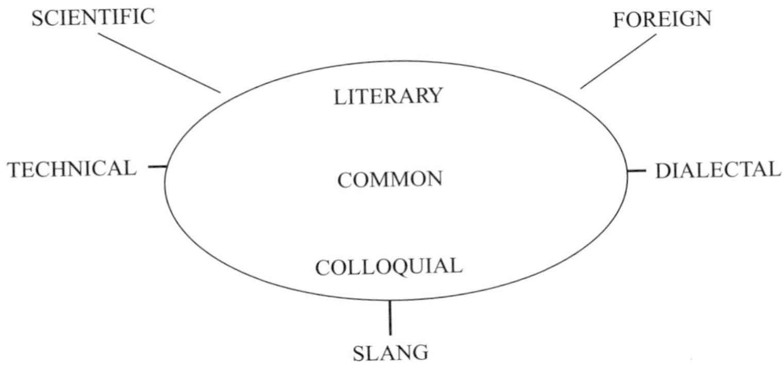

FIGURE 2.1
Reproduced with permission of Oxford University Press, James A.H. Murray et al. 1888. *A New English Dictionary on Historical Principles,* p. xvii

linguistic principles. All lexicographers face this conundrum, and each one makes a slightly different decision.

The OED is certainly the gold standard for English dictionaries today. Nevertheless, it has its own idiosyncrasies. For example, it contains a number of nonce words, words that are attested only once. Indeed there are quite a few nonce words that the OED includes, even though it is unable to define them. A search, using the key words "meaning obscure" and "of obscure meaning," turns up 87 words so labeled, including *smazky, squirgliting, val-dunk, vezon, uncape,* and *umbershoot*. Each bears an entry illustrated with one quotation, which unfortunately does not illuminate the word's meaning. Nevertheless, these and 81 others like them made it into the OED!

2.4.5 Modern dictionaries

Today, there are dozens of dictionaries available for English – unabridged dictionaries, college dictionaries, children's dictionaries, specialized dictionaries of music or architecture, an official Scrabble dictionary, not to mention on-line dictionaries in many varieties. Each one of these is edited by a team of individuals who make the judgment call whether *xyz* deserves to be in the dictionary. The decision is made on a number of grounds:

- the size of the dictionary, which determines the number of words it can hold;
- the intended audience of the dictionary (adults, children, language learners, etc.);
- whether a word has a sufficiently broad base of usage;
- whether it's likely to last;
- whether it's too specialized or technical for the intended audience;
- for a word borrowed from another language, whether it's assimilated enough to be considered part of English.

With respect to size, the number of words and the depth of entries (whether etymologies and illustrative quotes are included, for example) in print dictionaries are determined by the number of pages and the font size of the print used. On-line dictionaries do not have the sort of space constraints that print dictionaries do. As for audience, a dictionary intended for college-age adults will probably have more learned and technical words than a dictionary for children. On the other hand, words that a native speaker is unlikely to need defined might be more of a focus in a dictionary for English language learners; the meanings of prepositions and their idiomatic uses come to mind here. The type of dictionary also determines how broad a base of usage a word needs to have in order to be included. Dictionaries of slang, dialect, or of specialized fields obviously contain more narrowly used words than general dictionaries do (although you might be surprised at how much slang and technical terminology can be found in general dictionaries).

Perhaps the trickiest issue is how long a word has to have been around to merit inclusion in the dictionary. These days, words can appear in dictionaries fairly quickly, especially in on-line dictionaries. The OED already lists *google* as a verb, with its first illustrative quotation dated 1999. The word *bouncebackability* – allegedly coined by British sportscaster Iain Dowie in 2004 (Hohenhaus 2006) – already had a draft OED entry by June, 2006 (although interestingly, the OED has traced the word as far back as 1961!).

And there is more to consider in deciding whether a word goes into the dictionary. Take, for example, words formed with various prefixes and suffixes. If *happy* is in the dictionary (as it certainly would be), do we need to have an entry as well for *happiness*? Similarly, if *sad* has an entry, do we need *sadness*? If our audience is a learner of English, perhaps yes, but for native speakers who know intuitively how the suffix *-ness* is used, is there any need for these extra entries? Interestingly, dictionaries are often quite inconsistent on how many and which derivatives with particular suffixes get entries. The on-line OED has entries for *redness, blueness, pinkness, greenness,* and *yellowness*, but not *orangeness*. The word *purpleness* is used in the definition of the word *purplely*, but does not have its own entry. And not surprisingly, there is no entry for *mauveness* or *beigeness*. What is more surprising is that there are so many entries for color words with the suffix *-ness* attached.

Certainly, if a word derived with a prefix or suffix takes on an idiosyncratic or **lexicalized** meaning, the dictionary needs to include it. Take, for example, the word *transmission*, which can have the transparent meaning 'the act of transmitting' but probably more often is used to denote a part of a car. This second meaning probably deserves to be in the dictionary. But is it necessary to include all derived words whose meanings are perfectly clear from the meaning of the base plus the meaning of the affix? Probably not.

Until the last decade of the twentieth century lexicographers made their decisions by reading materials of all sorts, and in more recent decades by listening to radio, TV, and talk in general. Potential entries would be recorded with their context on small slips of paper. These slips would then be filed, and when a critical mass of usages accumulated for a word, it might be considered for entry in the dictionary. These days lexicographers are aided by **corpora** (singular **corpus**), large computerized databases that can be searched for words in the context of their use, and by the internet, which might be viewed as a vast corpus. Indeed the rise (and sometimes fall) of a new word can be traced by searching for its use on the internet.

Perhaps the most interesting recent development in lexicography is the rise of Wiktionary – an on-line collaborative dictionary created not by professional lexicographers, but by users themselves. In the instructions for submitting entries, Wiktionary asks that words be attested, by which it means they must be in widespread use, available in well-known works or refereed publications, used at least three times in at least three sources over more than a year. It does, however, have a category of what it calls 'protologisms' for "terms defined in the hopes that they will be used, but which are not actually in wide use."

One final note about the vagaries of dictionaries. Lest you think that lexicographers are humorless ("harmless drudges" as Johnson calls them in his dictionary), let's consider the issue of mountweazels mentioned briefly above. As Henry Alford reveals in the August 29, 2005 issue of *The New Yorker*, the editors of the *New Oxford American Dictionary* (2001) planted the non-existent word *esquivalience* (defined as "the willful avoidance of one's official responsibilities . . .") among the entries for the letter "e" to catch potential dictionary pirates. Such false words are called 'mountweazels', from the false entry for Lillian Virginia Mountweazel in the *New Columbia Encyclopedia*.[3] What is most interesting for our purposes is that once these fake words have been coined, they take on lives of their own. As of December 2006, there were 55,300 hits for *esquivalience* and 22,700 for *mountweazel* on Google, leading me to wonder whether these fakes have now become real words.

2.4.6 And other languages

I have concentrated here on the history of dictionary-making in English, but the same points might be made with respect to dictionaries of French, Italian, Russian, Chinese, or Central Alaskan Yup'ik. All dictionaries are products of individuals and all display the choices and idiosyncrasies of those individuals in some way or another.

Dictionaries of other languages might be organized quite differently from those of the Indo-European languages that we are most familiar with, however. For example, dictionaries of Mandarin Chinese are not alphabetized in the way that dictionaries of English and French are, because Chinese is not written in the Roman alphabet. Instead, the writing system (or **orthography**) of Chinese is **logographic** or word-based. Each word in Chinese is represented by a single character (or sometimes a combination of two characters). When you look up a word in a Chinese dictionary, you need to know how many strokes or lines make up that character. Dictionaries are organized from those characters made up of the fewest strokes to those containing the most strokes.

Dictionaries of other languages might include many fewer complex words than English dictionaries typically do. For example, if a language has very regular rules of word formation such that both the form and the resulting meaning of a complex word are perfectly predictable, the dictionary will have no need to list all complex words in separate entries. All it needs to do is list individual morphemes with their meanings (and perhaps some indication of how they combine). But the less predictable the form and meaning of complex words are, the greater the need to put them in the dictionary.

3. According to the *New Columbia Encyclopedia*, Lillian Virginia Mountweazel lived from 1942 to 1973. A fountain designer and photographer, she was supposedly well known for taking pictures of rural American mailboxes. She died tragically in an explosion while she was on assignment for *Combustibles* magazine.

Summary

In this chapter we have been concerned with the question of what constitutes a word. We have contrasted dictionaries with the mental lexicon. Dictionaries are written constructs that record words, along with their pronunciations, meanings, etymologies, and perhaps examples of use. On the one hand, they do not and cannot contain everything that a native speaker would recognize as words of her language – dictionaries have no need to record regularly inflected forms of words and words derived by very active rules of word formation, for example. On the other hand, dictionaries may include items that perhaps don't deserve to be considered real words – for example, nonce words that are undefinable, or artificially created words put in to check for copyright violations.

Our mental lexicons are something different, however. High-school educated adults may have vocabularies of 60,000 words. We acquire these words rapidly, and sometimes our mental representations are sketchy or incomplete. The evidence we have looked at from aphasia and genetic disorders, as well as studies using PET scans, allows us to begin to develop a picture of how these vast numbers of words are organized in our minds. Unlike dictionaries that list words alphabetically, our mental lexicon is organized as a complex web of entries that are linked in various ways, along with a system of rules for combining listed forms. It appears that entries and rules are at least to some extent wired into different parts of the brain.

Exercises

1. Go to the OED On-line website and search for words that are in the dictionary but have no known definition. To do this, click on Advanced Search (look towards the bottom of the OED home page), and type into the first open box "meaning obscure" or "of obscure meaning." Then choose three words and read through their entries. Do you think the OED was justified in including these words? If so, why? If not, why not?
2. Make a list of five words that you consider to be *slang*. Now look them up in your dictionary (you may use any dictionary at hand, whether print or on-line). First note whether or not you find them. If you do, is the dictionary definition the one that you had in mind? Does your dictionary list them as slang? If not, speculate on why they might not be listed as slang.
3. Make a list of at least ten words that come to mind that end in the suffix *-less*. Look these words up in a dictionary (you may use a standard college desk dictionary like the *American Heritage Dictionary* or you may use the on-line OED). How many of your words are in the dictionary? Is there any pattern that you can discern with respect to the words that are listed, as opposed to the words that are not?
4. Visit the Word Spy website (http://www.wordspy.com). Look at the list of new words and decide which ones, if any, are part of your own mental lexicon. If some of them are, compare your understanding of them with the definition that Word Spy gives.

CHAPTER

3 Lexeme formation: the familiar

CHAPTER OUTLINE

KEY TERMS

derivation
affixation
compounding
conversion
coinage
blending
backformation

In this chapter you will learn about common ways of creating new lexemes.

- We will look at derivational affixation, considering the distinction between affixes and bases, and between free and bound bases.
- We will learn how to segment words into morphemes, how to formulate word formation rules, and how to determine the structure of words.
- We will consider what morphemes mean.
- Beyond affixation, in this chapter we will learn about processes of compounding, conversion, and other ways of creating new words.
- And you will get your first taste of morphological analysis.

3.1 Introduction

Take a look at the words below:

- autoclave (v.)
- head bracelet (n.)
- conversate (v.)
- deBaathification (n.)
- oversuds (v.)
- McDonaldization (n.)
- unwipe (v.)

Have you ever heard these words before? Can you imagine what they mean?

Chances are that you haven't heard or read them before. Nevertheless, you probably didn't have much trouble figuring out at least roughly what their meanings might be. Assuming that you know that an autoclave is a device for sterilizing instruments, the verb *to autoclave* probably means something like 'to sterilize using an autoclave'. A *head bracelet* is probably something that goes around one's head. *DeBaathification* must have something to do with removing the Baath (the Iraqi political party associated with Saddam Hussein). And so on. You might not know exactly what they mean, but you can make a good guess.[1]

The reason you can make educated guesses about these words is that that they follow the rules of word formation in English. Once you know what the base – the central bit of the word – means, you can often figure out everything else. In this chapter, we're going to look at the most common ways of forming new lexemes in English and in other languages of the world. You'll learn how to analyze words into their component parts, see how those parts are organized, and how the various parts contribute to their meanings.

3.2 Kinds of morphemes

Most native speakers of English will recognize that words like *unwipe, head bracelet* or *MacDonaldization* are made up of several meaningful pieces, and will be able to split them into those pieces:

(1) un / wipe
head / bracelet
McDonald / ize / ation

As you learned in chapter 1, these pieces are called **morphemes**, the minimal meaningful units that are used to form words. Some of the morphemes

1. A *head bracelet* is a headband with sparkly decorations. *Conversate* means 'to have a conversation'. To *oversuds* is to put too much detergent in the washer. *McDonaldization* is the creation of vast chains of franchise stores. To *unwipe* is to restore deleted data to the hard disk of a computer (something which is, of course, impossible!).

in (1) can stand alone as words: *wipe, head, bracelet, McDonald*. These are called **free** morphemes. The morphemes that cannot stand alone are called **bound** morphemes. In the examples above, the bound morphemes are *un-*, *-ize*, and *-ation*. Bound morphemes come in different varieties. Those in (1) are **prefixes** and **suffixes**; the former are bound morphemes that come before the base of the word, and the latter bound morphemes that come after the base. Together, prefixes and suffixes can be grouped together as **affixes**.[2]

New lexemes that are formed with prefixes and suffixes on a base are often referred to as **derived** words, and the process by which they are formed as **derivation**. The **base** is the semantic core of the word to which the prefixes and suffixes attach. For example, *wipe* is the base of *unwipe*, and *McDonald* is the base of *McDonaldization*. Frequently, the base is a free morpheme, as it is in these two cases. But stop a minute and consider the data in the next Challenge box.

Challenge

Divide the following words into morphemes:

- pathology
- psychopath
- dermatitis
- endoderm

Chances are that you recognize that there are two morphemes in each word. However, neither part is a free morpheme. Do we want to call these morphemes prefixes and suffixes? Would this seem odd to you?

If you said that it would be odd to consider the morphemes in our Challenge as prefixes and suffixes, you probably did so because this would imply that words like *pathology* and *psychopath* are made up of nothing but affixes!

Morphologists therefore make a distinction between affixes and **bound bases**. Bound bases are morphemes that cannot stand alone as words, but are not prefixes or suffixes. Sometimes, as is the case with the morphemes *path* or *derm*, they can occur either before or after another bound base: *path* precedes the base *ology*, but follows the base *psych(o)*; *derm* precedes another base in *dermatitis* but follows one in *endoderm*. This suggests that *path* and *derm* are not prefixes or suffixes: there is no such thing as an affix which sometimes precedes its base and sometimes follows it. But not all bound bases are as free in their placement as *path*; for example, *psych(o)* and *ology* seem to have more fixed positions, the former usually preceding another bound base, the latter following. Similarly, the base *-itis* always follows, and *endo-* always precedes another base. Why not call them respectively a prefix and a suffix, then?

One reason is that all of these morphemes seem in an intuitive way to have far more substantial meanings than the average affix does. Whereas

2. We will see in chapter 5 that there are other types of affixes as well.

a prefix like *un-* (*unhappy, unwise*) simply means 'not' and a suffix *-ish* (*reddish, warmish*) means 'sort of', *psych(o)* means 'having to do with the mind', *-ology* means 'the study of', *path* means 'sickness', *derm* means 'skin' and *-itis* means 'disease'. Semantically, bound bases can form the core of a word, just as free morphemes can. Figure 3.1 summarizes types of morphemes. We'll look more carefully at the meanings of affixes in section 3.3.

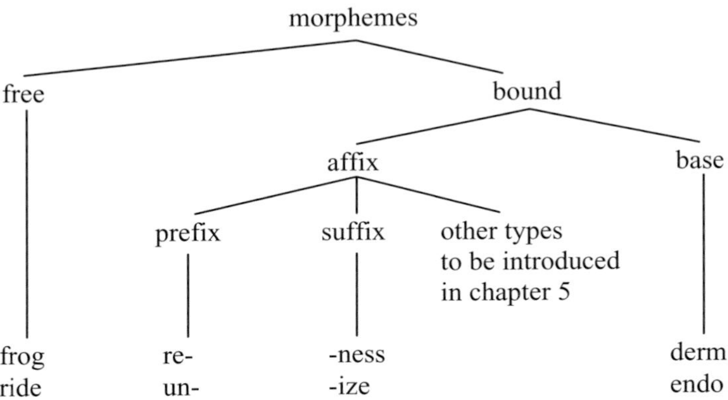

FIGURE 3.1
Types of morphemes

Another reason to believe that bound bases are different from prefixes and suffixes is that prefixes and suffixes tend to occur more freely than bound bases do. For example, any number of adjectives can be made negative by using the prefix *un-*, but there are far fewer words with the bound base *psych(o)*. This is perhaps not the best way of distinguishing between bound bases and affixes, though, as there are a few bound bases – *-ology* is one of them – that occur with great freedom, and there are some prefixes and suffixes that don't occur all that often (e.g. the *-th* in *width* or *health*). So we'll stick with the criterion of 'semantic robustness' for now. We'll return in the next chapter to the question of how freely various morphemes are used in word formation.

With regard to bases, another distinction that's sometimes useful in analyzing languages other than English is the distinction between **root** and **stem**. In languages with more inflection than English, there is often no such thing as a free base: all words need some sort of inflectional ending before they can be used. Or to put it differently, all bases are bound. Consider the data below from Latin:

(2)	*Latin*	*1st sg*	am + o 'I love'	*pl* am + a + mus	'we love'
			dic + o 'I say'	dic + i + mus	'we say'

In the singular, an ending signaling the first person ("I") can sometimes attach to the smallest bound base meaning 'love' or 'say'; this morpheme is the **root**. In the first person plural, and in most other persons and numbers, however, another morpheme must be added before the inflection goes on. This morpheme (an *a* for the verb 'love' and an *i* for the verb 'say') doesn't mean anything, but still must be added before the inflectional ending can be attached. The root plus this extra morpheme is the **stem**. Thought of another way, the stem is usually the base that is left when the inflectional endings are removed. We will look further at roots and stems in chapter 6, when we discuss inflection more fully.

3.3 Affixation

3.3.1 Word formation rules

Let's look more carefully at words derived by affixation. Prefixes and suffixes usually have special requirements for the sorts of bases they can attach to. Some of these requirements concern the phonology (sounds) of their bases, and others concern the semantics (meaning) of their bases – we will return to these shortly – but the most basic requirements are often the syntactic part of speech or **category** of their bases. For example, the suffix *-ness* attaches to nouns, as the examples in (3a) show, but not to verbs or adjectives (3b–c):[3]

(3) a. *-ness* on adjectives: redness, happiness, wholeness, commonness, niceness
b. *-ness* on nouns: *chairness, *ideaness, *giraffeness
c. *-ness* on verbs: *runness, *wiggleness, *yawnness

The prefix *un-* attaches to adjectives (where it means 'not') and to verbs (where it means 'reverse action'), but not to nouns:

(4) a. *un-* on adjectives: unhappy, uncommon, unkind, unserious
b. *un-* on verbs: untie, untwist, undress, unsnap
c. *un-* on nouns: *unchair, *unidea, *ungiraffe

We might begin to build some of the rules that native speakers of English use for making words with *-ness* or *un-* by stating their categorial requirements:

(5) Rule for *-ness* (first version): Attach *-ness* to an adjective.
Rule for *un-* (first version): Attach *un-* to an adjective or to a verb.

Of course, if we want to be as precise as possible about what native speakers know about forming words with these affixes, we should also indicate what category of word results from using these affixes, and what the resulting word means. So a more complete version of our *-ness* and *un-* rules might look like (6):

(6) Rule for *-ness* (second version): *-ness* attaches to adjectives 'X' and produces nouns meaning 'the quality of X'.
Rule for *un-* (second version): *un-* attaches to adjectives meaning 'X' and produces adjectives meaning 'not X'; *un-* attaches to verbs meaning 'X' and produces verbs meaning 'reverse the action X'.

3. Like other linguists, morphologists use the * before a word or sentence to indicate that it's ill-formed or unacceptable.

If we're really trying to model what native speakers of English know about these affixes, we might try to be even more precise. For example, *un-* does not attach to all adjectives or verbs, as you can discover by looking at the next Challenge box.

Challenge

Look at the following words and try to work out more details of the rule for *un-* in English. The (a) list contains some adjectives to which negative *un-* can be attached and others which seem impossible. The (b) list contains some verbs to which reversative *un-* can attach and others which seem impossible. See if you can discern some patterns:

(a) unhappy, *unsad, unlovely, *unugly, unintelligent, *unstupid
(b) untie, unwind, unhinge, unknot, *undance, *unyawn, *unexplode, *unpush

What the (a) examples in the Challenge box seem to show is that the negative prefix *un-* in English prefers to attach to bases that do not themselves have negative connotations. This is not true all of the time – adjectives like *unselfish* or *unhostile* are attested in English – but it's at least a significant tendency. As for the (b) examples, they suggest that the *un-* that attaches to verbs prefers verbal bases that imply some sort of result, and moreover that the result is not permanent. Verbs like *dance, push,* and *yawn* denote actions that have no results, and although *explode* implies a result (that is, something is blown up), it's a result that is permanent. In contrast, a verb like *tie* implies a result (something is in a bow or knot) which is temporary (you can take it apart).

We have just constructed what morphologists call a **word formation rule**, a rule which makes explicit all the categorial, semantic, and phonological information that native speakers know about the kind of base that an affix attaches to and about the kind of word it creates. We might now state the full word formation rules for negative *un-* as in (7):

(7) Rule for negative *un-* (final version): *un-* attaches to adjectives, preferably those with neutral or positive connotations, and creates negative adjectives. It has no phonological restrictions.

Now let's look at two more affixes. In English we can form new verbs by using the suffixes *-ize* or *-ify*. Both of these suffixes attach to either nouns or adjectives, resulting in verbs:

(8) *-ize* on adjectives: civilize, idealize, finalize, romanticize, tranquillize
-ize on nouns: unionize, crystallize, hospitalize, caramelize, animalize
-ify on adjectives: purify, glorify, uglify, moistify, diversify
-ify on nouns: mummify, speechify, classify, brutify, scarify, bourgeoisify

We might state the word formation rules for *-ize* and *-ify* as in (9):

(9) Rule for *-ize* (first version): *-ize* attaches to adjectives or nouns that mean 'X' and produces verbs that mean 'make/put into X'.
Rule for *-ify* (first version): *-ify* attaches to adjectives or nouns that mean 'X' and produces verbs that mean 'make/put into X'.

But again, we can be a bit more precise about these rules. Although *-ize* and *-ify* have almost identical requirements for the category of base they attach to and produce words with roughly the same meaning, they have somewhat different requirements on the phonological form of the stem they attach to. As the examples in (8) show, *-ize* prefers words with two or more syllables where the final syllable doesn't bear primary stress (e.g., ***TRAN**quil*, ***HOS**pital*). The suffix *-ify*, on the other hand, prefers monosyllabic bases (*pure, brute, scar*), although it also attaches to bases that end in a *-y* (*mummy, ugly*) or bases whose final syllables are stressed (*di**VERSE***, *bour**GEOIS***). Since we want to be as precise as possible about our word formation rules for these suffixes, we will state their phonological restrictions along with their categorial needs:

(10) Rule for *-ize* (final version): *-ize* attaches to adjectives or nouns of two or more syllables where the final syllable does not bear primary stress. For a base 'X' it produces verbs that mean 'make/put into X'.

I leave it to you to come up with the final version of the word formation rule for *-ify*.

3.3.2 Word structure

When you divide up a complex word into its morphemes, as in (11), it's easy to get the impression that words are put together like the beads that make up a necklace – one after the other in a line:

(11) unhappiness = un + happy + ness

But morphologists believe that words are more like onions than like necklaces: onions are made up of layers from innermost to outermost. Consider a word like *unhappiness*. We can break this down into its component morphemes *un* + *happy* + *ness*, but given what we learned above about the properties of the prefix *un-* and the suffix *-ness* we know something more about the way in which this word is constructed beyond just its constituent parts. We know that *un-* must first go on the base *happy*. *Happy* is an adjective, and *un-* attaches to adjectives but does not change their category. The suffix *-ness* attaches only to adjectives and makes them into nouns. So if *un-* attaches first to *happy* and *-ness* attaches next, the requirements of both affixes are met. But if we were to do it the other way around, *-ness* would have first created a noun, and then *un-* would be unable to attach. We could represent the order of attachment as if words really were onions, with the base in the innermost layer, and each affix in its own succeeding layer: see figure 3.2.

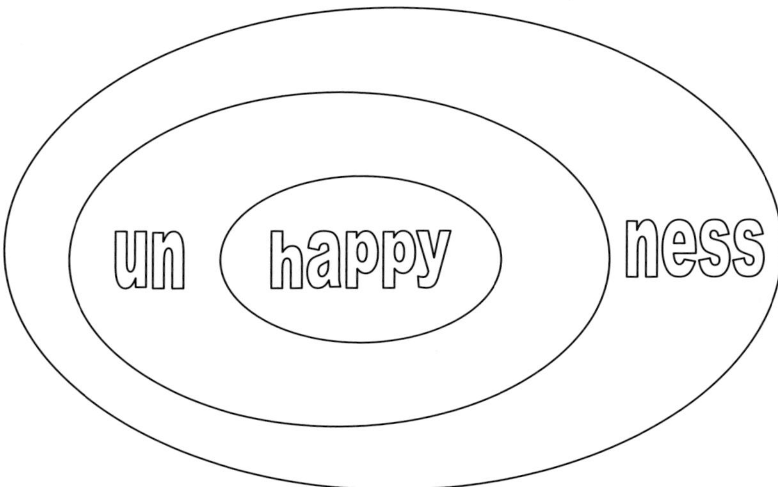

FIGURE 3.2
Words are like onions

But linguists, not generally being particularly artistic, prefer to show these relationships as 'trees' that look like this:

(12)

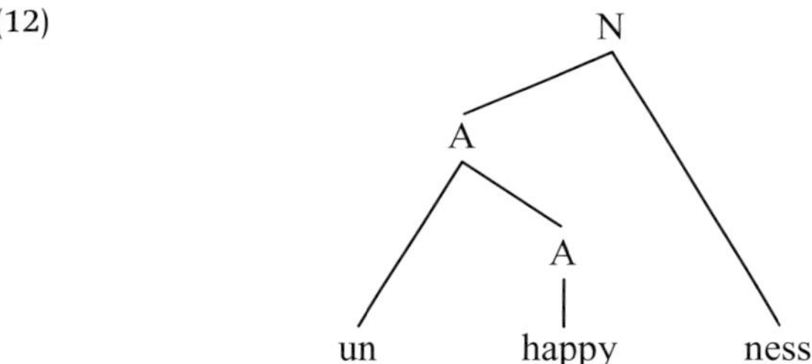

Similarly, we might represent the structure of a word like *repurify* as in (13):

(13)

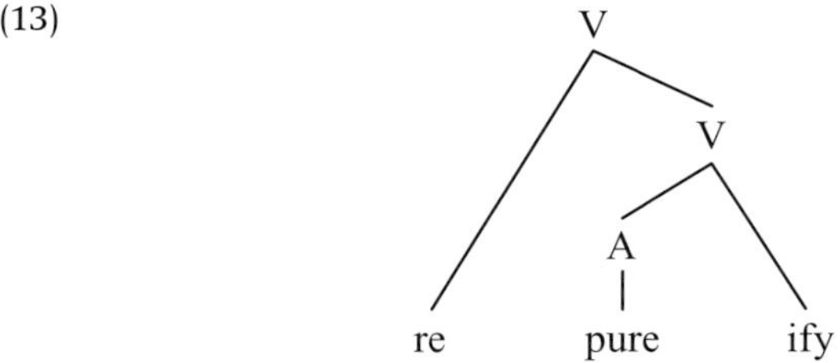

In order to draw this structure, we must first know that the prefix *re-* attaches to verbs (for example, *reheat, rewash*, or *redo*) but not to adjectives (**repure, *rehappy*) or to nouns (**rechair, *retruth*). Once we know this, we can say that the adjective *pure* must first be made into a verb by suffixing *-ify*, and only then can *re-* attach to it.

Challenge

In English, the suffix *-ize* attaches to nouns or adjectives to form verbs. The suffix *-ation* attaches to verbs to form nouns. And the suffix *-al* attaches to nouns to form adjectives. Interestingly, these suffixes can be attached in a recursive fashion: *convene* → *convention* → *conventional* → *conventionalize* → *conventionalization*.

First draw a word tree for *conventionalization*. Then see if you can find other bases on which you can attach these suffixes recursively. What is the most complex word you can create from a single base that still makes sense to you? Are there any limits to the complexity of words derived in this way?

3.3.3 What do affixes mean?

When we made the distinction between affixes and bound bases above, we did so on the basis of a rather vague notion of semantic robustness; bound bases in some sense had more meat to them than affixes did. Let us now attempt to make that idea a bit more precise by looking at typical meanings of affixes.

In some cases, affixes seem to have not much meaning at all. Consider the suffixes in (14):

(14) a. *-(a)tion* examination, taxation, realization, construction
-ment agreement, placement, advancement, postponement
-al refusal, arousal, disposal

b. *-ity* purity, density, diversity, complexity
-ness happiness, thickness, rudeness, sadness

Beyond turning verbs into nouns with meanings like 'process of X-ing' or 'result of X-ing', where X is the meaning of the verb, it's not clear that the suffixes *-(a)tion, -ment*, and *-al* add much of any meaning at all. Similarly with *-ity* and *-ness*, these don't carry much semantic weight of their own, aside from what comes with turning adjectives into nouns that mean something like 'the abstract quality of X', where X is the base adjective. Affixes like these are sometimes called **transpositional** affixes, meaning that their primary function is to change the category of their base without adding any extra meaning.

Contrast these, however, with affixes like those in (15):

(15) a. *-ee* employee, recruitee, deportee, inductee
b. *-less* shoeless, treeless, rainless, supperless
c. *re-* reheat, reread, rewash

These affixes seem to have more semantic meat on their bones, so to speak: *-ee* on a verb indicates a person who undergoes an action; *-less* means something like 'without'; and *re-* means something like 'again'.

Languages frequently have affixes (or other morphological processes, as we'll see in chapter 5) that fall into common semantic categories. Among those categories are:

- **personal affixes:** These are affixes that create 'people nouns' either from verbs or from nouns. Among the personal affixes in English are the suffix *-er* which forms **agent** nouns (the 'doer' of the action) like *writer* or *runner* and the suffix *-ee* which forms **patient** nouns (the person the action is done to).
- **negative** and **privative affixes:** Negative affixes add the meaning 'not' to their base; examples in English are the prefixes *un-*, *in-*, and *non-* (*unhappy, inattentive, non-functional*). Privative affixes mean something like 'without X'; in English, the suffix *-less* (*shoeless, hopeless*) is a privative suffix, and the prefix *de-* has a privative flavor as well (for example, words like *debug* or *debone* mean something like 'cause to be without bugs/bones').
- **prepositional** and **relational affixes:** Prepositional and relational affixes often convey notions of space and/or time. Examples in English might be prefixes like *over-* and *out-* (*overfill, overcoat, outrun, outhouse*).
- **quantitative affixes:** These are affixes that have something to do with amount. In English we have affixes like *-ful* (*handful, helpful*) and *multi-* (*multifaceted*). Another example might be the prefix *re-* that means 'repeated' action (*reread*), which we can consider quantitative if we conceive of a repeated action as being done more than once.
- **evaluative affixes:** Evaluative affixes consist of **diminutives**, affixes that signal a smaller version of the base (for example in English *-let* as in *booklet* or *droplet*) and **augmentatives**, affixes that signal a bigger version of the base. The closest we come to augmentative affixes in English are prefixes like *mega-* (*megastore, megabite*). The Native American language Tuscarora (Iroquoian family) has an augmentative suffix *-ʔoʔy* that can be added to nouns to mean 'a big X'; for example *takó:θ-ʔoʔy* means 'a big cat' (Williams 1976: 233). Diminutives and augmentatives frequently bear other nuances of meaning. For example, diminutives often convey affection, or endearment. Augmentatives sometimes have pejorative overtones.

Note that some semantically contentful affixes change syntactic category as well; for example, the suffixes *-er* and *-ee* change verbs to nouns, and the prefix *de-* changes nouns to verbs. But semantically contentful affixes need not change syntactic category. The suffixes *-hood* and *-dom*, for example, do not (*childhood, kingdom*), and by and large prefixes in English do not change syntactic category.

So far we have been looking at suffixes and prefixes whose meanings seem to be relatively clear. Things are not always so simple, though. Let's look more closely at the suffix *-er* in English, which we said above formed agent nouns. Consider the following words:

(16) a. writer
skater

b. printer
freighter

c. loaner
fryer (i.e., a kind of chicken)

d. diner

All of these words seem to be formed with the same suffix. Look at each group of words and try to characterize what their meanings are. Does *-er* seem to have a consistent meaning?

It's rather hard to see what all of these have in common. The words in (16a) are indeed all agent nouns, but the (b) words are instruments, in other words, things that do an action. In American English the (c) words are things as well, but things that undergo the action rather than doing the action (like the patient *-ee* words discussed above): a *loaner* is something which is loaned (often a car, in the US), and a *fryer* is something (a chicken) which is fried. And the word *diner* in (d) denotes a location (a *diner* in the US is a specific sort of restaurant). Some morphologists would argue that there are four separate suffixes in English, all with the form *-er*. But others think that there's enough similarity among the meanings of *-er* words in all these cases to merit calling *-er* a single affix, but one with a cluster of related meanings. All of the forms derived with *-er* denote concrete nouns, either persons or things, related to their base verbs by participating in the action denoted by the verb, although sometimes in different ways. This cluster of related meanings is called **affixal polysemy**.

Affixal polysemy is not unusual in the languages of the world. For example, it is not unusual for agents and instruments to be designated by the same suffix. This occurs in Dutch, as the examples in (17a) show (Booij and Lieber 2004), but also in Yoruba (Niger-Congo family), as the examples in (17b) show (Pulleyblank 1987: 978):

(17) a. *Dutch*

spel-er	'player'	(*spelen* 'play')
maai-er	'mower'	(*maaien* 'mow')

b. *Yoruba*

a-pànìà	'murderer'	(*pa* 'kill' *ènìà* 'people')
a-bẹ	'razor, penknife'	(*bẹ* 'cut')

The Dutch suffix *-er* is in fact quite similar to the *-er* suffix in English in the range of meanings it can express. The Yoruba prefix *a-* also forms both agents and instruments.

3.3.4 To divide or not to divide?

In chapter 1 we defined a morpheme as the smallest unit of language that has its own meaning. We have now looked at affixes and bases, both free and bound, and considered their meanings and how they combine into complex structures. We assume that affixes have meaning, but sometimes it's not completely clear whether they do. Consider words like *report, import, transport, deport, comport,* and *export*. They certainly seem to be made up of pieces, but is it clear what these pieces mean? In fact, English has dozens of words that are similar to what we might call the *-port* family. See how many cells of table 3.1 you can fill in.

Table 3.1.

	in-	ex-	con-	re-	trans-	de-
-port						
-mit						
-ceive						
-duce						
-cede						
-fer						
-scribe						
-gress						
-sist						

Challenge

Do you think that units like *-port, -mit, -ceive*, and the like should be considered morphemes? If so, what problems do they present for our definition of **morpheme**? If not, what should we do about the intuition that native speakers of English have that such words are complex?

One reason for our dilemma in analyzing these forms is that they are not native to English. They were borrowed from Latin (or from French, which in turn is descended from Latin), where they did have clear meanings: *-port* comes from the verb *portare* 'to carry', *-mit* from the verb *mittere* 'to send', *-scribe* from the verb *scribere* 'to write', and so on. But English speakers (unless they've studied Latin!) don't know this. Morphologists are left with an unsatisfying sense that the words above somehow ought to be treated as complex, but are nevertheless reluctant to give up the strict definition of morpheme.

Similar to these are word-pieces that are sometimes called **cran morphs**, from the word *cranberry*. The second part of the word *cranberry* is clearly a free morpheme. But when we break it off, what's left is a piece that doesn't seem to occur in other words (except in recent years, words like *cranapple* that are part of product names), and doesn't seem to mean anything independently. There are quite a few of these cran morphs in the names of other types of berries: *rasp-* in *raspberry*, *huckle-* in *huckleberry*. In cases such as these we are even more tempted than we were with *-port*, *-ceive*, and the like to divide words into morphemes, even though we know that one part of the word isn't meaningful in the way morphemes usually are.

3.4 Compounding

Derivation is not the only way of forming new words, of course. Many languages also form words by a process called compounding. **Compounds** are words that are composed of two (or more) bases, roots, or stems. In English we generally use free bases to compose compounds, as the examples in (18) show:

(18) *English compounds*
compounds of two nouns: windmill, dog bed, book store
compounds of two adjectives: icy cold, blue-green, red hot
compounds of an adjective and a noun: greenhouse, blackboard, hard hat
compounds of a noun and an adjective: sky blue, cherry red, rock hard

3.4.1 When do we have a compound?

How do we know that a sequence of words is a compound? Surprisingly, it's not that easy to come up with a single criterion that works in all cases. Spelling is no help at all; in English there is no fixed way to spell a compound word. Some, like *greenhouse*, are written as one word, others like *dog bed*, as two words, and still others, like *producer-director* are written with a hyphen between the two bases.

A better criterion is stress; compounds in English are often stressed on their first or left-hand base, whereas phrases typically receive stress on the right. Compare, for example, a ***green**house*, which is the place where plants are grown, to *a green **house***, that is, a house that's painted green. But it's not always the case that compounds are stressed on the left. For example, most people pronounce *apple pie* with stress on the second base, but *apple cake* with stress on the left one. Yet we have the feeling that both are compounds; it seems illogical to consider one a compound and not the other.

There is, however, one test for identifying compounds that is fairly reliable: we can test for whether a sequence of bases is a compound by seeing if a modifying word can be inserted between the two bases and still have the sequence make sense. If a modifying word cannot sensibly be inserted, the sequence of two words is a compound. This test confirms that both *apple pie* and *apple cake* are compounds, in spite of their differing stress. In neither case can we insert a modifier like *delicious* between the two stems; **apple delicious pie* and **apple delicious cake* are equally peculiar!

3.4.2 Compound structure

We can look at compounds as having internal structure in precisely the same way that derived words do, and we can represent that structure in the form of word trees. The compounds *windmill* and *hard hat* would have the structures in (19):

(19)

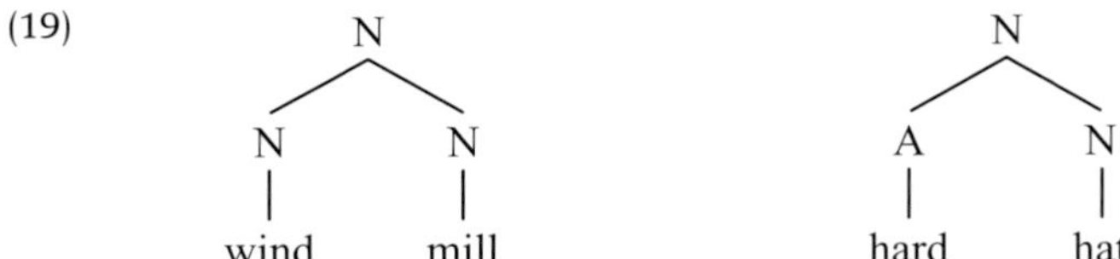

Compounds, of course, need not be limited to two bases. Compounding is what is called a **recursive** process, in the sense that a compound of two bases can be compounded with another base, and this compounded with still another base, so that we can eventually obtain very complex compounds like *paper towel dispenser factory building committee report*. As with derived words, it is possible to show the internal structure of complex compounds using word trees. Assuming that this compound is meant to denote a report from the building committee for the paper towel dispenser factory, we might give it the structure in (20):

(20)

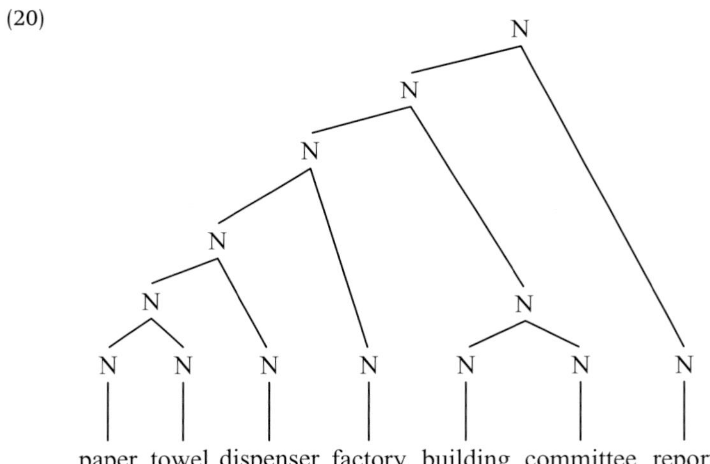

Some compounds can be ambiguous, and therefore can be represented by more than one structure For example, the compound *arctic cat observer*, might have this structure:

(21)

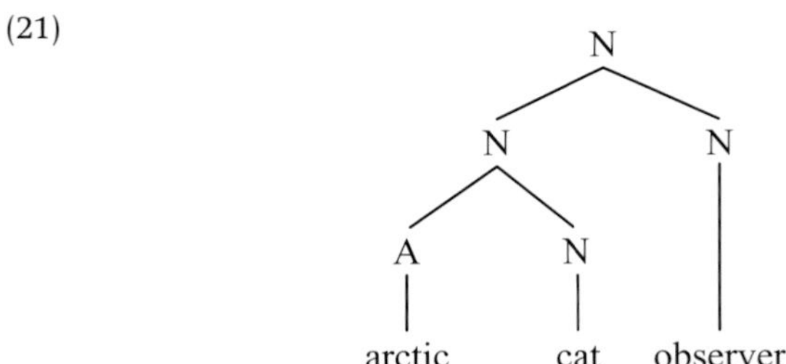

The way we've drawn this tree, the compound *arctic cat* has been compounded with the noun *observer* to make a complex compound. The compound as a whole then must mean 'an observer of arctic cats'. But if the compound *arctic cat observer* were intended to mean 'a cat observer who likes to do her observations in the arctic', the structure of the tree would be that in (22), where *cat observer* is first compounded, and then *arctic* added in:[4]

(22)

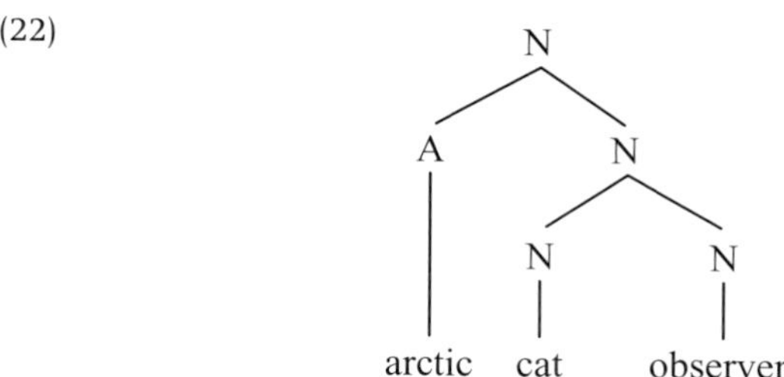

Often, the more complex the compound is, the greater the possibility of multiple interpretations, and therefore multiple structures.

Challenge

The compound *paper towel dispenser factory building committee report* could in fact have more than one meaning. See how many different meanings you can come up with, and draw a tree that corresponds to each of those meanings.

Languages other than English frequently construct compounds on free bases just as English does, although we can see in the French and Vietnamese examples in (23) that the order of elements in the compound is sometimes different from that in English, a fact we will return to in the next section:

(23) a. *French:*
timbre poste 'stamp-post = postage stamp'
chêne liège 'oak cork = cork oak'

b. *Dutch:*
boekhandel 'book shop'
zakgeld 'pocket money'

c. *Vietnamese:*
nhá thuong 'establishment be-wounded' = 'hospital'
nguói ọ̉' 'person be-located' = 'servant'

As we saw above, English has bound bases as well as free bases, and when we put two of them together, as in the examples in (24), we might

4. These two interpretations are sometimes distinguished in spoken speech by placement of stress.

call these forms compounds as well. Some linguists call them **neo-classical compounds**, as the bound bases usually derive from Greek and Latin:

(24) *English compounds on bound bases:* psychopath, pathology, endoderm, dermatitis

In languages like Latin where, as we saw, word formation often operates on roots or stems, rather than on free forms, all compounds are formed from bound bases. Specifically, the first parts of the compounds in (25) are formed from the roots of the nouns *ala* 'wing' and *capra* 'goat', (respectively *al-* and *capr-*) plus a vowel *-i-* linking the two parts of the compound together:

(25) *Latin compounds:*
ali-pes 'wing-footed'
capri-ficus 'goat fig' = 'wild fig'

The *-i-* that occurs between the two roots has no meaning, and is not the vowel that usually precedes the inflections (for these two nouns, that vowel would be *-a*). It is there solely to link the parts of the compound together, and is therefore sometimes called a **linking element** or alternatively an **interfix** (the latter term is less common).

3.4.3 Types of compounds

In English and other languages there may be a number of different ways of classifying compounds. In order to explain the various types of compounds, there is one indispensable term I need to introduce: the **head** of the compound. In compounds, the head is the element that serves to determine both the part of speech and the semantic kind denoted by the compound as a whole. For example, in English the base that determines the part of speech of compounds such as *greenhouse* or *sky blue* is always the second one; the compound *greenhouse* is a noun, as *house* is, and *sky blue* is an adjective as *blue* is. Similarly, the second base determines the semantic category of the compound – in the former case a type of building, and in the latter a color. English compounds are therefore said to be **right-headed**. In other languages, however, for example French and Vietnamese, the head of the compound can be the first or leftmost base. For example a *timbre poste* (23a) is a kind of stamp, and a *nguói ọ̉'* (23c) is a kind of person. French and Vietnamese can therefore be said to have **left-headed** compounds.

One common way of dividing up compounds is into **root** (also known as **primary**) compounds and **synthetic** (also known as **deverbal**) compounds. **Synthetic** compounds are composed of two lexemes, where the head lexeme is derived from a verb, and the nonhead is interpreted as an argument of that verb. *Dog walker, hand washing,* and *home made* are all synthetic compounds. **Root** compounds, in contrast are made up of two lexemes, which may be nouns, adjectives, or verbs; the second lexeme is typically not derived from a verb. The interpretation of the semantic relationship between the head and the nonhead in root compounds is quite free as long as it's not the relationship between a verb and its argument. Compounds like *windmill, ice cold, hard hat,* and *red hot* are root compounds.

We can also classify compounds more closely according to the semantic and grammatical relationships holding between the elements that make them up. One useful classification is that proposed by Bisetto and Scalise (2005), which recognizes three types of relation. The first type is what might be called an **attributive compound**. In an attributive compound the nonhead acts as a modifier of the head. So *snail mail* is (metaphorically) a kind of mail that moves like a snail, and a *windmill* is a kind of mill that is activated by wind. With attributive compounds the first element might express just about any relationship with the head. For example, a *school book* is a book used at school, but a *yearbook* is a record of school activities over a year. And a *notebook* is a book in which one writes notes. With a new compound (one I've just made up) like *mud wheel,* we are free to come up with any reasonable semantic relationship between the two bases, as long as the first modifies the second in some way: a wheel used in the mud, a wheel made out of mud, a wheel covered in mud, and so on. Some interpretations are more plausible than others, of course, but none of these is ruled out.

In **coordinative** compounds, the first element of the compound does not modify the second; instead, the two have equal weight. In English, compounds of this sort can designate something which shares the denotations of both base elements equally, or is a mixture of the two base elements:

(26) *Coordinative compounds:* producer-director, prince consort, blue-green, doctor-patient

A *producer-director* is equally a producer and a director, a *prince consort* at the same time a prince and a consort. In the case of *blue-green* the compound denotes a mixture of the two colors. Finally, there are also coordinative compounds that denote a relation between the two bases (like *doctor–patient* in *doctor–patient confidentiality*). We will return to these below. For coordinative compounds we can say that both elements are semantic heads.

We find a third kind of semantic/grammatical relationship in **subordinative** compounds. In subordinative compounds one element is interpreted as the argument[5] of the other, usually as its object. Typically this happens when one element of the compound either is a verb or is derived from a verb, so the synthetic compounds we looked at above are subordinative compounds in English. Some more examples are given in (27):

(27)	with *-er*	truck driver, hand mixer, lion tamer
	with *-ing*	truck driving, food shopping, hand holding
	with *-ation*	meal preparation, home invasion
	with *-ment*	cost containment

5. We will go into arguments in more depth in chapter 8. For now, it's enough to know that the arguments of the verb are its subject and its complements (direct object, indirect object, and so on).

It is easy to see that subordinative compounds are interpreted in a very specific way: that is, the first element of the compound is interpreted as the object of the verb that forms the base of the deverbal noun: for example, a *truck driver* is someone who *drives trucks*, *food preparation* involves *preparing food*, and so on.

Synthetic compounds are not the only subordinate compounds, however. A second type of subordinate compound is poorly represented in English, but occurs with great frequency in Romance languages like Spanish, French, and Italian:

(28) *English* pickpocket
Italian lava piatti (lit. 'wash dishes' = 'dishwasher')
Spanish saca corcho (lit. 'pull cork' = 'corkscrew')

In these compounds the first element is a verb, and the second bears an argumental relationship to the first element, again typically the complement relationship. We will return to these shortly.

We can further divide attributive, coordinative, and subordinative compounds into **endocentric** or **exocentric** varieties. In endocentric compounds, the referent of the compound is always the same as the referent of its head. So a *windmill* is a kind of mill, and a *truck driver* is a kind of driver. Endocentric compounds of all three types are illustrated in (29):

(29) *Endocentric compounds*
Atrributive: windmill, greenhouse, sky blue, icy cold
Coordinative: producer-director, blue-green
Subordinative: truck driver, meal preparation

The Dutch, French, and Vietnamese compounds in (23) are endocentric, as well, although as we pointed out above, the head occurs on the left in these compounds.

Compounds may be termed **exocentric** when the referent of the compound as a whole is not the referent of the head. For example, the English attributive compounds in (30) all refer to types of people – specifically stupid or disagreeable people – rather than types of heads, brains, or clowns, respectively. So an *air head* is a person with nothing but air in her head, and so on. Again, all three types of compounds may be exocentric:

(30) *Exocentric compounds*
Attributive: air head, meat head, bird brain, ass clown
Coordinative: parent-child, doctor-patient
Subordinative: pickpocket, cutpurse, lava piatti (Italian, lit. 'wash dishes')

In coordinative compounds like *parent-child* or *doctor-patient* the heads refer to types of people, but the compound as a whole denotes a relationship between its elements. We saw examples of exocentric subordinative compounds from English, Spanish, and Italian in (28). English has only a few examples: *a pickpocket* is not a type of pocket, but a sort of person (who picks pockets). Romance languages have many compounds of this type, however.

The different types of compounds are summarized in Figure 3.3.

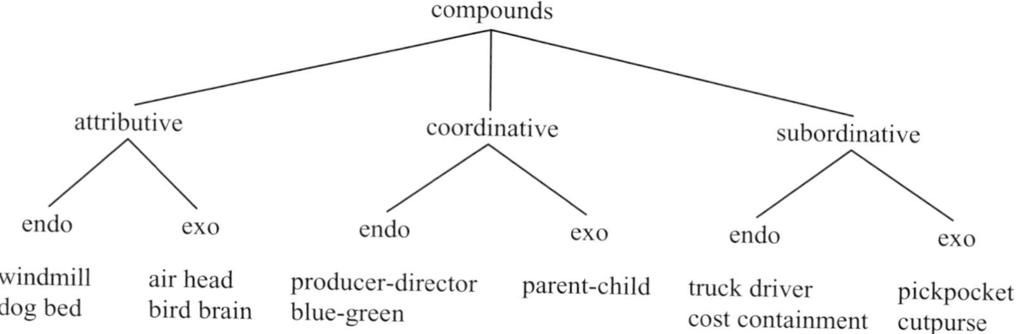

FIGURE 3.3
Types of compounds

3.5 Conversion

Although we often form new lexemes by affixation or compounding, in English it is also possible to form new lexemes merely by shifting the category or part of speech of an already existing lexeme without adding an affix. This means of word formation is often referred to as **conversion** or **functional shift**. In English, we often create new verbs from nouns, as the examples in (31a) show, but we also do the reverse (31b), and sometimes we can even create new verbs from adjectives (31c):

(31) a. table — to table
bread — to bread
fish — to fish

b. to throw — a throw
to kick — a kick
to fix — a (quick) fix

c. cool — to cool
yellow — to yellow

When we create new verbs from nouns, the resulting verbs may have a wide range of meanings. For example, *to bread* is 'to put bread (crumbs) on something', but *to fish* is 'to take fish from a body of water'. And *to clown* is 'to act like a clown' rather than to put a clown somewhere or take a clown from somewhere! Going in the opposite direction, the meaning of the new word is usually more predictable; that is, when we turn a verb into a noun, the result usually means something like 'an instance of

X-ing', where X is the denotation of the verb. So for example, *a throw* is 'an instance of throwing'.

English is, of course, not the only language with conversion. Noun to verb conversion occurs frequently in German and Dutch as well, as the examples in (32a–b) show, and verb to noun conversion is said to occur in French, as the examples in (32c) show:

(32) a. *German*

Antwort	'answer'	antwort-en	'to answer'
Holz	'wood'	holz-en	'to fell, cut wood'
Strick	'cord, string'	strick-en	'to knit'

b. *Dutch*

fiets	'bicycle'	fiets-en	'to bicycle'
hamer	'hammer'	hamer-en	'to hammer'
winkel	'shop'	winkel-en	'to shop'

c. *French*

gard-er	'to guard'	garde	'guard'
visit-er	'to visit'	visite	'visit'

There may appear to be a suffix added in the derivation of the verbs in the examples in (32a–b) and one deleted in (32c). But the *-en* suffix in German and Dutch and the *-er* suffix in French do not derive the verbs *per se* – they are inflectional morphemes that signal the infinitive form of the verb. If we assume that conversion involves only the base or root, these examples count as conversion.

3.5.1 What is conversion?

Morphologists have been divided on how to analyze conversion. Some argue that conversion is just like affixation, except that the affix is phonologically null – that is, it is unpronounced. When analyzed this way, conversion is called zero-affixation. It might be represented structurally as in (33):

(33)

Other morphologists argue that conversion is different from affixation, and treat it simply as change of category with no accompanying change of form, as we have done here. With this analysis, converted verbs like *to chair* would not have any internal structure, but would simply be regarded as having been relisted or recategorized in our mental lexicons. We will not decide between these analyses here.

Challenge

Is it possible in English for already compounded or affixed words to undergo conversion? Try to think of examples of words with prefixes or suffixes or compound words that can function as more than one part of speech (for example, as both nouns and verbs).

3.6 Minor processes

Affixation, compounding, and conversion are the most common ways of forming new words, at least in English (we will see in chapter 5 that there are other means of word formation that languages other than English use). In addition, there are a number of less common ways in which new lexemes may be formed. We provide a survey of them here, without going into great depth on any one of them.

3.6.1 Coinage

It is of course possible to make up entirely new words from whole cloth, a process called coinage. However, we rarely coin completely new words, choosing instead to recycle bases and affixes into new combinations. New products are sometimes given coined names like *Kodak, Xerox*, or *Kleenex*, and these in turn sometimes come to be used as common nouns: *kodak* was at one time used for cameras in general, and *xerox* and *kleenex* are still used respectively for copiers and facial tissue by some American English speakers. But it's relatively rare to coin new words. In hundreds of new words archived on the Word Spy website (www.wordspy.com), I was able to find only the following four apparent coinages:

(34) blivet ‘an intractable problem’
mung ‘to mess up, to change something so that it no longer works’
grok ‘to understand in a deep and exhaustive manner’
(from Robert Heinlein's *Stranger in a Strange Land*)
mongo ‘objects retrieved from the garbage’

Why are there so few coinages? Perhaps because the words themselves give no clue to their meaning. Context often clarifies what a word is intended to mean, but without a context to suggest meaning, the words themselves are semantically opaque. It is no wonder that many of the pure coinages that creep into English come from original product names: the association of the coined word with the product makes its meaning clear, and occasionally the word will then be generalized to any instance of that product, even if manufactured by a different company.

3.6.2 Backformation

Generally, when we derive words we attach affixes to bases; in other words, the base comes before the word derived by affixation. For example, we start with the verb *write* and form the agent noun *writer*. Sometimes, however, there are words that historically existed as monomorphemic bases, but which ended in a sequence of sounds identical to or reminiscent of that of certain affixes. When native speakers come to perceive these words as being complex rather than simple, they create what is called a **backformation**. For example, historically the word *burglar* was monomorphemic. But because its last syllable was phonologically identical to the agentive *-er* suffix, some English speakers have understood it to be based on a verb *to burgle*. Arguably for those speakers, then, *burglar* is no longer a simple word. Similarly, the verb *surveil* has been created from *surveillance* and the verb *liaise* from *liaison*. At least at first, some native speakers will find the backformations odd-sounding or objectionable. In January, 2007 I heard the governor of Iowa, Tom Vilsack, use the verb *incent* on National Public Radio; in context, it clearly was a backformation from the noun *incentive*, and it sounded quite odd at the time. But with time, that feeling of oddness will disappear. Indeed speakers are sometimes surprised to learn that the verb did not exist before the corresponding noun, so ordinary-sounding has the verb come to be. Such is the case for *peddle* and *edit*, both of which are historically backformations from *peddler* and *editor*, respectively.

3.6.3 Blending

Blending is a process of word formation in which parts of lexemes that are not themselves morphemes are combined to form a new lexeme. Familiar examples of **blends** (sometimes also called **portmanteau words**) are words like *brunch*, a combination of *breakfast* and *lunch*, or *smog*, a combination of *smoke* and *fog*. While not one of the major ways of forming new words, blending is used quite a bit in English in advertizing, product-naming, and playful language. The Word Spy website lists these blends:

(35) skitch — 'to propel oneself while on a skateboard or in-line skates by hanging onto a moving vehicle' (combination of *skate* and *hitch*)
spime — 'a theoretical object that can be tracked precisely in space and time over the lifetime of the object' (combination of *space* and *time*)
splog — 'a fake blog' (combination of *spam* and *blog*)
vortal — 'a vertical portal'
bagonize — 'to wait anxiously for one's bag to appear on the carousel at the airport' (combination of *bag* and *agonize*)
Chrismukkah — 'a holiday celebration that combines elements of Christmas and Hanukkah'

Indeed, the sheer number of words of this sort that can be found in the Word Spy archives suggests the vitality of this process. Note that while most of the time the parts that are fused together to form blends are not themselves morphemes, sometimes a whole base or affix will be used; for example, Word Spy also lists the word *celeblog* ('a blog written by a celebrity') which is made up of the chunk *celeb* from *celebrity* and the word *blog*; the latter part has become a free morpheme in English in the last few years.

3.6.4 Acronyms and initialisms

When the first letters of words that make up a name or a phrase are used to create a new word , the results are called **acronyms** or **initialisms**.

In acronyms, the new word is pronounced as a word, rather than as a series of letters. For example, **A**cquired **I**mmune **D**eficiency **S**yndrome gives us *AIDS*, pronounced [eɪdz]. And **s**elf-**c**ontained **u**nderwater **b**reathing **a**pparatus gives us *scuba*. Note in the case of *scuba*, the acronym has become so familiar to English speakers that many do not know that it's an acronym! My favorite current acronym is the *DUMP*, a term universally used in Durham, New Hampshire to refer to a local supermarket with the unwittingly unfortunate name 'the **D**urham **M**arket **P**lace'.

Initialisms are similar to acronyms in that they are composed from the first letters of a phrase, but unlike acronyms, they are pronounced as a series of letters. So most people in the US refer to the **F**ederal **B**ureau of **I**nvestigation as the *FBI* pronounced [ɛf bi ɑɪ]. Other initialisms are *PTA* for Parent Teacher Association, *PR* for either 'public relations' or 'personal record', and *NCAA* for National College Athletic Association.

3.6.5 Clipping

Clipping is a means of creating new words by shortening already existing words. For example, we have *info* created from *information*, *blog* created from *web log*, or *fridge* from *refrigerator*. Universities are fertile grounds for the creation of clippings: students study *psych*, *anthro*, *soc*, and even *ling* with one *prof* or another, and if they're taking a science class, may spend long hours in the *lab*, which might or might not involve running some *stats*. Although clippings are often used in a colloquial rather than a formal register, some have attained more neutral status. The word *lab*, for example, is probably used far more frequently in the US than its longer version *laboratory*. The word *mob* is a seventeenth-century clipping from the Latin term *mobile vulgus* 'the fickle common people'; the Latin phrase has long been forgotten, but the clipping persists as the normal word for an unruly throng of people.

3.7 How to: morphological analysis

So far we have looked mostly at English, where you already have a sense of how to divide words into morphemes. But morphologists are, of course, interested in all sorts of languages, and as this book progresses, you'll see that we devote increasing attention to languages that will likely be unfamiliar to you. You should therefore begin to get a sense of how to figure out how the word formation system of another language works.

How do linguists go about deciding what words are complex in an unfamiliar language, what sorts of processes are involved in creating complex words, and how to analyze individual words? Consider the words in (36), from the language Dyirbal, a language of the Pama-Nyungan family, formerly spoken in Australia, but now, according to Ethnologue, nearly extinct; data from Dixon (1972: 222–33):

(36) a. ɲalŋgaŋunu 'from a boy'
b. yaɽaŋaru 'like a man'
c. gugulaŋaru 'like a platypus'
d. banabaḑun 'proper water'
e. waŋalbaḑun 'proper boomerang'
f. yaɽabaḑun 'proper man'
g. yaɽagabun 'another man'
h. yaɽaḑaran 'two men'
i. baŋguyḑaran 'two frogs'
j. yugubila 'with a stick'
k. waŋalḑaranbila 'with two boomerangs'
l. miḑagabunŋunu 'from another camp'
m. gugulabaḑunŋaru 'like a proper platypus'
n. yaɽagabunḑaran 'two other men'

Just by looking at the Dyirbal words (36a) and (36b) and their glosses, you really can't tell anything. They might be simple or complex, but there's no way of knowing, because there are no parts of the two words that seem to overlap. But as soon as you look at example (36c) and its gloss, you will notice some overlap with (36b). Both examples share the gloss 'like a', and both have some characters at the end that overlap (*aŋaru*). So you might make a tentative hypothesis that these words are complex, and that they can be broken down into two morphemes, *yaɽ* + *aŋaru* and *gugul* + *aŋaru*, respectively. You might also hypothesize that *yaɽ* means 'man', *gugul* means 'platypus', and *aŋaru* means 'like a'. This is a good first guess, but you should always be prepared to revise your analysis as you look at more data.

If you then move on and look at examples (36d–f), you'll notice that they all share part of their meanings ('proper'), and the end of each word has the sequence *baḑun*. It's therefore reasonable to make the hypothesis that *baḑun* means 'proper', and that what's left over means 'water' in (36d), 'boomerang' in (36e), and 'man' in (36f). But now, we need to look back at our analysis of (36b), because our first hypothesis was that *yaɽ* meant 'man', and what's left over in (36f) is not *yaɽ* but *yaɽa*. We therefore need to go back and revise our analysis of examples (36b) and (36c) to be consistent with what we've learned from examples (36d–f). This means that (36b) should be divided into *yaɽa+ŋaru* and (36c) should be divided into *gugula+ŋaru*. What we've discovered so far is summarized in (37):

(37)				
	yaɽa	'man'	ŋaru	'like a'
	gugula	'platypus'	baḑun	'proper'
	bana	'water'	gabun	'another'
	waŋal	'boomerang'	ḑaran	'two'

We can now build on this hypothesis to analyze some more data. One strategy that's often good to use is to look for other words in which you already recognize a piece. Indeed it looks like examples (36g) and (36h) both have the piece yaṛa and a gloss that includes 'man'. If we subtract this piece, we are left with two more bits we can now identify: *gabun* probably means 'another' and *ḍaran* 'two'. This in turn suggests that we can identify the piece *baŋguy* as meaning 'frog'.

At this point, we have a good idea how to analyze examples (36b–i), but we still haven't cracked (36a). Example (36j) is still a problem as well, as so far, it doesn't overlap with any of the other examples. But as soon as we go on to (36k), we start to get a clue, because there are two morphemes that we can now recognize in this word 'boomerang' and 'two', leaving only the final bit *bila* which therefore must mean 'with'. We can now go back to (36j) and determine that *yugu* must mean 'stick'. Example (36l) finally leads us back to example (a): since we can identify a stretch in the middle of (36l) – the morpheme *gabun*, which we decided means 'another'– we can guess that *miḍa* means 'camp' and *ŋunu* means 'from'. Why not the opposite, by the way? The reason is that so far it looks like the more semantically contentful morphemes, like 'man' and 'frog' always come first, and the less contentful come after; we might therefore hypothesize that morphemes like 'from' and 'proper' are suffixes in Dyirbal. And now we can finally go back to example (36a) and decide that the morpheme for 'boy' is *ɲalŋga*. I leave it to you to analyze the last two examples, and check that our analysis so far is right.

I say 'so far' because we have only a tiny bit of data to work with here, and every morphological analysis is provisional on checking it against further data. Sometimes there are loose ends left after we've analyzed our data as much as we can. One loose end you might notice in our Dyirbal analysis is that it looks like there is no morpheme in any of our data that corresponds to a word like *a* in English. It's impossible to know from this little data set whether Dyirbal has anything that corresponds to indefinite articles.

Summary

In this chapter we have looked at a number of ways in which new words may be formed in languages. Affixed words are formed by word formation rules that make explicit the categorial, semantic, and phonological requirements of particular affixes, and specify the categorial, semantic, and phonological properties of the resulting words. Words formed by affixation have internal structure that may be represented in the form of trees. Similarly, compound words – words composed of two or more free morphemes or bound bases – have internal structure that can be represented in trees. Compounds may be attributive, coordinative, or subordinative, and within these categories compounds may be endocentric or exocentric. We have also looked at conversion, a shift in the category of a lexeme with no accompanying change in form. Finally, we have considered a number of forms of word formation – coinage, blending, clipping, backformation, acronyms and initialisms, that play a minor role, at least in English.

Exercises

1. Divide the following words into morphemes and label each morpheme as a *prefix, suffix, free base,* or *bound base.*

   hypoallergenic
   non-morphological
   telephonic
   overcompensation
   reheatability
   monomaniacal

2. On p. 37 we gave the word formation rules for *-ize.* Now consider the words below and discuss what other sorts of restrictions we would have to add to our rules for *-ize.*

   catechize, evangelize, antagonize, metabolize, epitomize

3. Using the data below, try to write a word formation rule for the suffix *-able.* Consider what category it attaches to, and what part of speech the resulting words belong to. Does it seem to have any phonological or semantic restrictions? Then draw the word trees for the words *unwashable* and *rewashable.*

washable	*yawnable
dryable	*arriveable
heatable	*fallable
readable	*blinkable
loveable	
knowable	

4. The word *unwindable* is potentially ambiguous. What are its two possible meanings? Draw two tree structures and show which meaning goes with each structure.
5. The linguist Laurence Horn has argued (2002) that the prefix *un-* really does attach to nouns, contrary to what we said in section 3.2. He has collected such examples as *undeath, uncountry, uncopier, unphilosophy,* and *unpublicity.* Can you think of or find other examples where *un-* has attached to nouns? What do you think these *un*-nouns mean? (You can use a dictionary to help think of examples.)
6. In section 3.3, we discussed the meanings (or lack thereof) of bases like *-ceive, -mit,* and *-port,* but not the meanings of the prefixes with which they combine. Consider the prefixes *re-* and *de-* in words like *report, deport, receive, deceive, remit,* and *demit.* Do these seem to be the same prefixes as the *re-* and *de-* in *rewash, rewind, reload* or *debug, de-ice, derail*? Why or why not?
7. How many meanings can you come up with for the complex compound *miniature poodle groomer manual*? Try to draw the trees that correspond to each meaning you've come up with.
8. Classify the compounds below as either root or synthetic, as attributive, coordinative, or subordinative, and as either endocentric or exocentric. Example: *book shelf* is an endocentric attributive root compound; *truck driver* is an endocentric subordinate synthetic compound.

oil burner
lighthouse
blue blood
hell raiser
scholar athlete
blue-eyed
pickpocket
house-hunting

9. Many languages use compounding as a strategy for forming new words. Consider the data below and try to determine: (a) which element is the head, (b) whether the resulting compounds are endocentric or exocentric.

   a. *Kannada (Dravidian) (Sridhar 1990)*

a: Du-ma:tu	'speak word'	'colloquial speech'
siDi-maddu	'explode chemical'	'explosive (i.e. chemical that explodes)'
maduve a:gu	'marriage become'	'to get married'
santo:Sa paDu	'happiness feel'	'rejoice'
kittaLe haNNu	'orange fruit'	'tangerine'

   b. *Maori (Polynesian) (Bauer 1993)*

ipu para	'container waste'	'rubbish bin'
apuru teepu	'cushion table'	'desk pad'
wai mangu	'water black'	'ink'
whaka-koi pene	'cause.sharp pen'	'pencil sharpener'

10. Consider the following noun/verb conversion pairs in English. In each case decide whether the noun was converted from the verb or *vice versa.* Give arguments based on meaning to support your choices.

bug	to bug
kick	to kick
saddle	to saddle
howl	to howl
yawn	to yawn
book	to book (e.g. a table in a restaurant)

11. Take a look at the words you (and your classmates) have collected so far in your Word Logs. Can you classify them according to the means of word formation used to create them? Does any one means of word formation predominate? If so, think about why this might be.

12. *Data analysis: Samoan (Mosel and Hovdhaugen 1992: 176).* Divide the following words into morphemes and propose a meaning for each morpheme:

fa'aga'o	'to apply grease to'
fa'amāsima	'to salt'
fa'apata	'to butter'
fa'apauta	'to apply power'
fa'asuka	'to sweeten, to apply sugar'
fa'atiapula	'to plant taro-tops'

CHAPTER

4 Productivity and creativity

CHAPTER OUTLINE

KEY TERMS

productivity
transparency
lexicalization
compositional
frequency
creativity

In this chapter you will learn about productivity – the extent to which word formation rules can give rise to new words.

- We will consider what factors contribute to productivity, what restricts the productivity of word formation processes, and how we can measure productivity.
- We will look at how the productivity of a word formation process can change over time.
- And we will consider how speakers of a language can use even unproductive word formation processes to create new words for humorous or playful effects.

4.1 Introduction

Consider the examples in (1):

(1) a. warm — warmth
true — truth

b. modern — modernity
pure — purity

c. happy — happiness
dark — darkness

In each case, we have adjectives and nouns that are derived from them (all cases of transposition, by the way). As a first pass, we might hypothesize the three rules of lexeme formation in (2):

(2) a. Rule for *-th*: *-th* attaches to adjectives, and creates nouns. For a base meaning 'X', the derived noun means 'the state of being X'.

b. Rule for *-ity*: *-ity* attaches to adjectives, and creates nouns. For a base meaning 'X', the derived noun means 'the state of being X'.

c. Rule for *-ness*: *-ness* attaches to adjectives, and creates nouns. For a base meaning 'X', the derived noun means 'the state of being X'.

Now consider the list of adjectives in (3). If you had to make a noun from each of these, which of the three suffixes would you choose (note that you might be able to use more than one in some cases)?

(3) lovely
cool
crude
evil
googleable
rustic
musty
inconsequential
feline
toxic
bovine

Chances are that there are some of these words that you would choose to use *-ity* with (I choose *crude, toxic, googleable, rustic, inconsequential*, maybe *feline*), and others that you would use *-ness* with (for me, *lovely, cool, evil, musty,* probably *bovine*). Your choices might be slightly different from mine, but I'd be willing to predict that you didn't choose to use *-th* with any of these adjectives.

What does this mean? In some cases, we can look at words, decide that they are complex, and isolate particular affixes. But when it comes to using those affixes to create new lexemes, we have the sense that they are no longer part of our active repertoire for forming new words. We have no trouble using other affixes, however, even if we've never seen them on particular bases; for example, you may never have seen a noun form of the word *bovine*, but you have no trouble forming the word *bovineness* (or maybe *bovinity*, or maybe even both). Processes of lexeme formation that can be used by native speakers to form new lexemes are called **productive**. Those that can no longer be used by native speakers, are **unproductive**; so although we might recognize the *-th* in *warmth* as a suffix, we never make use of it in making new words. The suffixes *-ity* and *-ness*, on the other hand, can still be used, although perhaps not to the same degree. Most morphologists agree that productivity is not an all-or-nothing matter. Some processes of lexeme formation, like affixation of *-th*, are truly unproductive, but for those processes that are productive, we have the sense that some are more productive than others. In this chapter we will explore in some detail what we mean by productivity, and look at a number of factors that contribute to productivity. We will also look at several ways in which productivity can be measured.

4.2 Factors contributing to productivity

A number of factors contribute to the degree to which we can use morphological processes to create new lexemes (see figure 4.1).

One factor is what is called transparency. Words formed with **transparent processes** can be easily segmented, such that there is a one-to-one correspondence between form and meaning. In other words, when we

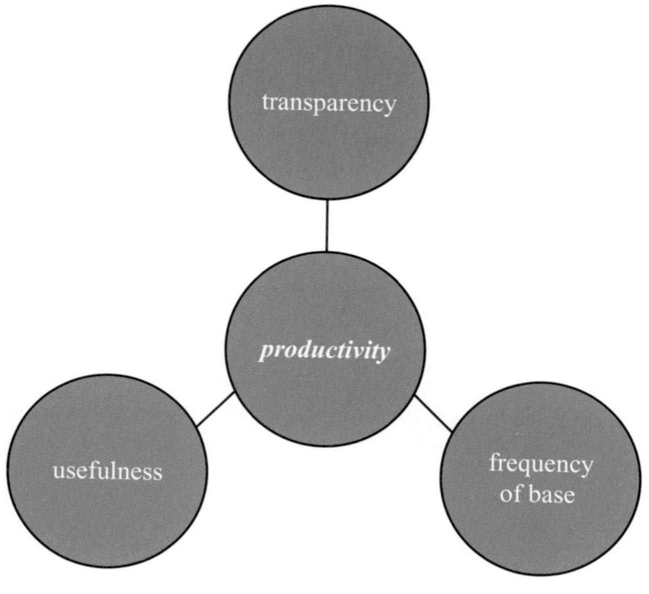

FIGURE 4.1
Factors contributing to productivity

attach an affix to a base, the phonological form (the pronunciation) of both morphemes stays the same, and the meaning of the derived word is exactly what we would expect by adding the meaning of the affix to that of the base. Let's look further at the case of *-ness* and *-ity*, this time considering the additional examples in (4):

(4)	a. candid	candidness
	pink	pinkness
	hardy	hardiness
	common	commonness
	ticklish	ticklishness
	cunning	cunningness
	horrible	horribleness
	pure	pureness
	odd	oddness
	b. crude	crudity
	odd	oddity
	pure	purity
	dense	density
	rustic	rusticity
	timid	timidity
	grammatical	grammaticality
	local	locality
	available	availability
	senile	senility

In all the *-ness* examples in (4a), it is easy to divide the complex words into base and suffix. The base is always pronounced in the derived word as it is in isolation. And the suffix always creates a noun meaning 'state of being "adjective"', whatever the adjective. Words formed with *-ness* are perfectly transparent. The suffix *-ity* is somewhat less transparent. Although you don't see this when words are written in English orthography, when you pronounce them, you see that *-ity* often has the effect of changing the phonological form of its base – sometimes its stress pattern, and sometimes both stress and phonological segments in the base. So *timid* in isolation is pronounced with stress on the first syllable (**TI**mid), but when *-ity* is added, stress shifts to its second syllable (ti**MID**ity). And with the base *rustic*, in addition to a shift in stress from first to second syllable, the final [k] of the base becomes [s] when *-ity* is added. Further, some of the words formed with *-ity* have meanings that cannot be arrived at by combining the meaning of the base with that of the suffix. An *oddity*, for example, is not merely 'the state of being odd' (we would probably prefer the word *oddness* for that meaning), but a person or thing that is odd. And a *locality* is not 'the state of being local', but a place or area. Finally, consider the examples in (5):

(5) verity
dexterity
authority

In the first two examples, *-ity* occurs on bound bases *ver, dexter*. In the third, it's not clear exactly how to analyze the derived word. Although it appears to be a combination of *author* and *-ity*, there are two problems with this analysis. First, as a free base *author* is a noun, and *-ity* typically attaches to adjectives, rather than nouns. And second, it's not clear what the independent meaning of the base is; certainly the meaning 'professional writer' does not seem to be part of the meaning of *authority*. We never find *-ness*, however, on bound bases, nor do we find it on bases that are not adjectives. All of this adds up to a conclusion that the suffixation of *-ness* is a much more transparent process than the suffixation of *-ity*, and this in turn suggests that *-ness* is a more productive affix than *-ity*.

Hand in hand with the notion of transparency comes the related notion of lexicalization. When derived words take on meanings that are not transparent – that cannot be made up of the sum of their parts – we say that the meaning of the word has become **lexicalized**. Meanings of complex words that are predictable as the sum of their parts are said to be compositional. Lexicalized words have meanings that are **non-compositional**. So the words *oddity* and *locality* that we looked at above have developed lexicalized or non-compositional meanings. Sometimes the meanings of derived words have drifted so far from their compositional meanings that it's quite difficult to imagine the compositional meaning for them. Consider, for example, the word *transmission*, which denotes a part of a car. It takes a bit of thought to realize that the car part in question is so-called because it transmits power from the engine to the wheels.

Transparency is not the only factor that contributes to productivity. Another factor that is important is what we might call frequency **of base type**. By this, I mean the number of different bases that might be available for affixes to attach to, thus resulting in new words. If an affix attaches only to a limited range of bases, it has less possibility of giving rise to lots of new words, and it will therefore be less productive. Consider, for example, the suffix *-esque* in English, which means something like 'having the style of' (Marchand 1969: 286). It attaches to nouns, but mostly to concrete ones (*statuesque*), and in fact, most often to proper names (*Kafkaesque, Reaganesque*). Indeed, although it attaches pretty freely to names, it seems most comfortable on names that have at least two syllables (*?Bushesque, ?Blairesque*). Compared to a suffix that could attach to any noun at all, *-esque* would be less productive.

The final factor that contributes to productivity is what we might call **usefulness**. A process of lexeme formation is useful to the extent that speakers of a language need new words of a particular sort. It's always useful, for example, to be able to form a noun meaning 'the state of being X' from an adjective, whatever X means, so both *-ness* and *-ity* are highly useful affixes. On the other hand, consider the suffix *-ess* in English. It used to be useful to be able to coin words referring to jobs performed by women or positions held by women (*stewardess, murderess, authoress*). But with the rise of feminism and efforts to promote gender-neutral language, such words have fallen into disuse, and the need for new words using this suffix has almost died out. Consequently the affix has become far less productive, perhaps completely unproductive.

4.3 Restrictions on productivity

As we saw above, the more limitations there are on the bases available to a lexeme formation process, the less productive it will be. In this section, we will explore different kinds of restrictions that may apply to lexeme formation processes.

We have actually looked at some such restrictions in chapter 3 (section 3.2), when we learned how to write lexeme formation rules. We learned that there could be different sorts of restrictions on what sorts of base an affix might attach to, including:

- *categorial restrictions:* Almost all affixes are restricted to bases of specific categories. For example, *-ity* and *-ness* attach to adjectives, *-ize* attaches to nouns and adjectives, or *un-* attaches to adjectives or verbs.
- *phonological restrictions:* Sometimes affixes will attach only to bases that fit certain phonological patterns. For example, *-ize* prefers nouns and adjectives that consist of two or more syllables, where the final syllable does not bear primary stress. The suffix *-en,* which forms verbs from adjectives, attaches only to bases that end in obstruents (stops, fricatives, and affricates). So we can get *darken, brighten,* and *deafen* but **slimmen* and **tallen,* which end in sonorant consonants, are impossible.
- *the meaning of the base:* For example, negative *un-* prefers bases that are not themselves negative in meaning. We find *unlovely* but not **unugly, unhappy* but not **unsad.*

To these sorts of restrictions we might add:

- *etymological restrictions:* Some affixes are restricted to particular subclasses of bases. For example, there are affixes in English that prefer to attach to bases that are native – for example the suffix *-en* that forms adjectives from nouns (*wooden, waxen* but not **metalen* or **carbonen*). On the other hand, another suffix *-ic* that forms adjectives from nouns (*parasitic, dramatic*) will not attach to native bases, only to bases that are borrowed into English from French or Latin.
- *syntactic restrictions:* Sometimes affixes are sensitive to syntactic properties of their bases. For example, the suffix *-able* generally attaches to transitive verbs, specifically verbs that can be passivized. So from the transitive verb *love* we can get *loveable,* but from the intransitive verb *snore* there is no **snorable.*
- *pragmatic restrictions:* Bauer (2001: 135) gives the following example. In Dyirbal, there is a suffix *-ginay* that means 'covered with'. Although there might conceivably be a use for a word meaning something like

'covered with honey', in fact, the suffix occurs in Dyirbal only on bases that denote things that are "dirty or unpleasant" (Dixon 1972: 223), like *gunaginay*, which means 'covered with feces'. What's considered dirty or unpleasant might to some extent be a function of cultural beliefs.

We might expect there to be an inverse correlation between the number of restrictions and the productivity of a lexeme formation process: the more restrictions apply, the fewer bases it will have available to it, and the fewer words it will be able to derive.

The restrictions above pertain to inputs to lexeme formation rules. But it's also possible for there to be restrictions specifically on the output of rules. For example, certain sorts of complex words can be restricted in register. Baayen (1989: 24–5) notes that the suffix *-erd* in Dutch forms "jocular and often slightly pejorative personal names." For example, from the adjective *bang* 'afraid' we get *bangerd* 'fraidy-cat' and from *dik* 'fat' we get *dikkerd* 'fatty'. Baayen points out that although there are a lot of adjectives that might give rise to pejorative names for people, words formed with the suffix are confined to use in spoken, as opposed to written, language and therefore the output of this lexeme formation process is restricted.

4.4 How to: finding words

Thinking about productivity requires us to look not just at a few examples of words that have a particular prefix or suffix, but at lots and lots of examples. You might wonder how morphologists go about finding all the words with one affix or another. For prefixes, of course, we can look in a dictionary and find words formed with that prefix alphabetized more or less together. I say "more or less" because sometimes non-prefixed words will intervene alphabetically between forms with a prefix (for example, *prelude* intervenes between *preloved* and *premarital* in the *Concise Oxford English Dictionary*). But in a normal dictionary, words with suffixes are alphabetized according to their bases. Nevertheless, there are at least two ways of finding all the words with a particular suffix.

The first is to look in a backwards word list like Lehnert (1971). A backwards word list gives words alphabetized starting with the last letter, rather than the first. So all the words with *-ity* or *-ness* can be found together. A few of the *-ity* words to be found in Lehnert (1971: 584) are shown in the sidebar. You'll notice that using a backwards word list is not a perfect tool: such word lists simply alphabetize words from the end to the beginning, so any word ending in *-ity* will occur in the list, not just words that really have the suffix *-ity*. In the list I give here, in addition to real *-ity* words like *oddity* and *rancidity*, we find 'junk' like *rumti-iddity* (spelled two different ways!); a bit earlier in the list we would have found the word *city* which of course also ends in the sequence of letters *ity*. In the list here, we also find the word *acidity*, plus four other derivatives of it (*subacidity, nonacidity, hypoacidity, hyperacidity*). So if you work with a backwards word list, be prepared to go through it word by word and check whether you really have an example

paucity
raucity
caducity
rumti-iddity
rumpt-iddity
quiddity
oddity
heredity
rabidity
morbidity
turbidity
acidity
subacidity
placidity
nonacidity
hypoacidity
hyperacidity
flaccidity
rancidity
viscidity
lucidity

of the suffix you're looking for, and whether you really just have one example, as opposed to several derivatives of the same word.

It is also possible to find words with a particular suffix by using the OED On line. To do so, instead of typing a whole word in the Find Word box, type the suffix preceded by *. The asterisk is what's called a 'Wild Card'. It stands for any characters that precede the ones that you're looking for. Again, you'll get a long list which contains many words with the suffix in question, plus a lot of 'junk'. As with the backwards word list, you'll need to be prepared to go through by hand and weed out those examples that don't really contain the suffix you're interested in.

4.5 Ways of measuring productivity

We have seen that the productivity of lexeme formation processes depends on a variety of factors, including restrictions on possible bases, usefulness of the words formed, and the transparency of the process. Looking at these factors can give us some sense of how productive a process might be, but can we do better and actually measure productivity? Is it possible to compare the productivity of different processes? If so, how might we go about making such measurements?

Challenge

One conceivable way of measuring the productivity of a lexeme formation process might be to count up all the items formed with that process that can be found in a good dictionary. Most morphologists think that this is not a good way of measuring productivity. Think of as many reasons as you can why they should think so.

It's not hard to think of reasons why counting items in a dictionary wouldn't be an accurate way of estimating productivity. For one thing, counting items that are already in the dictionary doesn't really tell us anything about how many new words might be created with a lexeme formation process, and it's the possibility of creating new forms that's most important in making processes productive. Further, the most productive of lexeme formation processes are ones that are phonologically and semantically transparent. If the words resulting from these processes are perfectly transparent in meaning, then it's unlikely that dictionaries will need to record them! On the other hand, less productive processes, as we've seen, frequently have outputs that are less transparent (more lexicalized), and therefore have more need to be listed in the dictionary. So simple counting might give a paradoxical result: less productive processes would be represented by more entries in the dictionary than more productive processes!

Morphologists have therefore tried hard to come up with other ways of measuring productivity. One suggestion (Aronoff 1976) was to make a ratio of the number of actual words formed with an affix to the number of bases to which that affix could potentially attach.

Challenge

Consider the suffix *-esque* that we mentioned in section 4.2 above. The *Oxford English Dictionary* lists approximately 220 words with this suffix. Can you come up with a ratio that would estimate the productivity of *-esque* using Aronoff's measure? Why not?

Most morphologists see several problems with Aronoff's way of measuring productivity. First, all of the problems we mentioned above with counting items in a dictionary (or corpus) apply to this measure as well. In addition, it's not clear that we can ever know for sure how many potential bases there are for a given lexeme formation process. If *-esque* can attach to any name (or at least to any name with two or more syllables), how would we ever know that we'd amassed all possible names?

A somewhat more sophisticated – but still not perfect – measure of productivity proposed by Baayen (1989) capitalizes on what we know about the **token frequency** of derived words. Remember from chapter 1 the distinction between types and tokens: if we're counting types in a corpus or language sample we look for each different word and count it once, no matter how many times it appears, but if we're looking at tokens we count up all the separate occurrences of that word in a particular corpus. The number of separate occurrences of a word in the corpus is the **token frequency** of that word.

An important observation that has been made about lexeme formation processes is that the less productive they are, the less transparent the words formed by those processes, and the less transparent the words, the higher their mean token frequency in a corpus. In other words, words formed with less productive suffixes are often more lexicalized in meaning and will often display many tokens in a corpus. The more productive a process is, the more new words it will give rise to and the more chance that these items will occur in a corpus with a very low token frequency, sometimes only once. One way of measuring the productivity of specific lexeme formation processes is to capitalize on this observation. To do so, we take a corpus, count up all tokens of all words formed with a particular affix, and then see how many of those words occur only once in the corpus (a type with token frequency of one in a corpus is called a **hapax legomenon** or sometimes just a **hapax**). The ratio of hapaxes to all tokens tells us something about productivity. Using this measure confirms, for example, our intuition that *-ness* is more productive that *-ity* (Baayen and Lieber 1991).

4.6 Historical changes in productivity

It should not come as a surprise at this point that lexeme formation processes may change their degree of productivity over time. Consider, for example, the suffix *-dom* in English, which attaches (mostly) to nouns and forms nouns. We find it in such words as *chiefdom, fandom,* and *stardom*. Not too much work has been done on methods of measuring productivity over time, but here is one very rough idea of how to do it. With some care, it's possible to find all the words in the OED with the suffix *-dom* and take note of when they were first cited (in other words, the year of the first quotation the OED gives for their use). We can then count up how many *-dom* words were first cited in each century. If we also know how many citations there are in the OED for each century (not every century has the same number of citations), we can calculate what percentage of them are first citations with *-dom*. For example, if the OED gives 28,698 citations dating from the thirteenth century, and seven of them are the first citations of words with *-dom*, then the *-dom* citations represent 0.0243% of all the citations. I've calculated these percentages for each century, and then plotted them on a graph, as you can see in figure 4.2.

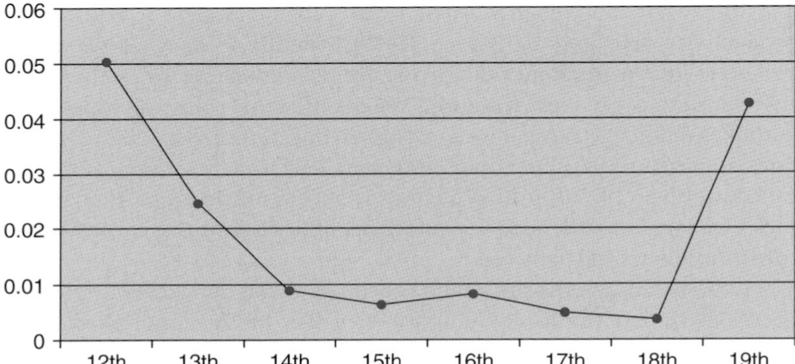

FIGURE 4.2 Comparative percentages of first citations of *-dom* per century

The suffix *-dom* is a very old one, going back to the beginnings of English, and indeed further back into the Germanic branch of the Indo-European family, from which English descends.[1] We can see that after an initially very productive period in the twelfth century, *-dom* seems to have dropped off in productivity from the fourteenth through the eighteenth centuries. But its productivity rises again precipitously in the nineteenth century. In fact, we can see from figure 4.3 that if we look in detail at the percentage of first citations per decade in the nineteenth century, the suffix gained steadily in productivity as the century progressed (with an odd blip in the 1870s), and peaked in the 1880s.

Exactly why the productivity of the suffix should start to rise after centuries of minimal productivity is unclear. Wentworth (1941) notices the same trend that I've shown here, and points out that particular

1. Figure 4.2 starts with the twelfth century because that is the first century for which we have the number of citations in the OED. Many thanks to Charlotte Brewer of Oxford University for sharing these data with me.

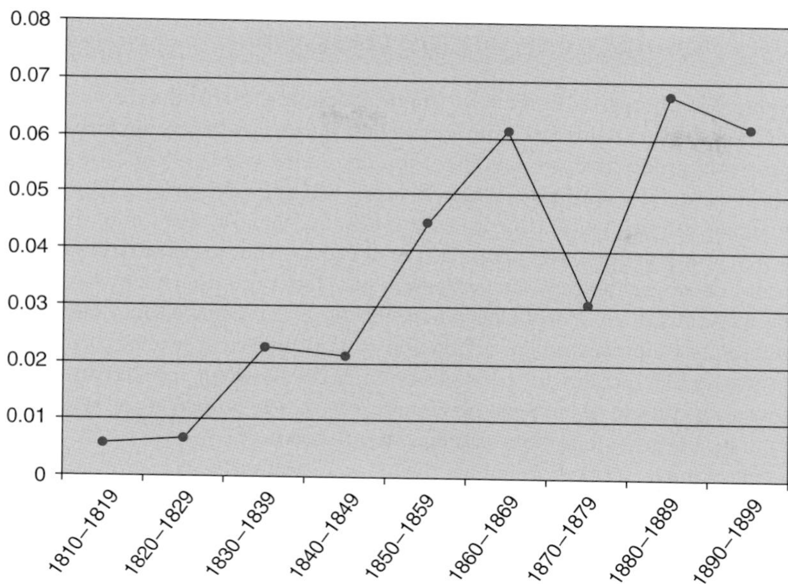

FIGURE 4.3 Comparative percentages of first citations of words with *-dom* per decade in the nineteenth century

nineteenth-century authors seem especially prone to coin new words with the suffix: Thomas Carlyle and William Makepeace Thackeray in Britain, Mark Twain and Sinclair Lewis in the United States. But whether they are the cause of the rise or a reflection of something that was happening in the language at large is impossible to say. Bauer (2001) points out that in the nineteenth century, the kind of bases available to the suffix *-dom* seemed to expand drastically. Where it was confined for many centuries to bases referring to important types of people (*lord, king, master, pope, earl,* but also *martyr* and *witch*) or a few adjectives (*wise, rich, free*), in the nineteenth century it began to appear with more frequency on names for animals (*puppy, dog, butterfly, centaur*) and a wide variety of common nouns (*school, twaddle, leaf, magazine, jelly, cotton, fossil*). But why, exactly, its range of bases expanded at this point is still a mystery.

By the way, when he wrote in the early 1940s Wentworth was convinced that the productivity of *-dom* did not drop from the turn of the twentieth century on, as figure 4.3 suggests: in addition to scrutinizing the OED, as I have done here, he checked through other dictionaries and collected his own examples, and his study turned up quite a few words. Still, the OED has not added a huge number of examples since Wentworth wrote his article, and it appears that although *-dom* is still quite productive, it does not now enjoy the enormous popularity it did during the 1880s.

This is just one suffix in just one language, but we would expect that other word formation processes could be tracked in a similar way, showing the different processes most active in a language at any given time.

4.7 Productivity *versus* creativity

Some morphologists make a distinction between morphological productivity and morphological creativity. When processes of lexeme formation are truly productive, we use them to create new words without noticing that we do so. Similarly, when hearers are exposed to a productively formed complex word, they understand it, but usually don't note that it's a new word (at least for them). This is not to say that speakers and hearers *never* notice productively formed new words, just that often such words slip by without notice. Morphological creativity, in contrast, is the domain of unproductive processes like suffixation of *-th* or marginal lexeme formation processes like blending or backformation. It occurs when speakers use such processes consciously to form new words, often to be humorous or playful or to draw attention to those words for other reasons.

For example, speakers might use the unproductive suffix *-th* to form an adjective like *coolth* (in contrast to *warmth*), consciously trying to be clever or witty. Another example might be the suffix *-some* that occurs in English in words like *twosome, threesome,* and *foursome*. Theoretically this suffix might be infinitely productive because its bases are cardinal numbers. But it's really only attached to the numbers *two* through *four* or *five*. We would probably only coin a new word like *seventeensome* if we were trying to be funny. Such a use would be creative, rather than productive use of this lexeme formation process.

Let's now look more closely at the case of blending in English. **Blending**, as we saw in Chapter 3, is the creation of new words by putting together parts of words that are not themselves morphemes. Relatively few blended words have become lexicalized words in English (*brunch, smog*), but the technique is frequently used for coining words by advertizers and the media, precisely because such words are noticeable. McDonald's, for example, creates a word like *menunaire* from *menu* and *millionaire* to catch your eye (or ear), and make you pay attention to their pitch.

Websites that track new words often have a disproportionate number of blends, and most of those words are culled from the popular press. For example, in the new words posted on the Word Spy website (www.wordspy.com) from May 28 to July 10, 2007, there were six blends:

(6) locavore — blend of *local* and *herbi-/carnivore* 'someone who likes to eat locally produced food'
carbage — blend of *car* and *garbage* 'the trash that accumulates in one's car'
blogebrity — blend of *blog* and *celebrity* 'a famous blogger'
boyzilian — blend of *boy* and *Brazilian* 'a kind of bikini wax for men'
gorno — blend of *gore* and *porno* 'extremely violent movie'
exergaming — blend of *exercise* and *gaming* 'activity combining exercise and gaming'

All six of these words were found in popular media – newspapers such as *Newsday* and *The Plain Dealer*, wire services (Associated Press), or magazines

(*The Economist*). All were intended to catch the reader's eye and therefore make for lively reading, and we might deem them successful because they found their way to Word Spy. In contrast, websites like Word Spy don't pick up other new words with *-ness*. Word-spotters are far less likely to notice new forms that come from truly productive lexeme formation processes than new blends or the sporadic creative coinages that still come from unproductive processes.

As Bauer (2001) points out, however, it is not always possible to draw a sharp line between productivity and creativity. Take the diminutive suffix *-let* in English (*booklet, wavelet, eyelet*). A look at the *Oxford English Dictionary* suggests that this suffix enjoyed a vogue in the nineteenth century (over 200 first attestations in this century), but declined markedly in its productivity in the twentieth century (only 21 first attestations). Although these numbers may be a function of the current state of the dictionary – the third edition, which is likely to add new forms, is as yet incomplete – the numbers are still suggestive.[2] The apparent marked decline in productivity may account for my sense that when a new form with *-let* is coined, it often sounds self-conscious. For example, in my household a very small poodle is referred to as a *poodlet* and a very small beagle as a *beaglet*; these forms are meant to be amusing, and I doubt that they would slip through unnoticed by anyone who heard us using them. Similarly, in a biography of Julia Child (great TV chef and cookbook author), her husband is quoted as referring to her as his *wifelet* – surely meant to be funny, as Julia was over six feet tall![3] If I'm right about this, this suffix may have slipped below the line of productivity, with new forms being marginal, and therefore perceived as creative.

Summary

In this chapter we have explored the notion of productivity – the extent to which lexeme formation processes can be used to create new words. We have seen that several factors contribute to productivity: the phonological and semantic transparency of the process, the size of the pool of bases it can apply to, and its usefulness. We have seen as well that there can be different sorts of restrictions on lexeme formation processes that result in a decrease in productivity. Among these are categorial, phonological, semantic, syntactic, etymological, and pragmatic restrictions. We have looked as well at ways in which we can measure productivity. Finally, we have seen that even unproductive and marginal processes can still give rise to occasional new formations, a phenomenon that we called creativity.

2. A check of the all the newly added entries from 2000–2007 shows no new forms with the suffix *-let*.
3. Laura Shapiro, *Julia Child*. Viking, 2007.

Exercises

1. Which of the following derived words with the suffix *-ity* have lexicalized (non-compositional) meanings. Hint: some have both. Fill in the grid below:

	Compositional? Yes/No	*Compositional meaning*	*Non-compositional meaning*
a. curiosity			
b. solidity			
c. publicity			
d. sexuality			
e. visibility			
f. facility			

2. Consider the examples in (a)–(c) below. Each set involves a lexeme formation process that takes nouns as base and produces adjectives. On the basis of these examples, compare the three lexeme formation processes in terms of their transparency. Remember that transparency involves both compositionality of meaning and the phonological stability of the base (that is, the base is pronounced the same way in isolation and in the derived word):

   a. *-ish* girlish
   kittenish
   sheepish
   loutish
   babyish

   b. *-ic* cyclic
   metallic
   economic
   totemic
   organic

   c. *-al* herbal
   global
   homicidal
   glacial
   clinical

3. In this chapter, we have looked exclusively at productivity as it concerns derivational processes. We can, however, also compare the productivity of various types of compounding. English has compounds that consist of two nouns (*dog bed, windmill*), two adjectives (*bittersweet, blue-green*), and two verbs (*blow dry, stir fry*). Are all three types of compounding equally productive? (Hint: one way to start is by thinking of examples of NN, AA, and VV, and seeing which type gives you the most difficulty.) Give as much evidence as you can for your answer.

4. Look at the words you've collected in your Word Log. How many of them are formed with affixes? Which affixes? How many are formed by compounding or conversion? What does this tell you about the productivity of various processes in present-day English?
5. The graph in figure 4.4 shows percentages of first citations in the OED with the suffixes *-esque, -ship, -let,* and *-hood.* Make some observations on the patterns that you observe in the graph. How good a view of the comparative productivity of these suffixes do you think this chart gives? Take into consideration what we have said in this chapter about basing estimates of productivity on material in a dictionary.

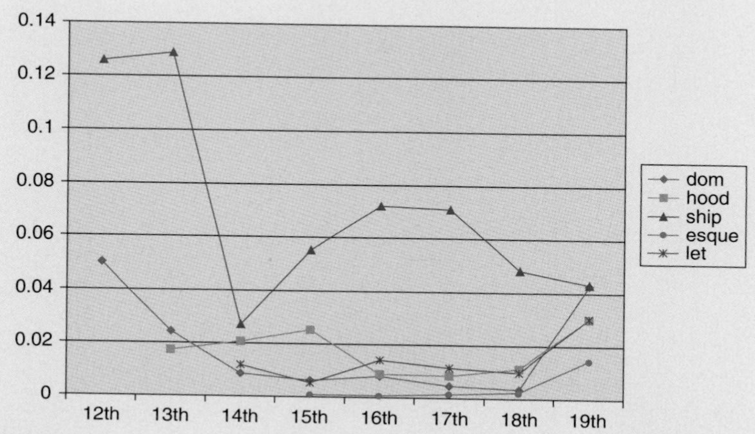

FIGURE 4.4
Percentages of first citations in the OED of suffixes *-dom, -esque, -ship, -let, -hood.*

6. Using the OED On-line, do a Wild Card search for words ending in the suffix *-eer* (as in *charioteer* or *mountaineer*). Look at the first 50 hits and divide them into two lists, one of words that you think really have the suffix *-eer*, and another of 'junk'. Then try to formulate a word formation rule for *-eer* on the basis of the examples you've gathered.

CHAPTER

5 Lexeme formation: further afield

CHAPTER OUTLINE

KEY TERMS

infix
circumfix
internal stem change
ablaut
consonant mutation
templatic morphology
reduplication

In this chapter you will learn about kinds of affixes other than prefixes and suffixes, including infixes and circumfixes.

- We will look at kinds of word formation that may be new to you: ablaut, umlaut, and consonant mutation, reduplication, and templatic morphology.
- And you will get further practice in morphological analysis.

5.1 Introduction

Take a look at the data in (1):

(1) a. *Tagalog (Schachter and Otanes 1972: 356)*

ganda	'beauty'	gumanda	'become beautiful'
hirap	'difficulty'	humirap	'become difficult'

b. *Manchu (Haenisch 1961: 34)*

haha	'man'	hehe	'woman'
ama	'father'	eme	'mother'
amila	'cock'	emile	'hen'

c. *Samoan (Mosel and Hovdhaugen 1992: 227)*

a'a	'kick'	a'aa'a	'kick repeatedly'
'etu	'limp'	'etu'etu	'limp repeatedly'
fo'i	'return'	fo'ifo'i	'keep going back'

These examples should look quite different from the kinds of morphology that we've concentrated on so far: prefixation, suffixation, compounding, and conversion. In (1a), it looks like a morpheme has been inserted right into a base to form a verb. In (1b), vowels have changed to form the female correlates of male nouns, and in (1c), segments of the base are repeated to form what's called the frequentative form of the verb (for a verb meaning X, this form means 'X repeatedly'). Prefixation, suffixation, compounding, and conversion may be the main ways of forming new words in English and many other languages, but there's a much wider world out there, and there are types of morphology that do not figure in English at all, or figure only in the most minor ways.

In this chapter we'll expand our horizons by surveying a number of morphological processes that we have not yet encountered: different kinds of affixes, internal stem changes to consonants and vowels, reduplication, and templatic morphology. Our concentration will be on the structural aspects of morphology – the kinds of rules that languages can make use of to form new words – as opposed to the semantic or grammatical aspects. Our aim here is to characterize a sort of universal toolbag of rules which languages may make use of in word formation.

5.2 Affixes: beyond prefixes and suffixes

As we saw in chapter 3, prefixes and suffixes are types of affixes that respectively go before or after a base. These are not the only positions in which affixes can occur. This section will look at these different sorts of affixes.

5.2.1 Infixes

Infixes are affixes that are inserted right into a root or base. We saw an example in (1a) above. In Tagalog, a Malayo-Polynesian language spoken in the Philippines, it is possible to form intransitive verbs meaning 'become X' from adjectives by inserting the morpheme *-um-* after the first consonant of the adjective root. Example (2) shows how the words can be broken down:

(2) g-um-anda become beautiful
h-um-irap become difficult

Another example of infixation can be found in Karok (a nearly extinct Hokan language, formerly spoken in northern California). In Karok, a form of verb called the intensive is created by infixing the morpheme *-eg-* after the first consonant or cluster of consonants in the root, as in (3):

(3) *Karok (Garrett 2001: 269)*

Base verb		*Intensive*
la:y-	'to pass'	l-eg-a:y
ɬkyorkʷ-	'to watch'	ɬky-eg-orkʷ
koʔmoy-	'to hear'	k-eg-oʔmoy
trahk-	'to fetch water'	tr-eg-ahk

Both examples of infixation that we've seen so far have had the infix right after the first consonant or consonant cluster of the base, but sometimes infixes can come near the end of the base as well. As the examples in (4) illustrate, in Hua, a Trans-New Guinea language, the negative infix *-'a-* comes before the last syllable of the verb root:

(4) *Hua (Haiman 1980: 195)*

zgavo	'embrace'	zga-'a-vo	'not embrace'
harupo	'slip'	haru-'a-po	'not slip'
rvato-	'be nigh'	rva-'a-to	'not be nigh'

Infixation in English?

English doesn't have any productive processes of infixation, but there's one marginal process that comes close, which is affectionately referred to by morphologists as "*fuckin'* infixation." In colloquial spoken English, we will often take our favorite taboo word or expletive – in American English *fucking*, *goddam*, or *frigging*, in British English *bloody* – and insert it into a base word:

abso-fuckin-lutely
fan-bloody-tastic
Ala-friggin'-bama

This kind of infixation is used to emphasize a word, to make it stronger.

What's particularly interesting is that we can't insert *fuckin* just anywhere in a word. In other words, there are phonological restrictions on the insertion of expletives. Try inserting your favorite expletive into the following words:

Winnepesaukee
elementary
onomatopoeia

Now think of some other words, and try to infix *fuckin'*. Can you begin to see a pattern to where the expletive is inserted?

Can you figure out what conditions the placement of the expletive?

5.2.2 Circumfixes

Another type of affix that occurs in languages is the **circumfix**. A circumfix consists of two parts – a prefix and a suffix that together create a new lexeme from a base. We don't consider the prefix and suffix to be separate, because neither by itself creates that type of lexeme, or perhaps anything at all. This kind of affixation is a form of **parasynthesis**, a phenomenon in which a particular morphological category is signaled by the simultaneous presence of two morphemes.

One example of a circumfix can be found in Dutch, although Booij (2002: 119) says that it's no longer productive. In Dutch, to form a collective noun from a count noun, the morpheme *ge-* is affixed before the base and *-te* after the base:

(5)	berg	'mountain'	ge-berg-te	'mountain chain'
	vogel	'bird'	ge-vogel-te	'flock of birds'

Neither *geberg* nor *bergte* alone forms a word – it's only the presence of both parts that signals the collective meaning. Another example can be found in Tagalog (Malayo-Polynesian), where adding *ka* before and *an* after a noun base X makes a noun meaning 'group of X':

(6) *Tagalog (Schachter and Otanes 1972: 101)*

Intsik	'Chinese person'	ka-intsik-an	'the Chinese'
pulo	'island'	ka-pulu-an	'archipelago'
Tagalog	'Tagalog person'	ka-tagalog-an	'the Tagalogs'

Again, neither *ka* + noun, nor noun + *an*, has its own meaning in these words.

Challenge

Remember that in chapter 3 we learned to draw word trees. Review chapter 3, section 2 and think about how we would have to draw word trees for words with circumfixes.

5.2.3 Other kinds of affix

Occasionally in the literature on morphology we find reference to several other types of affix. For the most part, in this book we use different terms for these particular morphological processes, so here I will just mention the terms and refer you to the sections of this book where they are discussed:

- **interfixes:** These are what we have called **linking elements**. See chapter 3, section 3.
- **simulfixes:** This is another term for **internal stem changes**, which we will discuss in section 5.3.
- **transfixes:** These are what we will call **templatic morphology**. See section 5.5 below.

5.3 Internal stem change

Most of the forms of lexeme formation that we've looked at so far have involved adding something to a base (or combining bases).[1] Some languages, however, have means of lexeme formation that involve changing the quality of an internal vowel or consonant of a base, root, or stem; sometimes this internal change occurs alone, and sometimes in conjunction with affixation of some sort. Such processes are called internal stem change or **apophony**.

5.3.1 Vowel changes: ablaut and umlaut

Example (7) gives some words where internal vowels change:

(7) a. *Manchu (Haenisch 1961: 34)*

haha	'man'	hehe	'woman'
ama	'father'	eme	'mother'
amila	'cock'	emile	'hen'

b. *Muskogee (Haas 1940: 143)*

nis	'to buy it'	Stem class I
ní:s	'to buy it'	Stem class III
ni:s	'to buy it'	Stem class IV

c. *German (Lederer 1969: 25)*

Bruder	'brother'	Brüderlein	'brother-dimin.'
Frau	'woman'	Fräulein	'woman-dimin.'

In Manchu, in forming the female equivalent of a male noun, back vowels become front vowels. In Muskogee, verb stems have five forms each of which can be used in a number of verbal contexts (completive, incompletive, durative, and so on). Three of these forms are differentiated by the length and tonal patterns on their vowels. For class I, stems have short vowels and no special tonal accent. Class III stems have long vowels and falling tonal accents, and class IV have long vowels and no special accent. Morphological processes that affect the quality, quantity, or tonal patterns of vowels are often referred to as ablaut.

A note on English

Ablaut figures in a minor way in the morphology of English as well, as we can see in the past and past participle forms of verbs like sing *(past* sang, *past pple.* sung*) or* sit *(past and past pple.* sat*). Since ablaut figures only in inflectional forms of English, though, we will postpone further discussion of it until chapter 6.*

1. The exception here is **conversion**, which we discussed in chapter 3.

Another note on English

You might be interested to know that a historical process of umlaut is responsible for such singular/plural pairs in English as foot ~ feet *or* goose ~ geese. *In earlier stages of English, the singular of the noun 'foot' was* fot *and its plural* foti *(similarly* gos sg. ~ gosi *pl.). The high front vowel of the plural suffix caused the vowel of the base to become front (so the singular and plural were then* fot ~ feti *and* gos ~ gesi*). The plural suffix was eventually lost, leaving the difference in vowels as the only signal of plurality in those words.*

In German, when certain suffixes like the diminutive suffix *-lein* are added to a stem, the stem vowel becomes a front vowel. Historically, this fronting was a phonological process that occurred when a following suffix itself contained a front vowel; this process is called **umlaut**. Over time, the front vowels were lost in some suffixes or became back vowels, as is the case with the diminutive suffix *-lein* (pronounced [laɪn]).

5.3.2 Consonant mutation

In some languages morphological processes are signaled by changes in consonants rather than vowels in the base, root, or stem. Such processes are called **consonant mutations**. As with the vowel processes noted above, consonant mutations may occur alone or in conjunction with prefixes or suffixes.

(8) a. *Seereer-Siin (McLaughlin 2000: 335)*

odon	'mouth'	o^{n}don	'mouth-dimin.'
okawul	'griot'	o^{ŋ}gawul	'griot-dimin.'
opaɗ	'slave'	o^{m}baɗ	'slave-dimin.'

b. *Chemehuevi (Press 1979: 21–2)*

punikai	'see'	navunika	'see-reflexive'
tɨka	'eat'	narɨka	'eat-reflexive'
koa	'cut'	naɣoa	'cut-reflexive'

In (8a), in the West Atlantic language Seereer-Siin, some noun diminutives are formed by replacing the first stop consonant in the stem, for example [p, k, d] in the words in (8a), with the corresponding prenasalized stop ([^{m}b, ^{ŋ}g, ^{n}d]). And in Chemehuevi, illustrated in (8b), the reflexive of a verb is formed by prefixing *na-* and changing the initial stop consonant of the root to a voiced continuant ([p] becomes [v], [t] becomes [r], and [k] becomes [ɣ]).

5.4 Reduplication

Reduplication is a morphological process in which all or part of the base is repeated. Some examples are given in (9):

(9) a. *Hausa (Newman 2000: 42)*

bāya	'behind'	bāya bāya	'a bit behind'
gàba	'forward'	gàba gàba	'a bit forward'
ƙasà	'below'	ƙasà ƙasà	'a bit below'

b. *Samoan (Mosel and Hovdhaugen 1992: 229)*

'apa	'beat, lash'	'apa'apa	'wing, fin'
au	'flow on, roll on'	auau	'current'
solo	'wipe, dry'	solosolo	'handkerchief'

(9a) and (9b) illustrate **full reduplication**, a process by which an entire base is repeated. In the case of Hausa, full reduplication is used to form what's called an **attenuative**, which is a form meaning 'sort of' or ' a little bit'. In Samoan full reduplication is used to form nouns from verbs. Samoan also has **partial reduplication** in which only part of the base is repeated:

(10) *Samoan (Mosel and Hovdhaugen 1992: 223)*

lafo	'plot of land'	lalafo	'clear land'
lago	'pillow, bolster'	lalago	'rest, keep steady'
pine	'pin, peg'	pipine	'secure with pegs'

In (10) you can see that partial reduplication in Samoan repeats the first consonant and vowel of the base; this process derives verbs from nouns. Partial reduplication need not repeat the initial part of a base; it may also in some languages repeat the final part of the base, as the example from Teton Dakota in (11) illustrates:

(11) *Dakota (Teton) (Shaw 1980: 321)*

wa+ksà	'cut with sawing motion'	wa+ksà-ksà	'slice up'
wač^{h}í	'dance'	wač^{h}íč^{h}i	'jump up and down'

In this dialect of Dakota, the final syllable of the verb root can be reduplicated to indicate iterative or repetitive action.

Challenge

Consider the following examples from English:

willy-nilly
hocus-pocus
mumbo-jumbo
hanky-panky
hodge-podge
handy-dandy
hoity-toity
helter-skelter

Can you think of more examples of this sort? Do you think that English has a process of reduplication? If so, is it productive? If not, why not?

5.5 Templatic morphology

Consider the data in (12):

(12) *Arabic (McCarthy 1979: 244; 1981: 374)*

katab	'wrote'
kattab	'caused to write'
kaatab	'corresponded'
ktatab	'wrote, copied'
kutib	'was written' (perfective passive)

All of the words in (12) have something to do with writing, and all share the consonants *ktb*, although in a couple of the forms, there's more than one *t*. All the active verb forms have the vowel *a*; the passive verb form has the vowels *ui*. Each word has a different pattern of vowels and consonants, and each expresses a slightly different concept. What we find in Arabic is called **templatic** or **root and pattern** morphology.

In Arabic, the root of a word typically consists of three consonants (like *ktb*), the **triliteral root**, which supply the core meaning. These three consonants may be interspersed with vowels in a number of different ways to modify the meaning of the root. The precise pattern of consonants and vowels – sometimes called the **template** – can be associated with specific meanings. For example, the pattern CVCVC simply means 'write', but the pattern CVCCVC adds a causative meaning, and the pattern CVVCVC a reciprocal meaning (we can take *correspond* to mean something like 'write to each other'). Each of these template patterns is called a **binyan** (a term which comes from traditional Hebrew grammar). The specific vowels that get interspersed between the consonants in these patterns can contribute inflectional meanings; so the vowel *a* is used in active forms, and the vowels *ui* in passive forms. Roots in Arabic are occasionally called **transfixes** because some morphologists look at them as affixes that occur discontinuously across the word.

Root and pattern morphology is very characteristic of the Semitic family of languages, which includes Arabic and Hebrew. But it can also be found in other languages, for example the Uto-Aztecan language Cupeño, a nearly extinct language of Southern California. Cupeño verbs can have a form called the **habilitative**, which means something like 'can V':

(13) *Cupeño (McCarthy 1984: 309)*

a.	čál	'husk'	čáʔaʔal	'can husk'
	téw	'see'	téʔeʔew	'can see'
	həl^{y}ə́p	'hiccup'	həl^{y}ə́ʔəʔəp	'can hiccup'
	kəláw	'gather wood'	kəláʔaʔaw	'can gather wood'
b.	páčik	'leach acorns'	páčiʔik	'can leach acorns'
	čáṣpəl	'mend'	čáṣpəʔəl	'can mend'

One way of looking at the habilitative forms in Cupeño is that they conform to templates like those in (14):

(14) *Template for Cupeño habilitatives*

a. (CV)CVʔVʔVC
b. CVC(C)VʔVC

If the only or the second vowel is the stressed vowel, as is the case in the examples in (13a), the habilitative form adds two more syllables, each of which start with [ʔ]. The final vowel of the stem is spread to the new syllables. The situation is slightly different if the first vowel of two is the stressed vowel, as the examples in (13b) show. In that case, the template has only one more syllable than the stem, again with the glottal stop as the consonant, and the vowel supplied by the last stem vowel.

A final example of templatic morphology comes from another Native American language, Sierra Miwok (Penutian family, spoken in California). In this language, new words can be derived by adding a suffix which then supplies a specific template for the base. Consider the examples in (15):

(15) *Sierra Miwok (Smith 1985: 365, 371–2)*

a.	peṭja	'drop several things'	peeṭaj -tee-ny	'string out'
	halki	'hunt'	haalik -tee-ny	'hunt along a trail'
b.	hulaw	'forget'	hulwaw-we	'be late'
	ʔokiih	'beg for food'	ʔokhih-he	'be pitiful'
c.	hywaat-	'run'	hywattatt	'run around'
	hyleet	'fly, be in the air'	hylettett	'flop about (fish)'

The examples in (15a) show that the suffix *-tee-ny*, which forms what Smith calls the 'linear distributive', makes the verb stem conform to a template of the form CVVCVC. The forms in (15b) have a suffix with the form Ce, where the C is the last consonant of the verb stem. In addition, the verb stem is made to conform to the pattern CVCCVC. Finally, in (15c) verb stems are made into derived forms that mean something like 'X around' just by making them conform to a template that looks like CVCVCCVCC, with no suffix added.

Summary

In this chapter we have completed our survey of the different types of rules that can be used in forming new lexemes in the languages of the world. We have gone beyond prefixation, suffixation, compounding, and conversion to add new types of affixes (infixes, circumfixes), and new processes like internal stem change (ablaut, umlaut, and consonant mutation), reduplication (full and partial), and templatic morphology.

Exercises

1. The Austronesian language Leti has a process that derives nouns meaning 'the act of V-ing' from verbs. Consider the data below (from Blevins 1999: 390):

kakri	'cry'	kniakri	'the act of crying'
pali	'float'	pniali	'the act of floating'
sai	'climb'	sniai	'the act of climbing'
teti	'chop'	tnieti	'the act of chopping'
vaka	'ask (for)'	vniaka	'the act of asking'
va-nunsu	'knead'	vnianunsu	'massage' = 'the act of kneading'

   a. Divide the Leti words in the second column into morphemes, and give the meaning of each morpheme.
   b. What is the morphological rule that creates nouns from verbs in Leti? What kind of a rule is it?

c. Now consider the following forms:

atu	'know'	niatu	'knowledge' = 'the act of knowing'
odi	'carry'	niodi	'the act of carrying'
osri	'hunt'	niosri	'hunt' = 'the act of hunting'

Divide these new words into morphemes and discuss what changes you need to make to the morphological rule you wrote for part (b) in order to account for this new data.

2. The examples below are from the Native American language Yurok (data from Garrett 2001: 274):

kep'eɬ	'housepit'	kep'kep'eɬ	'there are several housepits'
ket'ul	'there's a lake'	ket'ket'ul	'there's a series of lakes'
pegon	'to split'	pegpegon	'to split in several places'
siton	'to crack' (intrans.)	sitsiton	'to crack several times'
tekun	'to be stuck together'	tektekun	'to be stuck together in several places'

Write a word formation rule that derives the Yurok forms in the second column from the corresponding base in the first column. Make sure to include both the structural and semantic effects of the rule. What kind of a morphological rule is this?

3. Consider the data below from the Dravidian language Kannada (data from Sridhar 1990: 268):

a:Ta	'game'	a:Ta-gi:Ta	'games and the like'
huli	'tiger'	huli-gili	'tigers and the like'
sphu:rti	'inspiration'	sphu:rti-gi:rti	'inspiration, etc.'
autaNa	'banquet'	autaNa-gi:taNa	'banquet, etc.'

Try to write a morphological rule that derives the words in the second column from the bases in the first column. What kind of morphological rule is this? How does it differ from other morphological rules we've looked at in this chapter?

4. In the South Munda language Gtaʔ a number of different forms can be derived from a noun base, as the examples here show (data from McCarthy 1983):

kitoŋ	'god'
kataŋ	'being with powers equal to 'kitoŋ''
kitiŋ	'being smaller, weaker than 'kitoŋ''
kutaŋ	'being other than 'kitoŋ'' (e.g., spirits, ghosts)
kesu	'wrapper worn against cold'
kasa	'cloth equivalent to 'kesu' in size and texture'
kisi	'small or thin piece of cloth'
kusa	'any other material useable against cold'

Propose an analysis of this process. What kind of word formation rule is at work here?

5. The following words, taken from Yu (2004: 620) are characteristic of the speech of the character Homer Simpson from the animated TV show *The Simpsons.* In this data, Homer Simpson seems to display a process of infixation:

saxomaphone	'saxophone'	Missimassippi	'Mississippi'
telemaphone	'telephone'	Alamabama	'Alabama'

wondermaful	'wonderful'	diamalectic	'dialectic'
feudamalism	'feudalism'	Michamalangelo	'Michaelangelo'
secrematery	'secretary'		
terrimatory	'territory'		

Is this like real cases of infixation that we saw in this chapter? If so, why? If not, why not? Try to formulate a precise rule for Homer Simpson infixation.

6. The following examples from the Semitic language Amharic illustrate a form of language disguise or play language (like Pig Latin) used by young women in the Ethiopian capital, Addis Ababa (McCarthy 1984: 306):

gʷaro	'backyard'	gʷayrər
gɩn	'but'	gaynən
mətt'a	'come'	mayt'ət
kɩfu	'cruel'	kayfəf
həd	'go'	haydəd
man	'who'	maynən

Figure out the morphological rule that creates the play language version (the third column) of the Amharic words. What kind of morphological rule is this?

7. Consider the following, from the Muskogean language Alabama (Hardy and Montler 1988: 394):

salatli	'slide once'	salaali	'slide repeatedly'
haatanatli	'turn around once'	haatanaali	'turn around repeatedly'
noktiłifka	'choke once'	noktiłiika	'choke repeatedly'

Describe the word formation process that derives the words in the second column from those in the first column. What kind of morphological process is this?

8. The following data come from the Muskogean language Koasati (Kimball 1991: 351). Write a word formation rule for the process that they illustrate:

molápkan	'to gleam'	molalápkan	'to flash'
bolótin	'to shake'	bololótin	'to shake with fear'
wacíplin	'to feel a stabbing pain'	wacicíplin	'to feel repeated stabbing pains'
konótlin	'to roll'	kononó:tlin	'to quiver fatly'
watóhlin	'to clabber'	watotóhlin	'to jiggle like jello'

CHAPTER

6 Inflection

CHAPTER OUTLINE

KEY TERMS

person
number
gender
case
tense
aspect
inherent
contextual
paradigm

In this chapter you will learn about inflection, the sort of morphology that expresses grammatical distinctions.

- We will look at a wide variety of types of inflection, both familiar and unfamiliar, including number, person, gender and noun class, case, tense and aspect, voice, mood and modality.
- We will learn what morphologists mean by a 'paradigm' and look at patterns within paradigms.
- And we will consider whether it is always clear where to draw the line between inflection and derivation.

6.1 Introduction

At the outset of this book we divided morphology into two domains **inflectional** and **derivational** word formation. In the last three chapters, we have concentrated on derivational word formation – types of word formation that create new lexemes. In this chapter, we turn our attention to inflectional word formation.

Inflection refers to word formation that does not change category and does not create new lexemes, but rather changes the form of lexemes so that they fit into different grammatical contexts. As we'll see in detail below, grammatical meaning can include information about number (singular *vs.* plural), person (first, second, third), tense (past, present, future), and other distinctions as well. In this chapter, we will first survey different forms of inflection that can be found both in English and familiar languages, and further afield in the languages of the world, and then look at the ways in which inflection can work.

A word before we start though. We've seen that new lexemes can be derived using all sorts of different formal processes of word formation: affixation, compounding, conversion, internal stem change, reduplication, templatic morphology. Inflectional word formation makes use of almost all of these types of word formation rules as well, with the possible exception of compounding. That is, just as languages may have derivational affixes that form new lexemes, they may have inflectional affixes that make those lexemes suited for one grammatical context or another; similarly, languages may have rules of reduplication for either derivational purposes or inflectional purposes. In other words, we might say that *form* (the type of rule or process) is independent of *function* (derivation or inflection). Keep this in mind; many of the examples that I'll use to illustrate points below make use of affixation, but in many cases I could have chosen examples with reduplication or internal stem change as well.

6.2 Types of inflection

Native speakers of English are often surprised at the kinds of inflection that can be found in languages – English is a language that has relatively little inflection, as languages go. So we'll start by surveying some of the types of inflection that can be found in the languages of the world.

6.2.1 Number

Perhaps the most familiar inflectional category for speakers of English is number. In English, nouns can be marked as singular or plural:

(1) *Singular* cat, mouse, ox, child
Plural cats, mice, oxen, children

Although the vast majority of nouns pluralize in English by adding *-s* (or in terms of sounds, one of the variants [s], [z], or [əz]), some nouns form their plurals irregularly. We will return to the issue of regular *versus* irregular inflections shortly. In English, it is required to mark the plural on nouns in a context in which more than one of that noun is being discussed (*I have six beagles*). This is not the case in all languages, as our Mandarin Chinese example in chapter 1 illustrated.

Some languages distinguish a third category of number in addition to singular and plural. For example, in the Eskimo-Aleut language Yup'ik, nouns inflect not only for singular and plural, but also for what is called **dual**. This is a number-marking that means 'two':

(2) *Yup'ik (Mithun 1999: 79)*

qayaq	'kayak'	paluqtaq	'beaver'
qayak	'two kayaks'	paluqtak	'two beavers'
qayat	'three or more kayaks'	paluqtat	'three or more beavers'

As we'll see soon, some languages can make the singular/dual/plural distinction on verbs, as well as on nouns.

6.2.2 Person

Students of Indo-European languages like Latin or German, know that verbs in those languages are marked for the inflectional category of person: that is, verbs exhibit different endings depending on whether the subject of the sentence is the speaker (first person), the hearer (second person), or someone else (third person); frequently number is also expressed as well as person:

(3) a. *Latin:* amāre 'to love'

Singular	1st	amō	(-o)	*Plural*	1st	amāmus	(-mus)
	2nd	amās	(-s)		2nd	amātis	(-tis)
	3rd	amat	(-t)		3rd	amant	(-nt)

b. *German:* sagen 'to say'

Singular	1st	sage	(-e)	*Plural*	1st	sagen	(-en)
	2nd	sagst	(-st)		2nd	sagt	(-t)
	3rd	sagt	(-t)		3rd	sagen	(-en)

Speakers of Indo-European languages may, however, be less familiar with marking person on nouns. It is not unusual for languages to mark person on nouns to show possession, something we do in English with separate possessive pronouns. For example, the Iroquoian language Mohawk uses prefixes to mark person on nouns:

(4) *Mohawk nouns (Mithun 1999: 69)*

Singular	1st person	k-hnia'sà:ke	'my throat'
	2nd person	s- hnia'sà:ke	'your throat'
	3rd person	ie- hnia'sà:ke	'her throat'
		ra- hnia'sà:ke	'his throat'
Plural	1st person	iakwa- hnia'sà:ke	'our throats'
	2nd person	sewa- hnia'sà:ke	'your pl. throats'
	3rd person	konti- hnia'sà:ke	'their F. throats'
		rati- hnia'sà:ke	'their M. throats'

Mohawk, and other languages also show another kind of person marking that we don't have in English, making a distinction between the inclusive and exclusive forms of the first person plural. In an **inclusive** form, the speaker includes herself and the hearer. In the **exclusive** form, the speaker includes herself and others, but not the hearer. So the inclusive form of the first person could be thought of as a combination of first and second person marking, and the exclusive as a combination of first and third person marking. This distinction can be marked in Mohawk as well, specifically with prefixes on verbs:

(5) *Mohawk verbs (Mithun 1999: 70)*

1st person inclusive	tewa-hià:tons	'we all (you pl. and I) are writing'
1st person exclusive	iakwa- hià:tons	'we all (they and I) are writing'

As we mentioned above, it is also possible to mark verbs if the subject consists of exactly two people. So in addition to the inclusive and exclusive forms in (5), Mohawk also has first person dual inclusive and exclusive forms (Mithun 1999: 70):

(6)	*Dual inclusive*	teni- hià:tons	'we two (you and I) are writing'
	Dual exclusive	iakeni- hià:tons	'we two (s/he and I) are writing'

English verb forms are ambiguous with respect to these distinctions. If I say "we write," neither the form of the verb nor the form of the pronoun makes explicit whether the hearer is included or not, or how many other than the speaker are involved (although of course we can make the distinction in a round-about way, if we need to!).

6.2.3 Gender and noun class

If you've studied French, Spanish, German, Latin, Russian, or another Indo-European language, you're probably familiar with the concept of gender. In languages that have **grammatical gender** nouns are divided into two or more classes with which other elements in a sentence – for example, articles and adjectives – must agree. We use French and German as our examples here:

(7) a. *French*

Masculine		*Feminine*	
homme	'man'	femme	'woman'
rat	'rat'	souris	'mouse'
bureau	'desk'	table	'table'

b. *German*

Masculine		*Neuter*		*Feminine*	
Mann	'man'	Kind	'child'	Frau	'woman'
Tisch	'table'	Pult	'desk'	Mauer	'wall'
Hund	'dog'	Pferd	'horse'	Maus	'mouse'

French has two genders, masculine and feminine. German has three genders, masculine, feminine, and neuter. While sometimes the real-world sex of the noun's referent determines the **grammatical gender** of the noun – that is, the class that the noun belongs to – in many more cases nouns are assigned to genders with some degree of arbitrariness. So while the words for 'man' and 'woman' in both languages are masculine and feminine respectively, in accordance with **natural gender**, the assignment of various animal names to gender classes is quite arbitrary. Rats, mice, dogs, and horses of course have natural gender – in the real world they must be either male or female – but French and German grammar places them in a gender independent of their natural genders. In French, rats are masculine, but mice feminine. In German, dogs are masculine, horses neuter, and mice feminine. Inanimate nouns have no natural gender, but they are nevertheless classed as either masculine or feminine in French, and as any of the three genders in German.

Assignment to gender classes sometimes seems completely arbitrary, but it is not always as arbitrary as you might think. For example, in German all nouns derived with the derivational suffixes *-ung, -keit, -heit,* and *-schaft* are feminine, regardless of the gender of their bases. All of these suffixes form abstract nouns, so it's possible to say that derived abstract nouns are always feminine. Similarly, the diminutive suffixes *-chen* and *-lein* produce neuter nouns, regardless of the base they attach to. In other languages, nouns may be assigned to a gender based on their phonological shape. For example, the Afro-Asiatic language Hausa has masculine and feminine genders. Nouns for males are masculine and those for females are feminine in accordance with natural gender, but the rest of the nouns are assigned to one of the classes by the phonological form of the base: nouns that end in *-aa* are feminine, and everything else is masculine (Corbett 1991: 53).

For many nouns in French and German, neither the meaning of the noun nor its phonological form signals its gender. In other words, there are no suffixes or other marks right on the nouns to tell us their genders (life would be much easier for second language learners of these languages if there were!). Rather, we can tell what the gender of the noun is by other elements in a sentence that are in **agreement** with a noun. So in French, the definite article *le* is used with masculine nouns (*le bureau*), and *la* with feminines (*la table*). Similarly, in German the definite article *der* is used with masculines (*der Tisch*), *das* with neuters (*das Pferd*) and *die* with feminines (*die Maus*).

The gender systems we are most familiar with are typical of Indo-European languages, and occur in other language families as well, but there are many languages outside of Indo-European that exhibit genders or **noun classes** based on distinctions other than (or in addition to) masculine, feminine, and neuter. Languages may have human and nonhuman classes or classes for rational beings as opposed to everything else. In the Algonquian family of languages, noun classes are based not on masculine and feminine but on animacy. Words for people belong to the animate class, but so, for example, do spirits and animals. And while most words for inanimate things belong to the inanimate class, some belong to the animate class; for example the nouns for 'snowshoe' and 'button' in the Algonquian language Ojibwa belong to the animate noun class (Corbett 1991: 20). In other words, while there is a partial semantic basis for the two classes, assignment to the animate and inanimate classes can still be arbitrary.

Languages are not limited to two or three classes. Consider the language Yuchi, spoken in Oklahoma (Mithun 1999: 103):

(8) *Speaker*	*Class*
1. M	singular or plural Yuchi, except certain female relatives
2. M	singular female Yuchi relative, same or descending generation (sister, daughter, niece, granddaughter)
F	any female Yuchi of same or descending generation
3. F	singular male Yuchi relative, same or descending generation (brother, son, nephew, grandson)
4. M, F	singular female Yuchi relative, ascending generation (mother, aunt, grandmother)
5. F	singular male unrelated Yuchi, or plural Yuchis of same or descending generation
6. F	singular male Yuchi of ascending generation (father, uncle, grandfather, husband, or as a term of respect for Yuchis of ascending generation)
7. M, F	any non-Yuchi(s), animals
8. M, F	vertical inanimate objects
9. M, F	horizontal inanimate objects
10. M, F	round inanimate objects

In Yuchi, nouns fall into classes based on whether they denote humans, animals, or inanimate objects with certain shapes. For example, Class 1 contains nouns used by men to denote Yuchi people, except close female relatives. The gender of a noun is indicated by a number of things, one of which is the article suffix used with the noun. For example, *gɔnt̓ɛ-nǫ́* means 'the Yuchi man' and *gɔnt̓ɛ-wənǫ́* 'the non-Yuchi man'. 'The tree' is *yá-fa* but *ya-ʔɛ́* is 'the log'. Class 7 contains nouns used by either men or women to denote animals or people who are not Yuchi. Other classes distinguish Yuchis from other humans, and Yuchis related to the speaker from those unrelated to the speaker.

6.2.4 Case

Case is another grammatical category that may affect nouns (or whole noun phrases). In languages that employ the inflectional category of case, nouns are distinguished on the basis of how they are deployed in sentences, for example, whether they function as subject, direct object, indirect object, as a location, time, or instrument, or as the object of a preposition. In Latin, for example, nouns must be inflected in one of five cases, with singular and plural forms for each case:

(9) *Latin:*

Singular	*stella* 'star' (F)	*puer* 'boy' (M)
Nominative	stella	puer
Genitive	stellae	puerī
Dative	stellae	puerō
Accusative	stellam	puerum
Ablative	stellā	puerō
Plural		
Nominative	stellae	puerī
Genitive	stellārum	puerōrum
Dative	stellīs	puerīs
Accusative	stellās	puerōs
Ablative	stellīs	puerīs

The **nominative** case forms are used for the subject of the sentence. **Accusative** is generally used for the direct object and **dative** for the indirect object. **Genitive** is used for the possessor (for example, *the boy's shirt*). **Ablative** is used for the objects of prepositions (for example, *cum* 'with', *dē* 'from'), although some prepositions take objects in the accusative case (*ad* 'to', *post* 'after').

Latin displays what is commonly called a **nominative/accusative** case system. In this sort of system, subjects of verbs are nominative, whether the verbs are **transitive** (that is, they take an object) or **intransitive** (they don't take an object):

(10) a. Puer amat puellam
boy.NOM loves girl.ACC
'The boy loves the girl'

b. Puer it
boy-NOM goes
'The boy goes'

Less frequent is a kind of case marking system called an **ergative/absolutive** system. In this kind of system, the subject of a transitive verb gets a case called the **ergative**. The subject of an intransitive verb gets a case called the **absolutive**, which is also the case used for the direct object of a transitive verb. The examples in (11) from Georgian illustrate an ergative-absolutive case marking system (Whaley 1997: 163):[1]

(11) a. Student-i mivida
student-ABS went
'The student went'

b. Student-ma ceril-i dacera
student-ERG letter-ABS wrote
'The student wrote the letter'

1. Interestingly, Georgian has an ergative-absolutive case marking system in the perfect tense, but in the present tense it has a nominative-accusative system.

You can see the two systems compared schematically in (12):

(12)

	Nominative/Accusative	*Ergative/Absolutive*
Subject of transitive verb	Nominative	Ergative
Subject of intransitive verb	Nominative	Absolutive
Object of transitive verb	Accusative	Absolutive

Ergative/absolutive case systems are less frequent in the languages of the world than nominative/accusative systems, but they do occur in the Pama-Nyungan languages of Australia (for example Dyirbal), in the Tsimshianic languages of North America (e.g. Sm'algyax, spoken in British Columbia), in the language isolate Basque, as well as in Caucasian languages like Georgian.

6.2.5 Tense and aspect

Tense and aspect are inflectional categories that usually pertain to verbs. Both have to do with time, but in different ways.

Tense refers to the point of time of an event in relation to another point – generally the point at which the speaker is speaking. In **present** tense the point in time of speaking and of the event spoken about are the same. In **past** tense the time of the event is before the time of speaking. And in **future** tense the event time is after the time of speaking. This can be represented schematically as in (13), where S stands for the time of speaking and E for the time of the event:

(13) *Present* S = E
Past E before S
Future S before E

In English, we mark the past tense using the inflectional suffix *-ed* on verbs (*walked, yawned*), but there is no inflectional suffix for future tense. Instead, we use a separate auxiliary verb *will* to form the future tense (*will walk, will scream*). The use of a separate word to form a tense is called **periphrastic marking**. Strictly speaking, periphrastic marking is a matter of syntax rather than morphology. Unlike English, Latin marks both past and future inflectionally, that is, by means of morphology on the verb:

(14) *Present* amō 'I love'
Past amāvī 'I loved'
Future amābō 'I will love'

Past, present, and future are not the only possible tenses; some languages distinguish several kinds of past tense and several kinds of future tense, based on how close or distant the event spoken about is from the time of speaking. For example, in the nearly extinct Hokan language

Washo, there are four different past tenses and three different future tenses (Mithun 1999: 152–3):

(15)

-lul	distant past, before the lifetime of the speaker
-gul	distant past, but within the speaker's lifetime
-ayʔ	intermediate past, earlier than the same day, but not extremely distant
-leg	recent past, earlier on the same day or during the previous night
-áša?	near future, from the point of speaking until about an hour from that point
-tiʔ	intermediate future, after a short lapse of time (usually later in the day)
-gab	distant future, following day or later

Tense on nouns?

It may seem odd to think of putting tense marking on nouns; we don't do it in English, and it probably isn't done in any of the languages you've studied. But it's not uncommon in native languages of North America. For example, in Central Alaskan Yup'ik, both past tense and future tense can be marked on nouns (Mithun 1999: 154):

ikamraqa	'my sled'
ikamralqa	'my former sled'
ikamrarkaqa	'my sled to be'
nuliaqa	'my wife'
nulialqa	'my late/ex-wife'
nuliarkaqa	'my wife to be'

A past tense 'sled' might be a pile of junk in a shed, or something I used to own, now owned by someone else. If your 'wife' is past tense, she might be dead, or you might be divorced. A future tense 'sled' might also be a pile of material yet to be assembled, or something you might buy or get as a present. Your future tense 'wife' is your fiancée.

Aspect is another inflectional category that may be marked on verbs. Rather than showing the time of an event with respect to the point of speaking, aspect conveys information about the internal composition of the event or "the way in which the event occurs in time" (Bhat 1999: 43).

One of the most frequently expressed aspectual distinctions that can be found in the languages of the world is the distinction between perfective and imperfective aspect. With **perfective** aspect, an event is viewed as completed; we look at the event from the outside, and its internal structure is not relevant. With **imperfective** aspect, on the other hand, the event is viewed as on-going; we look at the event from the inside, as it were. English isn't the best language with which to illustrate this distinction, as tense and aspect are not completely distinct from one another, but I can give you a rough example from English. In English, when we say *I ate* *the apple*, we not only place the action in the past tense, but also look at it as a completed whole. But if we say *I was eating the apple*, although the action is still in the past, we focus on the event as it is progressing. The Iroquoian language Seneca has a much clearer distinction between perfective and imperfective aspect (Mithun 1999: 165):

(16) *Perfective* ǫkáhtaʔt 'I got full'
Imperfective akáhtaʔs 'I get full, I'm getting full'

Other forms of aspect focus on particular points in an event. **Inceptive** aspect focuses on the beginning of an event. **Continuative** aspect focuses on the middle of the event as it progresses, and **completive** on the end. We can illustrate these aspects with the following sentences from the Tibeto-Burman language Manipuri (Bhat 1999: 52):

(17) a. *Inceptive*
məhak-nə phu-gət-li
he-NOM beat-start-NON.FUT
'He began to beat it (and would continue to do so)'

b. *Continuative*
tombə layrik pa-rì
Tomba book read-CONT
'Tomba is reading the book'

c. *Completive*
yumthək ədu yu-rəm-mì
roof that leak-COMP-CONT
'That roof had been leaking (but not any more)'

A third category of aspectual distinction can be called **quantificational**. Quantificational aspectual distinctions concern things like the number of times an action is done or an event happens – once or repeatedly – or how frequently an action is done. Among the quantificational aspects are **semelfactive, iterative**, and **habitual** aspects. Actions that are done just once are called **semelfactive**. The Athapaskan language Koyukon has a special verb stem for actions that are done just once (Mithun 1999: 168), and West Greenlandic has suffixes that express **iterative** aspect for something that is done repeatedly and **habitual** aspect for something that is usually or characteristically done (Fortescue 1984: 280–2):

(18) a. *Koyukon semelfactive*
yeeltleɬ
'she chopped it once, gave it a chop'

b. *West Greenlandic iterative*
quirsur-tar-puq
cough-ITERATIVE-3rd.SG.INDIC
'He coughed repeatedly'

c. *West Greenlandic habitual*
qimmi-t qilut-tar-put
dog-PL. bark-HABITUAL-3rd.INDIC
'Dogs bark'

There are other sorts of aspectual distinctions that can be made as well, but these illustrate at least the main types of aspect that can be found in the languages of the world.

English can make some of the aspectual distinctions mentioned above, but it does so periphrastically, using a combination of extra verbs, prepositions, and adverbs to convey such nuances of meaning. In other words, many of these aspectual differences are expressed lexically rather than inflectionally:

(19) *Inceptive* She began to walk.
Habitual She always/usually walks.
Continuative She keeps on walking.
Iterative She reads over and over.

Tense and aspect can be and frequently are combined in languages, so for example, it is possible to speak of an event that is on-going in the past or the future. As mentioned above, tense and aspect are often combined in English. The past tense in English is also typically perfective: when we say *she walked* we generally speak of an event that is conceived of as completed. But when we use the past progressive, as in *she was walking*, we are talking about something that happened in the past, but which we are thinking of as on-going. The present tense in English can be used to signal the present moment (*At this very moment, a dog barks.*), or also to convey habitual aspect (*Dogs bark.*).

6.2.6 Voice

Voice is a category of inflection that allows different noun phrases to be focused in sentences. In the **active** voice in a sentence with an agent and a patient, the agent is focused by virtue of being the subject of the sentence:

(20) The cat chased the mouse.

But in the **passive** voice the patient is the subject of the sentence, and it gets the focus:

(21) The mouse was chased (by the cat).

In English the passive is expressed periphrastically by a combination of the auxiliary verb *be* plus the past participle, in example (19) *chased*, but in Latin active and passive forms of the verbs are distinguished by inflectional suffixes:

(22) *Active*

singular	1st	amō	*plural*	1st	amāmus
	2nd	amās		2nd	amātis
	3rd	amat		3rd	amant

Passive

singular	1st	amor	*plural*	1st	amāmur
	2nd	amāris		2nd	amāminī
	3rd	amātur		3rd	amantur

There is a great deal more to be said about voice distinctions like active and passive, and we will return to them in some detail in chapter 8.

6.2.7 Mood and modality

The inflectional categories of **mood** and **modality** have to do with a range of distinctions that include signaling the kind of **speech act** in which a verb is deployed. **Speech acts** are classically defined as things we can do with words, for example, making a statement, asking a question, or giving a command. Languages often have three moods: **declarative** for making ordinary statements, **interrogative** for asking questions, **imperative** for giving commands. But some languages can have other moods as well, for example, expressing a speaker's attitude about a statement, including whether it is necessary, possible, certain, or sometimes whether it is hearsay and not necessarily true.

The now-extinct language Tonkawa (Coahuiltecan) had eight suffixes signaling different moods/modalities (Mithun 1999: 171). Mood suffixes are shown in bold:

(23)			
	Declarative	naxadjganaw-**o**- 'o·'	'I married'
	Assertive	do·nan-**a'a**	'He lies!'
	Exclamatory	'awac'a·la hedoxa-**gwa**	'The meat is all gone!'
	Interrogative	yaxa-'-ga?	'Did you eat?'
	Intentive	heul-**a·ha'a**	'I shall catch him'
	Imperative	'andjo-**u**	'Wake up!'
	Potential	ya·dj-'**a**-n'ec	'I might see him'
	Exhortative	hama'amdo·xa·dew-**e·l**	'Let him be burned up.'

Another interesting distinction in mood/modality is the **realis/irrealis** distinction that is marked in some Native American languages. If the **realis** form is used, the speaker means to signal that the event is actual, that it has happened or is happening, or is directly verifiable by perception. The **irrealis** form, in contrast, signals something that can be imagined or thought.

In English, we have no special inflection that signals mood; questions are formed using syntactic means and intonation, imperatives deploy the uninflected verb stem without any special endings. We have a remnant of a **subjunctive** mood, which appears in counter-factual sentences (that is, sentences expressing something contrary to fact) like *If I were an aardvark, I'd eat insects*;

in such sentences the subjunctive verb form is the same as the plural form of the verb (so in the sentence just given, we have *were* rather than *was*).

Challenge

Go to your university library and browse the shelves where you can find grammars of unfamiliar languages. Find a grammar of a language that you've never heard of before and see what kinds of inflection (if any!) it has. Does it inflect nouns? Is there a case system? If so, what kind? What kind of verbal inflections do you find? Do you find any distinctions that we failed to cover in our survey, or other kinds of inflection that strike you as interesting? Share your findings with your classmates.

6.3 Inflection in English

6.3.1 What we have

As we've seen in passing in the sections above, English is a language that is quite poor in inflection. The distinction between singular and plural is marked on nouns:

(24)

Singular	cat, mouse, ox, child
Plural	cats, mice, oxen, children

English has only a tiny bit of case marking on nouns: it uses the morpheme *-s* (orthographically *-'s* in the singular, *-s'* in the plural) to signal possession, the remnant of the genitive case. Pronouns, however, still exhibit some case distinctions that are no longer marked in nouns:

(25) *Nouns*

singular non-possessive	mother	child
singular possessive	mother's	child's
plural non-possessive	mothers	children
plural possessive	mothers'	childrens'

Pronouns

singular subject	I	you	he/she/it
singular object	me	you	him/her/it
singular possessive	my	your	his/her/its
plural subject	we	you	they
plural object	us	you	them
plural possessive	our	your	their

In verbs, number is only marked in the third person present tense, where *-s* signals a singular subject. As we've seen, English verbs inflect for past tense, but not for future, and there are two participles (present with *-ing* and past with *-ed*) that together with auxiliary verbs help to signal various aspectual distinctions:

(26) *Verbs*

3rd person sg. present	walks, runs
all other present tense forms	walk, run
past tense	walked, ran
progressive	(be) walking, running
past participle	(have) walked, run

Distinctions in aspect and voice are expressed in English through a combination of auxiliary choice and choice of participle. The **progressive**, which expresses, among other things, on-going actions, is formed with the auxiliary *be* plus the present participle:

(27)		
	Present progressive	I am mowing the lawn.
	Past progressive	I was mowing the lawn.
	Future progressive	I will be mowing the lawn.

The **perfect** (note that the perfect is not the same as the perfective, which we discussed above) expresses something that happened in the past but still has relevance to the present. This is signaled in English with the past participle and a form of the auxiliary **have**:

(28) *Perfect* I have eaten the last piece of blueberry pie.

The passive voice in English is formed with the past participle as well, but the auxiliary *be* is used instead of *have*:

(29) *Passive* I was followed by a voracious weasel.

It is, of course, possible to combine various auxiliaries and participial forms to express tense/aspect distinctions that are quite complex, as in, for example, the past perfect progressive passive sentence *I had been being followed by a voracious weasel.*

As you can see in (25)–(29), English has both **regular** and **irregular** inflections. All of our regular inflections are suffixal, but irregular forms are often formed by internal stem change (ablaut and umlaut) or by a combination of internal stem change and suffixation. Examples of irregular forms are given in (30):

(30) a. *Irregular noun plurals*

foot	feet
mouse	mice
ox	oxen
child	children
alumnus	alumni
datum	data

b. *Irregular verb forms*

sing	sang	sung
sit	sat	sat
swing	swung	swung
write	wrote	written
hold	held	held
tell	told	told
bring	brought	brought

We could no doubt think of more examples as well. It is often said that the irregular plurals and past tenses in English form **closed classes**; that is, they constitute a fixed list from which particular forms can be lost, but to which no new forms can be added. The regular plural and past tense endings are considered **default endings**. In other words, when a new noun is added to English, its plural is formed with *-s* and when a new verb is added, its past tense is formed with *-ed*. So if we borrow a noun from another language or coin a completely new noun, their plurals will be formed with the regular suffix (*fajitas, wugs*). Similarly for new verbs (*googled*).

Why do we have irregular forms? In some cases, they are the remnants of ways of forming the plural or past tense that we no longer have today. We saw in chapter 5 that plurals like *foot* ~ *feet* and *mouse* ~ *mice* are the remnants of a rule of umlaut that was lost at the earliest stages of English. The irregular verbs are also a remnant of a way of inflecting verbs that goes all the way back to the Germanic ancestor of English and even beyond that to the way of inflecting verbs in proto-Indo-European. The details of how that kind of inflection worked need not concern us here, except to say that it involved internal vowel changes (ablaut). Suffice it to say that that form of inflection is no longer used to inflect new verbs in English.

Challenge

Is it really true that we can never form new irregular verbs? Here's an experiment that you and your classmates can do. Ask five friends to fill in the past tense of each nonsense verb in the following sentences:

Max likes to *plite*. Yesterday he _______ for two full hours.
Zelda *glings* very well. Years ago, her mother _______ professionally.
Sometimes we *trell* all night. Last weekend we _______ for two whole days.

Compile your data with that of your classmates and try to see if there are any patterns you can explain.

6.3.2 Why English has so little inflection

You might wonder why English has so little inflection. In fact, if you study the history of English, you'll find that at one time English had quite a bit more inflection than it now has. The earliest form of English, Old English, was spoken from about 450 to 1100 CE. Old English had three genders – masculine, feminine, and neuter – and a case system with four cases – nominative, accusative, dative, and genitive, see (31). Articles and adjectives agreed with nouns in case and number, as (32) shows:

(31) *Old English nouns*

	Masculine	*Feminine*	*Neuter*
Singular	'stone'	'gift'	'ship'
Nom.	stān	giefu	scip
Acc.	stān	giefe	scip
Gen.	stānes	giefe	scipes
Dat.	stāne	giefe	scipum
Plural			
Nom.	stānas	giefa	scipu
Acc.	stānas	giefa	scipu
Gen.	stāna	giefa	scipe
Dat.	stānum	giefum	scipum

(32) sē gōdan stān
the.MASC.NOM good.MASC.NOM stone.NOM

sēo gōde giefu
the.FEM.NOM good.FEM.NOM gift.NOM

ðæt gōde scip
the.NEUT.NOM good.NEUT.NOM ship.NOM

Verb inflection was also more complex in Old English than in Modern English. In Old English, verbs were inflected for person and number, and were different for present tense and past tense in both the indicative and the subjunctive. In addition, some verbs were **strong verbs**, which means that they show internal stem change – specifically ablaut – in some forms. For example, in the strong verb *drīfan* 'to drive' the present tense always has a long [i] vowel, but the past has the vowel [ɑ] in the first and third person singular and a short [i] in the plural form and the second person singular. Other verbs were called **weak verbs**; these inflected using suffixes rather than ablaut. As you can see with the weak verb *dēman* 'to judge' in (33), the vowel of the stem never changes, but in the past tense there is always a suffix *-d(e)*:

(33)

		Strong	*Weak*
Present		drīfan 'to drive'	dēman 'to judge'
singular	1st	drīfe	dēme
	2nd	drīf(e)st	dēm(e)st
	3rd	drīf(e)ð	dēm(e)ð
plural	1st	drīfað	dēmað
	2nd	drīfað	dēmað
	3rd	drīfað	dēmað

Past

singular	1st	drāf	dēmde
	2nd	drife	dēmdes(t)
	3rd	drāf	dēmde
plural	1st	drifon	dēmdon
	2nd	drifon	dēmdon
	3rd	drifon	dēmdon

Why did English lose all this inflection? There are probably two reasons. The first one has to do with the stress system of English: in Old English, unlike modern English, stress was typically on the first syllable of the word. Ends of words were less prominent, and therefore tended to be pronounced less distinctly than beginnings of words, so inflectional suffixes tended not to be emphasized. Over time this led to a weakening of the inflectional system. But this alone probably wouldn't have resulted in the nearly complete loss of inflectional marking that is the situation in present day English; after all, German – a language closely related to English – also shows stress on the initial syllables of words, and nevertheless has not lost most of its inflection over the centuries.

Some scholars attribute the loss of inflection to language contact in the northern parts of Britain. For some centuries during the Old English period, northern parts of Britain were occupied by the Danes, who were speakers of Old Norse. Old Norse is closely related to Old English, with a similar system of four cases, masculine, feminine, and neuter genders, and so on. The actual inflectional endings, however, were different, although the two languages shared a fair number of lexical stems. For example, the stem *bōt* meant 'remedy' in both languages, and the nominative singular in both languages was the same. But the nominative plural in Old English was *bōta* and in Old Norse *bótaR*.[2] The form *bóta* happened to be the genitive plural in Old Norse. Some scholars hypothesize that speakers of Old English and Old Norse could communicate with each other to some extent, but the inflectional endings caused confusion, and therefore came to be de-emphasized or dropped. One piece of evidence for this hypothesis is that inflection appears to have been lost much earlier in the northern parts of Britain where Old Norse speakers cohabited with Old English speakers, than in the southern parts of Britain, which were not exposed to Old Norse. Inflectional loss spread from north to south, until all parts of Britain were eventually equally poor in inflection (O'Neil 1980; Fennell 2001: 128–9).

6.4 Paradigms

If you've ever studied a foreign language – French, Latin, German, Russian – you probably know at least intuitively what a **paradigm** is. A **paradigm** consists of all of the different inflectional forms of a particular lexeme or class of

2. The *R* here is a runic character with a phonetic value close to [z].

lexemes. Each distinct form of a lexeme exhibits a specific combination of the inflectional properties that are expressed in that language. For convenience, you can think of a paradigm as a kind of table or grid with cells, one for each inflected form for a given lexeme. For example, in (31) and (33) above, I've shown you paradigms for the Old English nouns 'stone', 'gift', and 'ship', and for the verbs 'to drive' and 'to judge'; these paradigms show the various endings and stem changes that are exhibited by nouns of different genders in the singular and plural in different cases, and in the present and past of strong and weak verbs in different persons. Traditionally the paradigm of a noun or adjective was called its **declension** and that of a verb its **conjugation**.

6.4.1 Inflectional classes

Within a language, not all nouns or verbs may inflect in exactly the same way; all members of a particular category will typically make the same inflectional distinctions, for example, exhibiting case, number, or tense; but the actual forms for particular cases, numbers, or tenses might differ from one group of nouns or verbs to another. These different inflectional subpatterns are called **inflectional classes**. In Latin, for example, nouns generally belong to one of five inflectional classes that differ to some extent in their inflectional suffixes:[3]

(34)

	1	2	3	4	5
	'star'	'servant'	'father'	'hand'	'thing'
Stem form	stellā (F.)	servo (M.)	patr (M.)	manu (F.)	rē (F.)
Singular					
Nom.	stella	servus	pater	manus	rēs
Gen.	stellae	servī	patris	manūs	rĕī
Dat.	stellae	servō	patrī	manuī	rĕī
Acc.	stellam	servum	patrem	manum	rem
Abl.	stellā	servō	patre	manū	rē
Plural					
Nom.	stellae	servī	patrēs	manūs	rēs
Gen.	stellārum	servōrum	patrum	manuum	rērum
Dat.	stellīs	servīs	patribus	manibus	rēbus
Acc.	stellās	servōs	patrēs	manūs	rēs
Abl.	stellīs	servīs	patribus	manibus	rēbus

Nouns that belong to the first inflectional class, traditionally called first declension nouns, are usually feminine, and their stems always end in a long *-ā*. Second declension nouns are typically masculine or neuter and have stems ending in *-o*. In the third declension, nouns may be of any gender and stems typically end in a consonant. And so on.

Latin verbs fall into four inflectional classes or conjugations. Each conjugation is characterized by a particular vowel, called the **theme vowel**, which has no meaning, but is suffixed to the verb root to form a stem.

3. This is a slight simplification, because some of the Latin inflectional classes also have subclasses.

(35)

		1	2	3	4
		'love'	'warn'	'say'	'hear'
Root		am	mon	dic	aud
Stem (root+ theme vowel)		am + ā	mon + ē	dic + i	aud + ī
Present					
singular	1st	am+ō	mon+e+ō	dic+ō	aud+i+ō
	2nd	am+ā+s	mon+ē+s	dic+i+s	aud+ī+s
	3rd	am+a+t	mon+e+t	dic+i+t	aud+i+t
plural	1st	am+ā+mus	mon+ē+mus	dic+i+mus	aud+ī+mus
	2nd	am+ā+tis	mon+ē+tis	dic+i+tis	aud+ī+tis
	3rd	am+a+nt	mon+e+nt	dic+unt	aud+i+unt

The person and number endings are attached directly to the root in the first person singular of the first and third conjugations, and otherwise to the stem, which consists of the root plus the theme vowel.

6.4.2 Suppletion and syncretism

Suppletion and **syncretism** are terms that refer to relationships between inflected forms in a paradigm. **Suppletion** occurs when one or more of the inflected forms of a lexeme is built on a base that bears no relationship to the base of other members of the paradigm. Consider, for example, the verb *go* in English. In the present tense the base is *go*, of course: *I, you, we, they go; he/she/it goes*. The progressive participle is *going*, and the past participle *gone*, both built on the base *go* as well. The past tense of *go*, however, is a suppletive form *went* – that is, a base that is completely different from that of all the other forms. The Latin verb *ferō* is notorious for its suppletive forms. Its present stem is *fer* (so, for example, the first person plural form is *ferimus*). However, its past tense forms are built on the stem *tul-*, and some of its participles are built on yet a third stem *lāt*.

Syncretism is another relationship we can find between the members of a paradigm, specifically one in which two or more 'cells' in our inflectional grid or table are filled with precisely the same form. Consider, for example, the Old English verb paradigm we looked at earlier (repeated here for convenience):

(36)

Present		drīfan 'to drive'	dēman 'to judge'
singular	1st	drīfe	dēme
	2nd	drīf(e)st	dēm(e)st
	3rd	drīf(e)ð	dēm(e)ð
plural	1st	drīfað	dēmað
	2nd	drīfað	dēmað
	3rd	drīfað	dēmað

Although there are distinct forms for first, second, and third person in the singular, the same form is used for all three persons in the plural. These forms display **syncretism**. Another, more complex example of syncretism comes from the noun paradigms of a West Slavic language, Sorbian, spoken in parts of Germany (Baerman 2007):

(37)

	Singular	*Dual*	*Plural*
Nominative	žona	žone	žony
Accusative	žonu	žone	žony
Genitive	žony	žonow	žonow
Locative	žonje	žonomaj	žonach
Dative	žonje	žonomaj	žonam
Instrumental	žonu	žonomaj	žonami

The chart (37) illustrates the paradigm for the noun 'woman'. You can see that in the singular the accusative and instrumental cases are syncretic – they have exactly the same inflectional form – as are the dative and locative cases.[4] In the dual, nominative and accusative are syncretic, as are locative, dative, and instrumental. And in the plural, nominative and accusative are syncretic as well. Morphologists are interested in seeing if there are any patterns to syncretism across languages – for example, is it more typical in languages for plural forms of verbs to be syncretic than singular forms? Or is it more common for nominative and accusative forms of nouns to be syncretic than, say nominative and dative? As yet there is no definitive answer to these questions.

6.5 Inflection and productivity

It is often said that inflection differs from derivation in terms of productivity. We saw in chapter 4 that some rules of word formation are more productive than others. There are derivational affixes in English, as we saw, that are quite dead or nearly so, others that are relatively productive, and some that are fully productive. In contrast, rules of inflection are almost always fully productive: every verb in English, for example, has a progressive form with the suffix *-ing*, and just about every verb can form a past tense. I say "just about every verb" because there are occasional verbs that native speakers of English (at least of American English) are highly reluctant to use in the past tense: for example, I can use the verb *forgo/forego* in the present tense (*I forego dessert most nights*), but for the past tense *forwent* sounds too odd for most people to use either in spoken or written form (*??I forewent dessert last night*), and there's no alternative. Certainly not *foregoed*!

4. The instrumental case is used to mark 'instruments'; for example, in a sentence like *I cut the bread with a knife*, the noun *knife* would be in the instrumental case. The locative case is used to mark locations; for example, the phrase *in the trees* would be locative in *The birds were singing in the trees*.

Challenge

Are there any other verbs in English that you can't use in the past tense? Note that what I mean here are verbs for which you might find past tense forms in the dictionary, but would never actually use yourself. Find a list of irregular verbs in English, either in a dictionary, a grammar book, or on-line, and see if you can find some. Then compare your list of "no past tense" verbs with your classmates'. Is there any generalization you can make about the verbs for which we have no past tenses?

6.6 Inherent *versus* contextual inflection

Consider the Latin phrases in (38):

(38) bonus puer
good-MASC.SG.NOM boy-MASC.SG.NOM
'good boy'

bona puella
good-FEM.SG.NOM girl-FEM.SG.NOM
'good girl'

bonum dōnum
good-NEUT.SG.NOM gift-NEUT.SG.NOM
'good gift'

In each of these phrases the adjective and noun agree in number, gender, and case. As you can see, the adjective 'good' can occur in any of the three genders, depending on the context in which it occurs. The nouns 'boy', 'girl', and 'gift' are always, however, respectively masculine, feminine, and neuter nouns. In other words, the inflectional category of gender is **inherent** in nouns, whereas it is **contextual** in adjectives.

Put more generally, **contextual** inflection is inflection that is determined by the syntactic construction in which a word finds itself, whereas **inherent** inflection is inflection that does not depend on the syntactic context in which a word finds itself. Number is inherent in nouns and pronouns, as is gender. But the case of a noun always depends on its syntactic context. On the other hand, tense and aspect are inherent in verbs, but person and number depend on the nouns or pronouns with which a verb occurs in a sentence. So number can be **contextual** for one category (verbs) but **inherent** for another (nouns).

6.7 Inflection *versus* derivation revisited

We have now looked in some detail both at inflection and at derivation (or lexeme formation, more generally). Remember that we distinguished the two sorts of morphology in the following ways:

(39)

Inflection	*Derivation*
never changes category	sometimes changes category
adds grammatical meaning	often adds lexical meaning
is important to syntax	produces new lexemes
is usually fully productive	can range from unproductive to fully productive

One more thing we can add to these differences is that in words that have both inflectional and derivational affixes, the derivational affixes almost always occur inside the inflectional ones. Remember from chapter 3 that words are formed like onions, with successive layers added one by one. In these word structures, derivational affixes go closer to the base (or root or stem) than inflectional affixes do. For example, in English we can have words like *kingdoms* where the noun suffix *-dom* attaches to its base before the plural suffix *-s*, or *purified* where the verb-forming suffix *-ify* attaches to the adjective *pure* before the past tense suffix *-ed* is added:

(40)

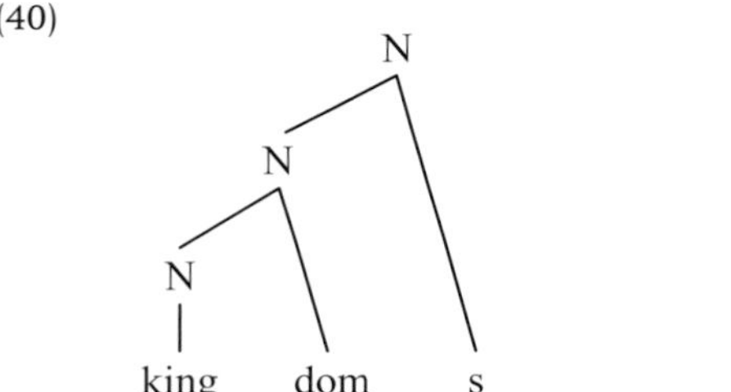

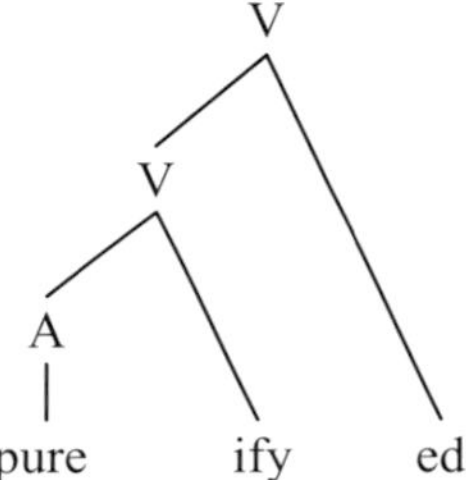

It's not possible in English to attach a plural or past tense suffix and then a derivational suffix; we never form words like **kingsdom* or **walkeder*.

Challenge

We have seen that in words that have both derivational affixation and inflection derivation occurs "inside" inflection. Now consider compounding. Is it possible for the first element in a compound in English to bear an inflection, like a plural or a possessive suffix? You'll have to think carefully here. Collect relevant examples and see if you can make up some yourselves. What do you think: can inflection occur "inside" compounds?

We've seen that the differences between inflection and derivation are usually quite clear, in terms of function, meaning, and position in word structures. In most cases, when we look at the morphology of languages it's not too hard to distinguish inflection from derivation. There are cases, however, where the distinction doesn't seem so clear-cut. One puzzling case is that of nouns in the West Atlantic language Fula (Lieber 1987: 74; Arnott 1970: 75). Each noun in Fula belongs to up to seven different noun classes. One of those classes is a singular class, another a plural class, and the remainder are classes for singular and plural diminutives, pejorative diminutives (meaning something like 'nasty little X'), augmentatives, and pejorative augmentatives. The various noun class forms for 'monkey' are shown in (41):

(41)	Fula	*waa*	'monkey'
	11	waa-ndu	singular
	25	baa-ɗi	plural
	3	baa-ŋgel	diminutive singular
	5	baa-ŋgum	pejorative diminutive singular ('nasty little monkey')
	6	mbaa-kon	diminutive plural
	7	mbaa-ŋga	augmentative singular
	8	mbaa-ko	augmentative plural

As (41) illustrates, noun class is marked in Fula not only by different suffixes, but also by mutation of the initial consonant of the noun stem. So in class 11, for example, the initial consonant of the stem is a continuant [w], in classes 25, 3, and 5, the initial consonant is a stop [b] that corresponds in point of articulation to the continuant, and in classes 6, 7, and 8 it is a prenasalized stop [mb], again corresponding in point of articulation. Singular and plural, of course, are number distinctions, and thus belong to the realm of inflection. Augmentatives and diminutives, however, are expressive morphology (look back to chapter 3, section 2), and are usually considered derivational. The whole list in (41) has the look of a paradigm, though, and even more perplexing, adjectives and articles agree with Fula nouns, even in the noun classes that form augmentatives and diminutives. Agreement, of course, is a hallmark of inflection. The point here is that it's not at all clear in the case of Fula whether to count augmentatives and diminutives as inflectional or derivational, or just to concede that in this particular case the distinction just doesn't make sense.

An equally perplexing case can be found in the Bantu language Sesotho. Like Fula, Sesotho has noun classes. Classes 1 and 2 are classes that contain human nouns. Interestingly, agent nouns can be derived from verbs by putting them into classes 1/2:

(42) *Sesotho (Demuth 2000: 278)*

Infinitive of verb		*Corresponding agent noun (class 1)*	
ho-pheha	'to cook'	mo-phehi	'cook'
ho-ruta	'to teach'	mo-ruti	'teacher'

Formation of agent nouns from verbs certainly looks like derivation. Yet in Sesotho, as in Fula, articles and adjectives must agree with the nouns they modify, in that they must bear the class prefixes corresponding to those nouns. And agreement, of course, is part of inflection.

We leave this issue unresolved here – although it may not seem particularly satisfying to a beginning student of morphology to know that the distinction between inflection and derivation is not always crystal clear, it is precisely cases like these that most intrigue morphologists!

6.8 How to: morphological analysis

In this chapter, I have tried to expose you to some of the sorts of inflectional distinctions that you might expect to find outside of English. Reading about inflectional morphology is not the same as analyzing it though. As a student morphologist you should be ready to figure out what sorts of inflectional distinctions are expressed in an unfamiliar language and how they are expressed. In this section, we will simulate such an experience for you, and take you through the process of trying to analyze the inflectional morphology of a language you otherwise know little or nothing about. Our example comes from the Papuan language Yimas, spoken in New Guinea (Foley 1991: 217):

(43) *Yimas verb forms*

a.	nakatay	'I see him'
b.	nantay	'you see him'
c.	nantay	'he sees him'
d.	impakatay	'I see those two'
e.	impantay	'you see those two'
f.	impantay	'he sees those two'
g.	pukatay	'I see them (more than two)'
h.	puntay	'you see them'
i.	puntay	'he sees them'
j.	naŋkratay	'we two see him'
k.	naŋkrantay	'you two see him'
l.	nampɨtay	'those two see him'
m.	impaŋkratay	'we two see those two'
n.	impaŋkrantay	'you two see those two'
o.	impampɨtay	'those two see those (other) two'
p.	puŋkratay	'we two see them (more than two)'
q.	puŋkrantay	'you two see them'
r.	pumpɨtay	'those two see them'
s.	nakaycay	'we (more than two) see him'
t.	nanantay	'you (more than two) see him'
u.	namputay	'they (more than two) see him'
v.	impakaycay	'we (more than two) see those two'
w.	impanantay	'you (more than two) see those two'
x.	impamputay	'they (more than two) see those two'
y.	pukaycay	'we (more than two) see them (more than two)'
z.	punantay	'you (more than two) see them (more than two)'
aa.	pumputay	'they (more than two) see them (more than two)'

Analyzing the inflectional system of an unfamiliar language is not very different from analyzing the sort of derivational data we looked at in chapter 3. What we do to start off is to look at glosses, and compare forms for areas of overlap.

If you glance even casually at the data in (43), you'll see that I've given you part of a verb paradigm, namely the verb 'to see' in Yimas. You might therefore expect to find something that occurs in every form that would correspond to the root meaning 'see'. Scanning the data, you will see that almost every form except s, v, and y ends in the sequence *tay*. The three forms that don't end in *tay* end in *cay*. It would be a good initial guess, then, that the morpheme for 'see' is *tay*. Since *cay* looks a lot like *tay*, we might hypothesize that it also means 'see', although we don't yet know why those three forms are different. At this point, let's set aside the three forms with *cay* to think more about later.

The next thing we notice about the forms in (43) is that they vary in the person and number of the subject: there are examples with first, second, and third person subjects, not only in singular and plural, but also apparently in the dual. So Yimas makes a three-way number distinction in its verb forms. We notice as well that the examples differ from one another in the number of their object (again singular, dual, and plural), although all of the object forms in these examples happen to be in the third person. Given that we already suspect that the verb root comes at the end, we would guess that subject and object are marked on the verb with prefixes. So our next task is to start comparing the various forms that have the same number object or the same person and number subject to see if we can find separate prefixes for subject and object.

Let's start with the object forms. If you look at (43a–c), you'll notice that all three forms begin with *na-*, but that (43a) has *ka-* after the *na-*, whereas in (43b, c), there's an *n-* after *na-*. We can hypothesize, then, that *na-* must mean 'he-object', but we need to check ourselves to make sure that other forms in (43) with third person singular objects begin with *na-*. If we look at (43j, k, l), you'll see that our hypothesis is confirmed, and if you look further down the data, you'll also see *na-* at the beginning of (43s, t, u). Now, looking at (43d, e, f), you'll notice that all three forms begin with *impa-*; in (43d) this is followed by *ka-* and in (43e–f) by *n-*. We can guess then that *impa-* must mean third person dual object. Finally (43g, h, i) all begin with *pu-*; again in (43g) *pu-* is followed by *ka-* and in (43h–i) by *n-*. It looks like *pu-* is used for a third person plural object.

If *na-* is the third person object marker, then what's left over between it and the verb stem must be the subject marker: in (43a, b, c), this would leave *ka-* as the first person singular subject marker, and *n-* for both the second and third person singular subject markers (syncretism!). Now, if you peel off the other object markers *impa-* and *pu-* from the beginnings of the words, and *tay/cay* from the end of the words, what you have left should be all the subject markers. This is what we get:

(44) *Yimas subject markers*

1 sg.	ka-
2 sg.	n-
3 sg.	n-
1 dual	ŋkra-
2 dual	ŋkran-
3 dual	mpɨ-
1 pl.	kay-
2 pl.	nan-
3 pl.	mpu-

Beginning students might have the impulse to call the subject markers 'infixes', because they occur between the object markers and the verb root, but they are not infixes. Remember that we only call an affix an infix if it occurs within another morpheme. What we have here instead is a sequence of two prefixes before the verb root. So the structure of the Yimas verb is:

(45)

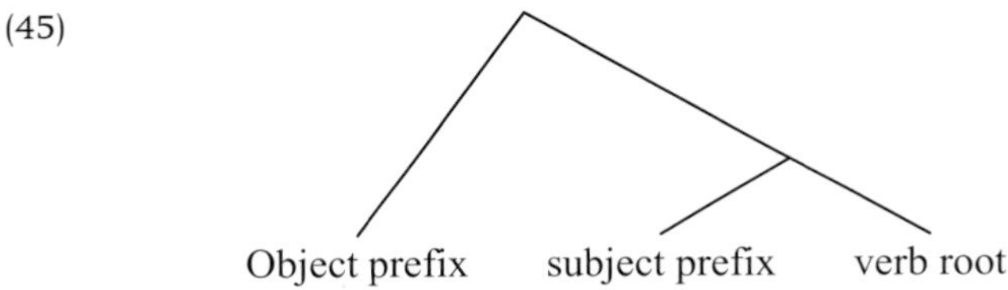

A note about the Yimas data: we still haven't explained why the verb root appears to be *tay* in most verb forms but *cay* in (41s, v, and y). With the data I've given you, it's actually impossible to say anything more about these forms. This is a point at which you, as the morphologist studying an unfamiliar language, must go looking for more data in the hope that they will explain what's going on. So here's a cautionary note: linguistic data can sometimes be a bit messy. Introductory text books have a tendency to sanitize data so that the student linguist will not be confronted with bits that can't be explained. But keep in mind that in the real world data are rarely perfectly sanitary. You often see a pattern, but it's not always perfect. This may be frustrating, but it isn't a bad thing – every bit of mess – or *apparent* mess – forces us, as linguists, to keep looking for more data and to look more carefully at the data we have.

A final note: if you look carefully in Foley's (1991) grammar of Yimas, it appears that there is a phonological rule that turns [t] to [c] if it is preceded by [y].[5] So we were right to guess that *tay* and *cay* are the same morpheme. In chapter 9, we'll see more data like this, and learn how to handle them.

5. This is a rough statement of the rule.

Summary

In this chapter we've first surveyed quite a few sorts of inflection that can be found in the languages of the world, looking at person, number, gender and noun class, tense and aspect, voice, mood, and modality. We've looked in some detail at the sorts of inflections that are found in English, and considered the historical reasons why English has relatively little in the way of inflection. We've then looked at paradigms and important relationships between forms in paradigms, such as suppletion and syncretism, and at the distinction between inherent and contextual inflection. We have revisited the distinction between inflection and derivation to see that the line between them can be blurred. And finally, we've looked at a set of data to see how to figure out how the inflection in an unfamiliar language works.

Exercises

1. Look at the following data. In each case, identify the form of the morphological rule (that is, prefixation, suffixation, infixation, reduplication, internal stem change, templatic) and its function (inflection or derivation):

   a. *Turkish (Kornfilt 1997: 446)*

silâh	'weapon'	silâhlı	'armed person'
at	'horse'	atlı	'horseman'
yaş	'age'	yaşlı	'aged person'
Londra	'London'	Londralı	'person living in London'

   b. *Musqueam (Suttles 2004: 139)*

p'ét'ᶿ	'sew'	p'ép'ət'ᶿ	'be sewing'
k'ʷéc	'look'	k'ʷék'ʷəc	'be looking'
łás	'fish with a net'	łáłəs	'be fishing with a net'

   c. *Hausa (Newman 2000: 454)*

tsā̀kō	'chick'	tsā̀kī	'chicks'
kwā̀ɗō	'frog'	kwā̀ɗī	'frogs'
zā̀bō	'guinea-fowl'	zā̀bī	'guinea-fowls'

2. In the two columns below, you find verb bases and imperfective forms for a number of verbs in Tagalog, an Austronesian language spoken in the Philippines (Schachter and Otanes 1972: 365):

   a.

Verb base		*Imperfective*	
lagyan	'put in/on'	nilalagyan	'is putting in/on'
regaluhan	'give a present to'	nireregaluhan	'is giving a present to'
walisan	'sweep'	niwawalisan	'is sweeping'

   Write a rule that shows how the imperfective is formed in Tagalog.

   Now consider these data:

   b.

Verb base	*Imperfective*
lagyan	linalagyan
regaluhan	rineregaluhan
walisan	winawalisan

Apparently the imperfective forms in (b) are less preferred, but possible, imperfective forms for the same verbs. Write an alternative rule that accounts for these forms.

Finally, what are the two imperfective forms that you might expect from the verb stem *yapakan* 'step on'?

3. Consider the following data from Swahili (Corbett 1991: 43–4):

kikapu	kikubwa	kimoja	kilianguka
basket	large	one	fell
vikapu	vikubwa	vitatu	vilianguka
baskets	large	three	fell

Describe how number marking works in Swahili. On which categories is number marking inherent and on which is it contextual?

4. In Russian, both the noun *student* 'student' and the noun *dub* 'oak' are masculine, but there are slightly different declensions for animate and inanimate nouns. Discuss the paradigms below in terms of the patterns of syncretism they display (data from Corbett 1991: 166):

Singular

student	'student'	*dub*	'oak'
Nominative	student	dub	
Accusative	studenta	dub	
Genitive	studenta	duba	
Dative	studentu	dubu	
Instrumental	studentom	dubom	
Locative	studente	dube	

Plural

Nominative	studenty	duby
Accusative	studentov	duby
Genitive	studentov	dubov
Dative	studentam	dubam
Instrumental	studentami	dubami
Locative	studentax	dubax

5. Consider the data below from Syrian Arabic (Cowell 1964: 173–4). Segment the words into morphemes, and identify the meanings/functions of the morphemes. What word formation processes are represented in these data? (Hint: Assume that the form for 'he ate' is *ákal*, that this form has neither prefixes nor suffixes, and that a glottal stop always occurs before a vowel-initial stem.)

ʔákal	'he ate'	byaakol	'he eats'
ʔáklet	'she ate'	btaakol	'she eats'
ʔákalu	'they ate'	byaaklu	'they eat'
ʔakált	'you (masc.) ate'	btaakol	'you (masc.) eat'
ʔakálti	'you (fem.) ate'	btaakli	'you (fem.) eat'
ʔakáltu	'you (pl.) ate'	btaaklu	'you (pl.) eat'
kol	'eat! (masc.)'		

6. Below are the Latin verb paradigms for the verbs 'love' and 'warn' in the future and perfect tenses. Identify the morphemes in each form (root, stem, suffixes) and discuss how the future and perfect tenses differ from one another, and how the first and second conjugation verbs differ from one another.

amābō	'I will love'	monēbō	'I will warn'
amābis	'you will love'	monēbis	'you will warn'
amābit	'he/she will love'	monēbit	'he/she will warn'
amābimus	'we will love'	monēbimus	'we will warn'
amābitis	'you (pl.) will love'	monēbitis	'you (pl.) will warn'
amābunt	'They will love'	monēbunt	'they will warn'
amāvī	'I loved'	monuī	'I warned'
amāvistī	'you loved'	monuistī	'you warned'
amāvit	'he/she loved'	monuit	'he/she warned'
amāvimus	'we loved'	monuimus	'we warned'
amāvistis	'you (pl.) loved'	monuistis	'you (pl.) warned'
amāvērunt	'they loved'	monuērunt	'they warned'

7. Dutch makes a distinction between weak and strong verbs. Below are the paradigms for the past tense of a weak verb (*werken* 'to work') and a strong verb (*binden* 'to tie'). Discuss differences in the ways that weak and strong past tenses are formed in Dutch. Are the patterns of syncretism the same or different in the weak and strong forms?

ik werkte	'I worked'	ik bond	'I tied'
jij werkte	'you worked'	jij bond	'you tied'
hij, zij werkte	'he/she worked'	hij/zij bond	'he/she tied'
wij werkten	'we worked'	wij bonden	'we tied'
jullie werkten	'you (pl.) worked'	jullie bonden	'you (pl.) tied'
zij werkten	'they worked'	zij bonden	'they tied'

8. Consider the sets of verbs below from the Yuman language Diegueño (Langdon 1970: 80–7).

a.	a·ap	'to lay down a long object'
	a·kaṭ	'to cut with a knife'
	a·mał^y	'to sweep'
	a·naṛ	'to lower a long object, to drown'
	a·maṛ	'to cover over a long object, to bury someone'
	a·uł	'to lay a long object on top of'
b.	cu·kaṭ	'to bite off'
	cu·paṛ	'to emit a victory yell'
	cu·kuw	'to bite'
	cu·ya·y	'to hum'
	cu·sip	'to smoke' (e.g. a pipe)
	cu·k^{w}is	'to chatter (like squirrel)'
c.	tu·kaṭ	'to cut with scissors or ax, to cut in chunks'
	tu·mił	'to hang (small round object)'
	tu·pa·	'to crack acorns'
	tu·uł	'to put on (e.g. a hat)'
	tu·maṛ	'to cover over a small object'
	tu·yum	'to put a round small object in sun'

a. Divide the words above into prefixes and roots and try to assign meanings to each morpheme.
b. Is the process you see illustrated here one of inflection or derivation? Give evidence to support your answer.

CHAPTER

7 Typology

CHAPTER OUTLINE

KEY TERMS

isolating
analytic
agglutinative
fusional
polysynthetic
index of synthesis
index of fusion
head-marking
dependent-marking
implicational universal

In this chapter you will learn about morphological typology: how morpholgists characterize the morphological systems of languages.

- We will begin by describing the morphological systems of five very different languages, looking at the kinds of lexeme formation and inflection that they display.
- Then we will discuss both traditional ways of classifying the morphology of languages and more contemporary ways of doing so.
- Finally, we will look at how both the family a language belongs to and the geographic area in which it is spoken can influence its typological classification.

7.1 Introduction

In this book, we have focused so far on formal processes of morphology that occur in many languages of the world; we have provided a sort of toolkit for forming new words from which languages can pick and choose. What we haven't looked at yet is what we could call "the big picture": how does word formation work overall in specific languages and how can the morphological systems of particular languages vary from one another? In other words, rather than looking at specific processes and how they work, we can look at how languages exploit different parts of our toolkit to constitute their own unique systems of morphology. We can try to characterize the morphological systems of languages according to the sorts of morphological processes that they exploit. We can compare languages to each other to see if characteristics of their morphological systems correlate in any way with other parts of their grammars, say their syntax or their phonology. And we can look at the distribution of morphological patterns in terms of genetic relationships (language families) or areal tendencies (where languages are spoken in the world). Studying language from this sort of global perspective is the subject of **linguistic typology**.

7.2 Universals and particulars: a bit of linguistic history

The history of linguistics has for centuries seen a tug of war between theories that emphasize universals – those things that are common to all human languages, perhaps because they are part of our common biological endowment – and particulars – those things that look unique and appear to distinguish languages from one another.

At the turn of the twentieth century, partly as a legacy of colonialism, linguists started studying indigenous languages of Africa, Asia, and North America more seriously. In North America, the tradition of American Structuralism stressed the uniqueness of languages, not surprising, considering the linguistic diversity of native North American languages and their prodigious differences from one another and from more familiar and better studied Indo-European languages. With the advent of Generative Grammar in the middle of the twentieth century, the pendulum has swung in the other direction. Chomskians stress what's universal in languages, and search for ways to explain linguistic differences as the result of small choices that languages make from a universal set of options that our biological make-up, our hard-wiring for language as it were, makes available.

Understanding this universal set of options is ever more important today, with renewed efforts among linguists to study the many languages that are endangered. Universals and particulars are both important: until we have a sense of the full range of particulars, we can only begin to confront the issue of universals. That's why studying the widest range of languages possible is so important.

Do we know anything about morphological universals? Yes – and you've gotten a taste of what we know here. We know, for example, that there is a range of word formation strategies that appear in the languages of the world. And there are some conceivable sorts of word formation strategies that never occur. We know, for example, that there's no language so far that forms one sort of word from another – say nouns from verbs or verbs from nouns – by reversing the sounds of the words, or by infixing [p] after every third sound. But there are a lot of things we don't know – what are possible forms of reduplication or infixing, for example, and what is impossible. So the search for particulars and universals goes on in tandem.

7.3 The genius of languages: what's in your toolkit?

Students of linguistics often have a sense of excitement when they come upon data from languages they've never heard of before and discover how very different languages can look from one another. Although linguists in the generative tradition are always quick to stress that languages are more alike underlyingly than they seem superficially, what often strikes students first are the wonderfully exuberant ways in which languages can do things differently. Some of what gives this impression of difference is the unique way in which the morphology of languages can package different concepts in different forms.

The linguist Edward Sapir, writing at the turn of the twentieth century, had a rather romantic name for the unique combination of processes that characterize the grammar of each language – he called it the "genius" of the language (Sapir 1921: 120):

> For it must be obvious to anyone who has thought about the question at all or who has felt something of the spirit of a foreign language that there is such a thing as a basic plan, a certain cut, to each language. This type or plan or structural "genius" of the language is something much more fundamental, much more pervasive than any single feature of it that we can mention, nor can we gain an adequate idea of its nature by a mere recital of the sundry facts that make up the grammar of the language.

These days, linguists might find quaint Sapir's idea that each language is imbued with something like a special spirit or soul that embodies its 'basic plan'. But Sapir's idea of "genius" comes close to that feeling that students have that the new languages they encounter are in some sense new creatures.

In this section we take a brief look at five very different languages – Turkish, Mandarin Chinese, Samoan, Latin, and Nishnaabemwin – to try to see something of this unique combination of morphological processes that constitutes at least one part of the genius of each language. All of these languages use morphology in one way or another, but each makes different choices from the universal toolbag of rule types that we have surveyed so far in this book. Some use predominantly one strategy, others many; some have lots of inflection, others almost none. But each has its own unique pattern.

7.3.1 Turkish (Altaic)

Imagine one word that means 'were you one of those whom we are not going to be able to turn into Czechoslovakians?' This may seem highly unlikely, but it's possible in Turkish: the word is *çekoslovakyalılaştıramayac aklarımızdanmıydınız*, and it's possible because Turkish is a language that delights in suffixation:

(1) *Turkish (Inkelas and Orgun 1998: 368)*[1]

çekoslovakya - lı - laş - tır - ama - yacak - lar - ımız -
Czechoslovakia - from - become - CAUSE – unable - FUT - PL - 1PL -

dan - mı - ydı - nız
ABL INTERR - PAST - 2PL

Let's look in detail at the pieces that make up this word. Note first that Turkish has a phonological rule called 'vowel harmony' which makes the vowels of suffixes agree with the preceding vowels in the base in backness and sometimes roundness (we'll look more closely at this rule in chapter 9). The first suffix that we encounter after the base is a suffix *-li*, which attaches to nouns to make personal nouns. With vowel harmony, the suffix *-li* will show up as *-lu* after the front round vowel ö:

(2) *-li (-lu) personal nouns (Lewis 1967: 60)*

şehir	'city'	şehir-li	'city dweller'
köy	'village'	köy-lu	'villager'

The next suffix *-laş* forms intransitive verbs from adjectives. Again, taking vowel harmony into account, the suffix can appear as *-leş* if it is preceded by a base with front vowels, and *-laş* if preceded by back vowels:

(3) *-laş (-leş) intransitive verbs (Lewis 1967: 228–9)*

ölmez	'immortal'	ölmez-leş	'become immortal'
garp-lı	'West-from'	garp-lı-laş	'become Westernized'

Next we have the suffix *-dir*, which forms causative verbs from intransitive verbs. Note that the [d] in the suffix shows up as the corresponding voiceless stop [t] if the preceding consonant is voiceless:

(4) *-dir (-dur, -dür, -tir, etc.) causative (Lewis 1967: 144–5)*

don	'freeze'	don-dur	'cause to freeze'
öl	'die'	öl-dür	'kill' (= 'cause to die')

1. Inkelas and Orgun (1998) give this word in phonetic transcription. Here it is rewritten in Turkish orthography, as nothing hinges on the pronunciation.

The following suffix is called the 'impotential', which essentially means 'not able':

(5) *-eme (-ama) impotential (Lewis 1967: 151)*

gel-eme	'unable to come'
anlı-ama	'unable to understand'

Next is the future suffix *-ecek*:

(6) *-ecek (-acak) future (Lewis 1967: 114)*

bul-acak	'will find'
tanı-acak	'will recognize'

Then the plural suffix *-ler*:

(7) *-ler (-lar) plural (Lewis 1967: 29)*

kız	'girl'	kız-lar	'girls'
el	'hand'	el-ler	'hands'

And then, we get the first person possessive suffix *-ımız*, the ablative marker *-dan* (which essentially means 'from'), the question marker *-mı*, the locative marker *-dı* (which means 'at'), and the second person plural verb marker *-nız*. As you can see, each of these suffixes can occur in simpler words, but they can all be used together to form the enormously long and complex word we started with. If we put it all back together again, we get something like (8):

(8)

çekoslovakya-lı	'someone from Czechoslovakia' = 'Czechoslovakian'
çekoslovakya-lı-laş	'become Czech'
çekoslovakya-lı-laş-tır	'cause to become Czech'
çekoslovakya-lı-laş-tır-ama	'unable to cause to become Czech'
çekoslovakya-lı-laş-tır-ama-(y)-acak	'will be unable to cause to become Czech'
çekoslovakya-lı-laş-tır-ama-(y)-acak-lar	'will be unable to cause to become Czech-pl.'
çekoslovakya-lı-laş-tır-ama-(y)-acak-lar-ımız	'we will be unable to cause to become Czech.-pl'
çekoslovakya-lı-laş-tır-ama-(y)-acak-lar-ımız-dan	'from (those) we will be unable to cause to become Czech-pl'
çekoslovakya-lı-laş-tır-ama-(y)-acak-lar-ımız-dan-mı-ydı-nız	'were you from (those) we will be unable to cause to become Czech-pl.'

Although the predominant way of forming words in Turkish is through suffixation, it also has a process of compounding, as the examples in (9) show:

(9) *Turkish compounds (Lewis 1967: 231–3)*

Noun + noun	baba + anne father mother	babaanne paternal grandmother
	baş + bakan head minister	başbakan prime minister
Adjective + noun	kırk + ayak forty foot	kırkayak centipede
	büyük + anne great mother	büyükanne grandmother

As the examples in (9) show, Turkish compounds are right-headed.

We can see from our lengthy discussion of the example in (1) that Turkish uses suffixation for both derivation and inflection. In addition to marking number on nouns, Turkish also marks case, as the paradigm in (10) shows:

(10)

ev	'house'
evi	Definite-accusative
evin	Genitive
eve	Dative
evde	Locative
evden	Ablative

Turkish verbs are inflected for person and number, and can appear in a number of different tenses, including present, past, future, and conditional. There are affixes to make verbs negative or interrogative, and verbs can mark other distinctions as well. All of these inflections are suffixes; verb forms can be quite long and complex.

What this brief description of Turkish morphology shows is that a language can have wildly abundant morphology, and yet use no more than a couple of tools from our universal toolkit. Turkish is an overwhelmingly, exuberantly suffixing language, using suffixes for both lexeme formation and inflection, but it has no processes of prefixation to speak of. What few prefixes can be found in Turkish are always on borrowed words, and essentially are not part of the native system of word formation of Turkish.

7.3.2 Mandarin Chinese (Sino-Tibetan)

Where the genius of Turkish morphology lies in the exuberance of its processes of suffixation, Mandarin Chinese makes entirely different choices from our universal toolkit, although it too concentrates on just a few tools.

According to Li and Thompson (1971), Mandarin has no processes of prefixation to speak of, and it has only a tiny handful of suffixes, among them the three in (11):[2]

2. Li and Thompson give a few examples of prefixes, but it's not clear why they treat them as prefixes rather than as the first elements of compounds.

(11) *Li and Thompson (1971: 41–3)*

-xué	dòngwù-xué	'animal-ology' = 'zoology'
	shèhuì-xué	'society-ology' = 'sociology'
	zhé-xué	'philosophy-ology' = 'study of philosophy'
-jiā	kēxué-jiā	'science -ist' = 'scientist'
	yùndòng-jiā	'athletics-ist' = 'athlete'
	zhèngzhì-jiā	'politics-ist' = 'politician'
-huà	gōngyè-huà	'industry-ize' = 'industrialize'
	tóng-huà	'similar-ize' = 'assimilate'

The suffix *-xué* attaches to nouns to make nouns meaning 'the study of X', and *-jiā* makes personal nouns, also from other nouns. Notice that in the example *kēxué-jiā*, both suffixes occur. The third suffix *-huà* makes verbs from nouns and adjectives. Suffixation is quite limited in Mandarin though: there are relatively few suffixes, and we certainly do not find words of the complexity of those in Turkish or even of words in English.

Mandarin also has full reduplication, which it uses for two purposes. Verbs can be reduplicated to form derived verbs meaning 'X a little':

(12) *Li and Thompson (1971: 29)*

jiāo	'teach'	jiāo-jiāo	'teach a little'
shuō	'say'	shuō-shuō	'say a little'
xiē	'rest'	xiē-xiē	'rest a little'

And some adjectives can be reduplicated to make intensive adjectives, that is, adjectives that mean 'very X':

(13) *Li and Thompson (1971: 33)*

pàng	'fat'	pàng-pàng	'very fat'
hóng	'red'	hóng-hóng	'very red'
yuán	'round'	yuán-yuán	'very round'

Though Mandarin is relatively poor in affixation and reduplication, it is incredibly rich in compounding. Mandarin has not only compound nouns and compound adjectives, as English does, but also all sorts of compound verbs, as the examples in (14) show:

(14) *Examples from Li and Thompson (1971: 49–55), Ceccagno (undated ms. 3–8), and Li (1995: 256)*

a. $[N + N]_N$	hè-mǎ	'river-horse' = 'hippopotamus'
	hǎi-gǒu	'sea-dog' = 'seal'
	chún-gāo	'lip-ointment' = 'lipstick'
b. $[N + N]_N$	shū-guǒ	'vegetable-fruit' = 'vegetables and fruit'
c. $[A + A]_A$	liàng-lì	'bright-beautiful' = 'bright and beautiful'
d. $[A + N]_N$	hēi-chē	'black-vehicle' = 'illegal vehicle'
	zhǔ-yè	'main-page' = 'home page'

e. $[V + N]_N$	jiān-shì	'supervise-matter' = 'supervisor'
	wén-xiōng	'hide-breast' = 'bra'
f. $[V + N]_V$	dài-gǎng	'wait for-post' = 'wait for a job'
	jìn-dú	'prohibit-poison' = 'ban (sale/use of) drugs'
g. $[A + V]_V$	gōng-shī	'public-show' = 'make public'
h. $[V + V]_V$	dǎ-pò	'hit-broken'
	lā-kāi	'pull-open'
	zhui-lei	'chase-tired'

As the examples in (14) show, Mandarin has many different types of compound, indeed, many more types than English, which as we've seen has very productive compounding processes. In Mandarin, some compounds are attributive, for example those in (14a) and (14d). The examples in (14b, c) are coordinative compounds. And some are subordinative, for example those in (14e, f, g). Most of these compounds are endocentric (14a, b, c, d, f, g, h), but those in (14e) are exocentric. Some are right-headed (14a, c, d, f, g), some have two heads (the coordinate compounds in (14b, c)), and some are left-headed (14h).

The examples we have given above all concern lexeme formation in Mandarin because Mandarin has rather little in the way of inflection. Nouns are not inflected for number, nor do verbs inflect for person or number. Tense is not marked morphologically and aspect is marked only by separate particles that appear after the verb. Mandarin does have a system of noun classifiers that are used when counting or otherwise quantifying nouns, but again separate particles rather than affixes are used to mark the class of particular nouns. So we can return to the sentences we looked at in chapter 1 and see them in the wider context of Mandarin morphology:

(15) Wo jian guo yi zhi chang jing lu.
I see EXP[3] one CLASSIFIER giraffe

(16) Wo jian guo liang zhi chang jing lu
I see EXP two CLASSIFIER giraffe

The verb *jian* 'see' doesn't change its form from one aspect to another, nor does the noun *chang jing lu* 'giraffe' change from singular to plural. In order to signal more than one giraffe, one needs to signify a specific number or quantity.

What this shows us is that Mandarin is just as able as Turkish to come up with new words and to express grammatical distinctions, but its strategy for doing so makes use of different means.

3. In chapter 1 we translated *guo* as 'past', but this was not quite right. The morpheme *guo* marks what Li and Thompson (1971: 226) call "experiential aspect," which signals that the speaker has experienced the event. It is, however, often used in the context of an event that has already happened.

7.3.3 Samoan (Austronesian)

What makes Samoan an interesting contrast to Turkish and Mandarin is that it uses a wide variety of word formation processes without seeming to favor one over another. To pursue our mechanical metaphor, its toolbag is chock-full of different tools. In this language we can find prefixation, suffixation, and circumfixation, both partial and full reduplication, and also to some extent compounding. There's also even a bit of internal stem change in the form of a morphological process of vowel lengthening. Here are some examples:

(17) *Prefixation: fa'a 'causative' (Mosel and Hovdhaugen 1992: 175–6)*

alu	'go'	fa'aalu	'make go'
goto	'sink'	fa'agoto	'make sink'
ga'o	'fat'	fa'aga'o	'apply grease to'
māsima	'salt'	fa'amāsima	'salt' = 'put salt on'

The prefix *fa'a* can be put on either verbs or nouns to make verbs meaning 'cause X' or 'make X' or 'put X on'.

(18) *Circumfixation: fe- -a'i 'reciprocal' (Mosel and Hovdhaugen 1992: 182)*

fīnau	'quarrel'	fefīnaua'i	'quarrel with one another'
logo	'inform'	felogoa'i	'consult with one another'
mata	'look'	femātaa'i	'look at one another'

Although Mosel and Hovdhaugen say that prefixes are usually mutually exclusive – that is, there can only be one in a word – the circumfix *fe- -a'i* can occur outside the prefix *fa'a-*, as you see in the word in (19):

(19) fe - fa'a - māfanafaa - a'i
RECIP - CAUSE - warm - RECIP
'be of comfort to one another'

In addition to prefixes and circumfixes, Samoan can also form words by suffixation:

(20) *Suffixation: -ga forms abstract nouns from verbs (Mosel and Hovdhaugen 1992: 195)*

amo	'carry'	amoga	'carrying'
a'o	'learn'	a'oga	'education'
savali	'walk'	savaliga	'a walk'

Suffixing *-ga* to a verb and lengthening the first vowel of the verb stem forms another kind of derived noun which can be concrete and often, according to Mosel and Hovdhaugen (1992: 195) has a flavor of plurality:

(21) *Suffixation of -ga and vowel lengthening*

amo	'carry'	āmoga	'person(s) carrying loads on yokes'
a'o	'learn'	ā'oga	'school'
savali	'walk	sāvaliga	'people on march'

The vowel lengthening that occurs in this process can be considered a form of internal stem change.

Samoan is also rich in processes of reduplication, as we already saw in section 5.4. As we saw there, Samoan has a process of partial reduplication that forms verbs from nouns. To repeat example (10) from chapter 5:

(22) *Partial reduplication: N → V*

lafo	'plot of land'	lalafo	'clear land'
lago	'pillow, bolster'	lalago	'rest, keep steady'
pine	'pin, peg'	pipine	'secure with pegs'

Partial reduplication can also be used to make ergative verbs from nonergative verbs:

(23) *Partial reduplication:* $V_{nonergative} \rightarrow V_{ergative}$ *(Mosel and Hovdhaugen 1992: 222–3)*

lo'u	'bent'	lolo'u	'bend'
motu	'break (non-erg.)'	momotu	'break (erg.)'
sa'e	'overturn'	sasa'e	'cause to capsize'

In both cases, partial reduplication copies the first consonant and vowel of the base.

New words are also formed in Samoan by full reduplication. We saw one example (9b) in section 5.4, which is repeated in (24), and another example is given in (25):

(24) *Full reduplication: V → N (Mosel and Hovdhaugen 1992: 229)*

'apa	'beat, lash'	'apa'apa	'wing, fin'
au	'flow on, roll on'	auau	'current'
solo	'wipe, dry'	solosolo	'handkerchief'

(25) *Full reduplication: frequentative/intensive*

a'a	'kick'	a'aa'a	'kick repeatedly'
'emo	'blink, flash'	'emo'emo	'twinkle'
fo'i	'return'	fo'ifo'i	'keep going back'

In (25) we see a process of full reduplication that takes verbs and makes them into **frequentatives**, that is, forms that mean 'X repeatedly', or **intensives**, forms that mean 'X a lot'.

Finally, Samoan also has compounding, as the examples in (26) show:

(26) *Compounding (Mosel and Hovdhaugen 1992: 241–3)*

alagā	'source'	'oa	'valuable goods'	alagā'oa	'source of wealth'
'aliti	'bed'	tai	'sea'	'alititai	'seabed'
fāsi	'piece of'	moli	'soap'	fāsimoli	'piece of soap'
suā	'liquid'	esi	'paw paw'	suāesi	'paw paw soup'

These examples are all left-headed endocentric attributive compounds. As we can see, although compounding in Samoan is possible, this language has nowhere near the richness of compound types that can be found in Mandarin.

Interestingly, although Samoan sentences express case relations (ergative/absolutive) and clauses are marked for tense, aspect, and mood, Samoan has no inflectional paradigms (Mosel and Hovdhaugen 1992: 169). In fact. relations like case, tense, aspect, and mood are expressed by independent particles, rather than by prefixes, suffixes, or reduplication, in this language; hence most of our examples here have been derivational.

7.3.4 Latin (Indo-European)

Like Turkish, and unlike Mandarin and Samoan, Latin is a heavily inflected language. And like Turkish, its inflections are almost entirely suffixal.[4] However, its inflection looks rather different from Turkish inflection in that often several meanings are combined into a single inflectional morpheme in Latin. Its toolbag is somewhat larger for derivation than for inflection, with some prefixation and compounding in addition to suffixation. Indeed, you will probably recognize elements of Latin derivational morphology, as many of them have been borrowed into English. We will look at inflection first, then derivation.

Latin nouns are inflected for case, number, and gender, and adjectives are inflected to agree with them. (27) shows the paradigm for the feminine noun *puella* 'girl', and (28) a noun phrase with an agreeing adjective:

(27)	*'girl'*	*Singular*	*Plural*
	Nom.	puella	puellae
	Gen.	puellae	puellārum
	Dat.	puellae	puellīs
	Acc.	puellam	puellās
	Abl.	puellā	puellīs

(28)	bona puella	good-NOM.SG. girl-NOM.SG	'good girl'
	bonae puellae	good-NOM.PL. girls-NOM.PL	'good girls'

Each inflection carries a combination of meanings that includes case, number, and gender. For example, the morpheme *-ārum* is used in the genitive plural, and in addition, signals that this noun belongs to the first Latin declension, almost all of whose members are feminine in gender.

Verbs have a number of different stems which form the basis of inflectional paradigms that show aspect (imperfect *vs.* perfect) and voice (active *vs.* passive), as well as person and number. A portion of the paradigms for the verbs 'love' and 'warn' are shown in (29) (these are the same examples you looked at in exercise 6 of chapter 6):

4. Latin has a small amount of reduplication and infixation in its verbal paradigms, but both processes occur only in a small set of verbs, so we will not go into them here.

(29)

amābō	'I will love'	monēbō	'I will warn'
amābis	'you will love'	monēbis	'you will warn'
amābit	'he/she will love'	monēbit	'he/she will warn'
amābimus	'we will love'	monēbimus	'we will warn'
amābitis	'you (pl.) will love'	monēbitis	'you (pl.) will warn'
amābunt	'They will love'	monēbunt	'they will warn'
amāvī	'I loved'	monuī	'I warned'
amāvistī	'you loved'	monuistī	'you warned'
amāvit	'he/she loved'	monuit	'he/she warned'
amāvimus	'we loved'	monuimus	'we warned'
amāvistis	'you (pl.) loved'	monuistis	'you (pl.) warned'
amāvērunt	'they loved'	monuērunt	'they warned'

These verb forms are built on one of the stem forms, called the Theme Vowel stem (*amā-, monē-*) to which a future suffix *-bi-* or a perfect suffix *-v-* is attached. Then person and number suffixes are attached. Interestingly, different person and number affixes are used in the past than in other tenses:

(30) *Person and number suffixes in Latin verbs*

Non-past

singular	1	-ō	plural	1	-imus
	2	-s		2	-itis
	3	-t		3	-unt

Past

singular	1	-ī	plural	1	-imus
	2	-istī		2	-istis
	3	-it		3	-ērunt

In the non-past, the suffixes combine person and number; in some sense, however, the second set of suffixes also signals past tense in addition to person and number, since they are only used in the past tense.

Latin has both derivational suffixes and prefixes. For example, it forms abstract nouns from verb roots by adding the suffix *-or*:

(31)

timor	'fear'	timēre	'to fear'
amor	'love'	amāre	'to love'

The suffix *-men* attaches to either roots or theme vowel stems to form nouns that denote the result of an action:

(32)

agmen	'line of march, band'	agere	'to lead'
certāmen	'contest, battle'	certāre	'to contend'

The prefix *amb-* attaches to verbs and means 'around' and the prefix *in-* attaches to adjectives to form negative adjectives:

(33)	īre	'to go'	amb-īre	'to go about'
	sānus	'sane'	in-sānus	'insane'

Latin does not use compounding as much as English and Germanic languages do, but it does have some compounds:

(34)	flōs, flōris	'flower'	coma	'hair'	flōri-comus	'flower-crowned'
	āla	'wing'	pēs	'foot'	āli-pēs	'wing-footed'

When two roots are put together into a compound, the linking vowel *-i-* is used between them.

7.3.5 Nishnaabemwin (Algonquian)

The final language we will look at is Nishnaabemwin, an Algonquian language spoken in southern Ontario, Canada (Valentine 2001). It makes heavy use of affixation, especially suffixation, and has an extremely rich system of inflection. What's most interesting about Nishnaabemwin, however, is the way that it combines bound morphemes to form new lexemes.

Let's look first at inflection. Nouns have either animate or inanimate gender. They can be inflected for number, and have different forms for diminutive, pejorative, and what is called 'contemptive', a suffix that adds a negative meaning, but one that is less strongly negative than the pejorative suffix. Nouns can also occur in a locative form, and what is called the 'obviative' form, which serves to distance a noun from the speaker in a narrative. Finally, there are prefixes and suffixes that indicate possession of a noun. Some of the relevant forms for the noun *zhiishiib* 'duck' are given in (35):

(35)	zhiishiib	'duck'
	zhiishiib-ag	Plural
	zhiishiib-an	Obviative
	zhiishiib-enh	Contemptive[5]
	zhiishiib-ens	Diminutive
	zhiishiib-ish	Pejorative
	zhiishiib-ing	Locative
	n-zhiishiib-im	'my duck'

These inflections are not mutually exclusive. If they occur in combination, the diminutive, for example, must precede the pejorative, which in turn precedes the suffix that occurs in the possessive. Nor are these the only inflections that can appear on nouns: this is just a small selection!

Verb inflection is even more complex than noun inflection, and we cannot really do justice to it here. But just to give you a taste of how very

5. I have constructed this form and the next one. Valentine (2001) does not cite these forms himself.

intricate the inflection of verbs is in Nishnaabemwin, consider Valentine's (2001: 219) description of the inflectional possibilities of intransitive verbs that take animate subjects:

For the INDEPENDENT and CONJUNCT ORDERS, there are theoretically nine person/number/obviation categories, four MODES (and ITERATIVES in the conjunct), two POLARITIES, three TENSES, and two functions (VERBAL and PARTICIPIAL in the conjunct) creating 882 inflectional combinations. For the IMPERATIVE ORDER, there are three person/number combinations, and three modes, creating theoretically nine inflectional combinations, making a total of roughly 890 forms for the animate intransitive verb.

The independent form of the verb is used in main clauses, and differently inflected forms are used in subordinate clauses (the conjunct form) and in imperatives. By polarities, Valentine means that verbs have different forms for positive and negative. Compare this to the four forms of the verb *walk* in English (*walk, walks, walked, walking*); English uses the same forms of the verb in main and subordinate clauses, and uses a separate word for negation.

Derivation is no less complex than inflection in this language: words rarely consist of a single root morpheme. Instead, various bound morphemes are joined together to form words. Intransitive verbs, for example, frequently consist of two or three pieces. The last piece, called the 'final', expresses a verbal concept. The first piece, called the 'initial', expresses something that modifies the verbal concept; in English we would express similar concepts with separate adjectives, adverbs, or prepositions:

(36) *Examples from Valentine (2001: 327) with initial giin- 'sharp'*
giin'zi 'be sharp (of tongue)-ANIM. SUBJ. giinaa 'be sharp-INANIM.SUBJ.

Verbs may also have a third piece that occurs between the initial and the final; this is called the 'medial' and corresponds to what in English would usually be a nominal concept (Valentine 2001: 330, 334):

(37) dewnike 'have an ache in one's arm' dew 'sore' + nik 'arm' + e 'have'
bookjaane 'have a broken nose' book 'broken' + jaan 'nose' + e 'have'
gaagiijndbe 'have a sore head' gaagiij 'sore' + ndib 'head' + e 'have'

Such forms can undergo further derivation by adding another final element, so from *gaagiijndbe* 'have a sore head' we can get *gaagiijndbekaazo*, which means 'pretend to have a sore head' by adding the final *-kaazo*, which means 'pretend to'. And of course each of these verbs can then take various inflectional elements.

Nouns can be made up of several bound morphemes as well. For example, the nouns in (38a) are made up of an initial bound element that has an adjectival sort of meaning, and a second bound element that means 'thing'. Those in (38b) have an initial element that is a free form, and a bound final element that means 'building, habitation':

(38) a. *From Valentine (2001: 484)*

gete hii	'old thing'	gete-	'old'	-hii	'thing'
shkihii	'new thing'	oshk-	'new'	-hii	'thing'

b.

bzhikiiwgamig	'cowshed'	bizhikiw	'cow'	-gamigw	'building'
gookooshgamig	'pig sty'	gookoosh	'pig'	-gamigw	'building'

Valentine uses terms like 'initial', 'medial', and 'final', rather than calling the bound morphemes that make up these forms 'prefixes' or 'suffixes', probably because these morphemes are much more like roots than like affixes in their meanings. We might therefore think of them as bound bases.

There are some derivational suffixes in Nishnaabemwin, however. For example the suffix *-aagan* creates nouns from one class of transitive verbs:

(39)

naabkawaagan 'scarf, necklace'	naabkaw 'wear anim. noun around neck'
noodaagan 'employee'	noodaw 'hire anim. noun'

And Nishnaabemwin also has compounds, which differ from the forms in (38) by being composed of two independent stems (Valentine 2001: 516–17):

(40)

jiibaakwe-kik	'cooking pot'	(cook + pot)
shkode-daaban	'train'	(fire + vehicle)
waasgamg-kosmaan	'bell pepper'	(pepper + squash)

One thing that is striking about the morphological system of Nishnaabemwin is the overall complexity of words: words rarely consist of a single morpheme, and frequently consist of many morphemes.

7.3.6 Summary

Comparing these languages, we can see a bit of what Sapir means about the "genius" of a language. Although we don't need to romanticize the unique character of each language, studying morphology opens our eyes to the different mixture and balance of word formation processes to be found in individual languages. Each language has a different combination of word formation processes that gives the language its unique character. But we should keep in mind as we wonder at all this diversity that we should always be on the lookout for the commonalities or universals that mark all these languages as human languages.

Challenge

Go to your university library and look for a grammar of a language you know nothing about. Make sure the grammar you choose has a section on morphology. Write a two- or three-page description of the sorts of inflection and derivation that your chosen language displays, thinking about both inflection and derivation, and about the different kinds of word formation rules your language displays. We will look at these again shortly.

7.4 Ways of characterizing languages

Up to this point we have viewed the morphological systems of languages in an impressionistic way, looking at the combination of inflectional and derivational processes that give the language its overall morphological pattern. Morphologists continually seek to go beyond simple descriptions, however. In looking at the morphological systems of individual languages, we are always looking for patterns. We are interested in what sorts of morphological rules we might expect to find in languages and what that tells us about the general faculty of human language. We are also interested in classifying languages by looking at whether particular sorts of traits cluster together, and whether those clusters tell us something deeper about the nature of language. We will return to the first of these considerations in the last chapter of this book. Here, we will look more closely at different ways we may classify the morphology of languages, and how various classifications illuminate the nature of language. This latter enterprise is called **typology**. We start this section by looking at a very traditional way of classifying languages, and then look at more contemporary schemes of morphological typology.

7.4.1 The fourfold classification

Morphological typology has a long history, going back at least to the early nineteenth century in the work of Wilhelm von Humboldt (1836; reference in Comrie 1981/1989). In this tradition, also developed by the linguist Edward Sapir, who we mentioned above, it was common to divide languages into four morphological types: isolating (or analytic), agglutinative, fusional, and polysynthetic.

An **isolating** or **analytic** language is one in which each word consists of one and only one morpheme. Vietnamese is often cited as an example of an isolating language. For example, nouns do not inflect for plurality. The noun *đồng hồ* means 'watch' or 'watches'. If one wants to be specific about how many watches are in question, it is possible to use a numeral and then a noun classifier before the noun (Nguyen and Jorden 1969: 119), as (41a) shows:

(41) a. hai cái đồng hồ
two CL watch
'two watches'

b. Mai tôi làm cái đó
tomorrow I do CL that
'I will do that tomorrow'

Tôi làm cái đó hôm qua.
I do CL that yesterday
'I did that yesterday'

Similarly, as (41b) illustrates, verbs do not inflect for tense in Vietnamese. Instead, if one wants to be specific about the time of an event, it is necessary to use specific adverbs like 'tomorrow' or 'yesterday'.

Of the languages we have profiled in section 7.3, Mandarin comes closest to being an isolating language. Although Mandarin has abundant compounding, it has little that would count as morphological inflection. Like Vietnamese, plurality, tense, and aspect are all expressed by separate words.

Unlike isolating languages, **agglutinative** languages have complex words. Furthermore, those words are easily segmented into separate morphemes and each morpheme carries a single chunk of meaning. In our grammatical sketches in 7.3, Turkish is the language that comes closest to an agglutinative ideal. For example, we gave the various case forms of the Turkish noun 'house' in (10), repeated here (42):

(42)	ev	'house'
	evi	Definite-accusative
	evin	Genitive
	eve	Dative
	evde	Locative
	evden	Ablative

To form the plurals of these nouns, all one needs to do is add the morpheme *-ler*, which goes after the root and before the case endings:

(43)	evler	'house-PLURAL'
	evleri	Plural definite-accusative
	evlerin	Plural genitive
	evlere	Plural dative
	evlerde	Plural locative
	evlerden	Plural ablative

The two sorts of morphemes are easily separated in terms of both form and meaning.

A **fusional** language, like an agglutinative language, allows complex words, but its morphemes are not necessarily easily segmentable: several meanings may be packed into each morpheme, and sometimes it may be hard to decide where one morpheme ends and another one starts. Latin is a good example of a fusional language. We can, for example, compare the noun paradigm in Latin with that in Turkish. Whereas it is easy in Turkish to separate off one morpheme that means 'plural' and another that means 'genitive', it is not possible find separate morphemes that go with those concepts in Latin. Let's look again at the paradigm for 'girl' in Latin in example (27), repeated here:

(44)	*'girl'*	*Singular*	*Plural*
	Nom.	puella	puellae
	Gen.	puellae	puellārum
	Dat.	puellae	puellīs
	Acc.	puellam	puellās
	Abl.	puellā	puellīs

If we assume that the root for the noun 'girl' is *puell*, the best we can do is to say that the morpheme that means genitive singular is *-ae* and the one that means genitive plural is *-ārum*. Each of these also carries gender information (remember that nouns with these endings are most often feminine) as well. But there is no way of separating part of these morphemes into smaller pieces that mean 'genitive' or 'singular' or 'plural' or 'feminine'). This is the hallmark of fusional morphology.

The final morphological type is called **polysynthetic**. In a polysynthetic language words are frequently extremely complex, consisting of many morphemes, some of which have meanings that are typically expressed by separate lexemes in other languages. In our grammatical sketches in section 7.3, Nishnaabemwin is a language that could easily be characterized as polysynthetic. Remember that it not only has an intricate inflectional system, but forms complex words out of two or more bound bases. We repeat the examples from (37) here as an illustration of polysynthesis (Valentine 2001: 330, 334):

(45)	dewnike 'have an ache in one's arm'	dew 'sore' + nik 'arm' + e 'have'
	bookjaane 'have a broken nose'	book 'broken' + jaan 'nose' + e 'have'
	gaagiijndbe 'have a sore head'	gaagiij 'sore' + ndib 'head' + e 'have'

These forms can then act as bases for all the inflectional affixes that attach to intransitive verbs in Nishnaabemwin.

7.4.2 The index of synthesis and the index of fusion

The problem with the traditional fourfold classification is that languages rarely fall neatly into one of the four classes. For example, English is not quite an isolating language – it has some inflection – but it is certainly not an agglutinating or a fusional language (Old English was much closer to being a fusional language, though). Another problem is that sometimes the inflectional system of a language falls into one category, but the derivational system fits better into another. English again can serve as an illustration: English derivational morphology is actually not that far from being agglutinating, as an example like *operationalizability* (*operat-ion-al-iz-able-ity*) suggests.

One way of dealing with these problems is to give up the fourfold classification in favor of two different scales, which Comrie (1981/1989: 51) calls the 'index of synthesis' and the 'index of fusion'. The **index of synthesis** looks at how many morphemes there are per word in a language. Isolating languages will have few morphemes per word – in the most extreme cases, only one morpheme per word. Agglutinative or polysynthetic languages, on the other hand, will typically have many morphemes per word. And because this is a scale, languages like Samoan, or English can fall somewhere in-between the extremes.

The **index of fusion**, in a rough sense, measures how many meanings are packed into each morpheme in a language. High on the index of fusion would be Latin inflection, where at least three different concepts (for example, gender, number, and case in nouns, person, number, and tense in verbs) can be packed into a single morpheme. Low on the index of fusion would be an agglutinative language like Turkish, where each morpheme carries only one inflectional concept (for example, case or number, but not both together).

There is no reason why we could not look at the derivational and inflectional morphologies of a language separately and see where they fit on these two scales. In terms of inflection, English would be low on the index of synthesis, but we might place it higher on that scale if we're looking at English derivation, since many words in the language are formed by compounding, prefixation, or suffixation. Similarly, we might class English higher on the index of fusion if we're looking at verbal inflection (the suffix *-s* carries the meanings 'third person', 'present', and 'singular' packed together in a form like *walks*) than if we're looking at derivation, where each morpheme typically has one distinct meaning.

Challenge

Take a look at the grammatical sketch of an unfamiliar language that you made earlier in this chapter. How would you characterize your language in terms of the fourfold classification? Where would you place it in terms of the index of synthesis and the index of fusion? Does your language pose any special problems for these means of classification?

7.4.3 Head- *versus* dependent-marking

Above, we have looked at the morphologies of languages in terms of the ease with which words can be segmented and the relationship between meaning and form in morphemes. There are other things we can look at, however, in classifying and comparing languages.

One thing we can look at is the way that morphology signals the relationship between words in phrases. The main element in each syntactic phrase is called its **head**; the head of a noun phrase (NP) is the noun, the head of a verb phrase (VP) is the verb, and so on. The other elements that combine with the head to become a phrase might be called the **dependents** of the head. Dependents of a noun can be adjectives, determiners, or possessives, and dependents of a verb can be its subject or object. Languages can choose to mark relationships between the head and its dependents in different ways: the relationship can be marked exclusively on the head, or exclusively on the dependent, or on both or neither. If the relationship is marked by some morpheme on the dependent, this is called **dependent-marking**, and if it is marked on the head, it is called **head-marking**.

As illustrated in (46a), the relationship between the head noun and its possessor is marked on the possessor in English, but on the head in Hungarian (46b) (examples from Nichols 1986: 57):

(46) a. *English*
the man's house
dependent head

b. *Hungarian*

as	ember	ház-a
the	man	house-3SG.
dependent		head

'the man's house'

The NP in English therefore shows dependent-marking between a possessor and the head noun, whereas the NP in Hungarian shows head-marking.

Whole clauses may also exhibit either dependent-marking or head-marking. In Dyirbal, NPs are case-marked to show their relationship to the verb:[6]

(47) *From Nichols (1986: 61)*

balan	ḍugumbil	baŋul	yaɽangu	baŋgu	yuguŋu	balgan
ART.NOM	woman.NOM	ART.ERG	man.ERG	ART.INSTR	stick.INS	hit
dependent		dependent		dependent		head

'The man is hitting the woman with a stick.'

Dyirbal would therefore be considered a dependent-marking language within clauses.

In contrast, the Mayan language Tzutujil shows head-marking within clauses: the verb is marked for the person and number of its subject and object, but there is no marking on the subject and object themselves to show their function in the clause (Nichols 1986: 61):

(48)

x- ∅- kee- tij	tzyaq	ch'ooyaa7
ASP-3SG.-3PL.- ate	clothes	rats
head	dependent	dependent

'Rats ate the clothes'

As I mentioned above, it is also possible for languages to show neither head-marking nor dependent-marking. For example, a language that is isolating and has no inflection would have neither head- nor dependent-marking. On the other hand, it is possible for a language to have inflectional markings on both the head and its dependents. Turkish, for example, marks both the possessor and the possessed noun in an NP:

(49)

ev-in	kapı-sı
house-GEN	door-3SG
dependent	head

'the door of the house'

When the relationship between the dependent and the head is marked on both constituents, we have what is called **double-marking**.

6. Nichols (1986) considers the verb to be the head of a clause, but not all linguists agree with her on this.

7.4.4 Correlations

In the last sections we have seen various ways in which the morphologies of languages can be classified. Typologists are interested in more than classification, however. They are also interested in seeing whether there are any predictable correlations between particular morphological characteristics or between morphological characteristics and other (syntactic or phonological) aspects of grammar. In other words, they seek to find whether there are any patterns to the kinds of morphology one finds in a language, and if there are, why those patterns might exist.

For example, as Whaley (1997: 131) points out, isolating languages usually have rigidly fixed word orders. This correlation makes perfect sense: if a language has no morphological way of marking the *function* of noun phrases in a sentence, those functions must be signaled by the *position* of a noun phrase in a sentence.

Linguists such as Joseph Greenberg (1963) and Joan Bybee (1985) have looked at many languages and observed that there are several other correlations to be found. For example, Greenberg noted the two patterns in (50):

(50) If a language has inflection, it will also have derivation.

If a language has separate morphemes for number and case, and if both are either prefixes or suffixes, the number morpheme almost always occurs closer to the base than the case morpheme.

Observations such as these are called **implicational universals**. Based on observations of lots of languages, they are not true in every language, but they are true in a statistically significant number of languages.

Bybee (1985) also observed a statistically significant trend in the ordering of inflectional affixes in the languages of the world. What she noticed is that in languages with a number of different inflectional affixes on verbs, those affixes tended to come in a particular order. For example, if a language exhibits both tense and person/number affixes, the tense affix usually comes closer to the verb stem than the person/number affix. And if there are aspectual affixes, these tend to precede tense affixes.

We must still ask, however, why these particular correlations should exist. Bybee, for example, claims that the order of inflectional morphemes on verbs has something to do with their relevance to the verb itself. We might think of this in terms of the concepts of inherent and contextual inflection that we discussed in section 6.6. For example, tense and aspect are inherent categories for verbs, but person and number are contextual: they signal agreement with one or more of a verb's arguments (its subject or object, for example). So inherent inflection comes closer to the verb stem than contextual inflection. The second of Greenberg's implicational universals might be explained in the same way. Number is an inherent inflection on nouns, but case is contextual, and inherent marking comes closer to the noun stem than contextual marking. Whether this is generally the case, however, is something that will require looking at many more languages.

7.5 Genetic and areal tendencies

In addition to classifying languages on the basis of specific structural characteristics that they display in their morphologies, we can look at typological patterns in a more global way. There are two ways to do this. We can look at whether there are sorts of morphology that tend to be prevalent in particular language families or sub-families. And we may look at whether there are specific sorts of morphology that tend to be found in certain geographic areas even among languages that belong to different language families.

We can give several examples of genetic tendencies. If we look, for example, at compounding in two different branches of the Indo-European family, Italic (Romance) and Germanic, we can see an interesting pattern: although both branches make use of compounds, the sorts of compounds they favor are quite different. Germanic languages like English tend to favor endocentric attributive and subordinate compounds like those in (51a), whereas Italic languages seem to prefer exocentric subordinate compounds, and have few attributive compounds (see 3.4 for these terms):

(51) a. *English*
endocentric attributive: dog bed, windmill
endocentric subordinate: dishwasher, hand made

b. *Italian*
exocentric subordinate: lavapiatti 'wash-dishes' = 'dishwasher'

Another example comes from the Bantu sub-family of languages. It is relatively rare in the languages of the world for inflectional morphology to be accomplished predominantly by prefixing. Nevertheless, there is a large concentration of such languages in the central and southern parts of Africa. This is the area of Africa in which we find the Bantu languages which are in turn part of the larger Niger-Congo family. Bantu languages frequently inflect nouns and verbs by adding prefixes. A nice illustration of this can be found in the World Atlas of Language Structures On-line; go to http://wals.info and take a look at the map that accompanies chapter 26.

As for areal tendencies, Whaley (1997: 13) gives a fascinating example. He points out that three languages spoken in close proximity in the Balkan region of Europe all mark the definiteness of nouns by adding a suffix:

(52)	*Albanian*	mik-u	'friend-the'
	Bulgarian	trup-at	'body-the'
	Rumanian	om-ul	'man-the'

What makes this example so interesting is that these three languages belong to completely different sub-families of Indo-European – Albanian forms its own branch; Bulgarian is Balto-Slavic; and Rumanian is Italic – and none of the other languages in these three branches show definiteness with suffixes! Geographic proximity can be the only explanation for the distribution of this morphological trait.

Another example of a morphological pattern that is especially prevalent in a particular geographic region is verbal compounding. We saw in chapter 3 that English rarely compounds two verbs (although there are a few examples like *stir-fry* or *slam-dunk*). In contrast, verbal compounds are not at all unusual in Asia, even in genetically unrelated languages. For example, although Japanese is thought to be a language isolate (it is not related to any language family), and Mandarin Chinese is a member of the Sino-Tibetan family, both display verbal compounds, as the examples in (53) show:

(53) *Japanese (Fukushima 2005: 570–85)*
naki-saken   cry-scream   'cry and scream'

Mandarin (Li and Thompson 1971: 55)
mai-dao   buy-arrive   'manage to buy'

It would be interesting to explore the historical and social forces that lead languages in the same geographic area to develop similar morphological patterns, but we will not do so here.

Summary

In this chapter we have surveyed five languages to see what morphological resources they make use of. Turkish is an agglutinative language that largely relies on suffixing. Mandarin Chinese is an inflectionally isolating language that makes heavy use of compounding to form new lexemes. Samoan makes use of a wide range of different word formation processes to derive new lexemes, but is rather poor in inflection. Latin has heavily fusional inflection, and primarily derives new lexemes using prefixes and suffixes. And Nishnaabemwin is a polysynthetic language. We also looked at the traditional fourfold morphological classification of languages into isolating, agglutinative, fusional, and polysynthetic types, and at more useful typological tools such as the indexes of synthesis and of fusion, and at the distinction between head- and dependent-marking. Finally, we looked briefly at genetic and areal tendencies in morphological patterning.

Exercises

1. On the basis of the data below, try to classify these languages as isolating, agglutinative, fusional, or polysynthetic.

   a. *Swahili (Vitale 1981: 18)*
   Juma a-li-wa-piga watoto
   Juma 3.SG.SUBJ-PST-3PL.OBJ-hit children
   'Juma hit the children'

   Watoto wa-li-m-piga Juma
   Children 3.PL.SUBJ-PST-3.SG.OBJ-hit Juma
   'The children hit Juma'

   b. *Yay (Whaley 1997: 127)*
   mi^4 ran^1 tua^4 ŋwa^1 lew^6
   not see CLASS snake CMPLT
   'He did not see the snake'[7]

   c. *Musqueam (Suttles 2004: 28)*
   xʷ-qʷé-nəc-t-əs
   inward-penetrate-bottom-TR-3TR[8]
   '[She] punches holes in the bottom of it'

   d. *Old English (Baugh and Cable 1993: 62)*
   On þyss-um ēaland-e cōm ūp sē
   on this-NEUT.DAT.SG island-NEUT.DAT.SG came up the.MASC.NOM.SG

   God-es þēow Augustinus
   God-MASC.GEN.SG. servant.MASC.NOM .SG Augustine

   and his gefēr-an.
   and his companion-MASC.NOM.PL
   'God's servant Augustine and his companions came up on this island.'

   e. *Náhuatl Puebla Sierra (Nida 1946: 171 – called Zacapoaxtla Aztec there)*
   nan-čoka-to-skih-h
   2PL- cry-DUR-COND-PL
   'you all would keep crying'

2. Consider the following paradigms from the Mayan language Tzutujil (Dayley 1985: 87):

waraam	*'to sleep'*	
Perfect	1sg.	in warnaq
	2sg.	at warnaq
	3sg.	warnaq
	1pl.	oq warnaq
	2pl.	ix warnaq
	3pl.	ee warnaq
Completive	1sg.	xinwari
	2sg.	xatwari
	3sg.	(x)wari
	1pl.	xoqwari
	2pl.	xixwari
	3pl.	xeewari

7. The superscript numerals on the original Yay sentence in (b) above are tone markings.
8. TR means 'transitive suffix'; 3TR means 3rd person transitive subject.

Incompletive	1sg.	ninwari
	2sg.	natwari
	3sg.	nwari
	1pl.	noqwari
	2pl.	nixwari
	3pl.	neewari

Identify all the morphemes in the paradigms above. On the basis of your analysis, how would you classify Tzutujil using the traditional fourfold classification system?

3. On the basis of the data below, try to classify these languages as head-marking, dependent-marking or double-marking.

   a. *Chechen (Nichols 1986: 60)*
   de:-n a:xča
   father-GEN money
   'father's money'

   b. *Huallaga Quechua (Nichols 1986: 72)*
   hwan-pa wasi-n
   John-GEN house-3
   'John's house'

   c. *Abkhaz (Nichols 1986: 60, from Hewitt 1979: 116)*
   à-č'k°ən yə-y°nə̀
   the-boy his-house
   'the-boy's house'

4. Review the sections of chapter 5 where we discussed morphological processes like reduplication, infixation, internal stem change, and templatic morphology. Do they present any problems for the traditional fourfold classification? Choose two examples from chapter 5 and discuss whether they are easily classified or not.
5. Look at the World Atlas of Language Structures On-line (http://wals.info). At the WALS website click on "Features," and then click on article 24. "Locus of Marking in Possessive Noun Phrases." Which is more prevalent in the languages of the world, head-marking or dependent-marking? Now click on the accompanying map. Can you notice any areal tendencies in head-marking and dependent-marking in possessive noun phrases?
6. Look at the Universals Archive website (http://typo.uni-konstanz.de/archive/intro/index.php). Click on "Search" and at the search screen, type "morphology" in the box next to "Original," and then click on "Submit Query." You should get about 25 hits. From these hits, find five implicational universals.
7. Consider the following examples from the Otomanguean language Mixtec (Macaulay 1996: 79):

   a. a-ni-ka-žesámá-rí
   TEMP-CP-PL-eat-1
   'We already ate'

   b. a-ni-ka-kã́ʔã-ró xĩ́ maestro
   TEMP-CP-PL-talk-2 with maestro
   'You (PL) already talked with the teacher'

TEMP stands for temporal, CP for completive, and PL for plural. 1 and 2 stand for first person and second person respectively.

What problem does this example raise for Bybee's implicational universal?

CHAPTER

8 Words and sentences: the interface between morphology and syntax

CHAPTER OUTLINE

KEY TERMS

valency
argument
active
passive
anti-passive
causative
applicative
noun-incorporation
clitic
phrasal verb
phrasal compound

In this chapter you will learn about the intersection between morphology and syntax, which is the study of sentence structure.

- We will examine morphological processes like passivization and causativization that change the number of arguments of a verb.
- We will look at phenomena that sit on the borderline between word formation and syntax: clitics, phrasal verbs like *call up* in which the two parts can sometimes be separated in sentences, and compounds that contain whole phrases or even whole sentences.

8.1 Introduction

As you've learned so far in this book, morphology is concerned with the ways in which words are formed in the languages of the world. Syntax, in contrast, is concerned with identifying the rules that allow us to combine words into phrases and phrases into sentences. Morphology and syntax, then, are generally concerned with different levels of linguistic organization. Morphologists look at processes of lexeme formation and inflection such as affixation, compounding, reduplication, and the like. Syntacticians are concerned, among other things, with phrase structure and movement rules, and rules concerning the interpretation of anaphors and pronouns. Nevertheless, there are many ways in which morphology and syntax interact.

We saw in chapter 6 that inflectional morphology is defined as morphology that carries grammatical meaning; as such it is relevant to syntactic processes. Case-marking, for example, serves to identify the syntactic function of an NP in a sentence. Inflectional markers like tense- and aspect-affixes identify clauses of certain types, for example, finite or infinitive, conditional or subjunctive. Person and number markers often figure in agreement between adjectives and the nouns they modify, or between verbs and their subjects or objects. In some sense, inflection can be viewed as part of the glue that holds sentences together.

In this chapter we will first look in more detail at several types of verbal morphology that affect sentence structure by changing what is called the valency of verbs. **Valency** concerns the number of **arguments** in a sentence, where arguments are noun phrases like the subject and object selected by the verb of the sentence. In section 8.3 we will look at the borderline between morphology and syntax. While it is usually clear to linguists which phenomena belong to which level of organization, the boundary between the two levels is not always crystal clear. There are cases in which derivational morphemes appear to attach to whole phrases, for example, or elements that seem not quite bound enough to be affixes, but not quite free enough to be viewed as independent words.

8.2 Argument structure and morphology

Above, we defined the **valency** of a verb as the number of arguments it takes. **Arguments**, in turn, are defined as those phrases that are semantically necessary for a verb or are implied by the meaning of the verb. Generally, arguments occur obligatorily with a verb, as the examples in (1) show:

(1) a. Fenster snores.
*Snores.[1]

1. Here we use the convention of marking an unacceptable sentence with an asterisk.

b. Fenster devoured the pizza.
   *Fenster devoured.
   *Devoured the pizza.

c. Fenster put the wombat in the bathtub.
   *Fenster put the wombat.
   *Fenster put in the bathtub.
   *Fenster put.

The verb *snore* has only one argument, its subject noun phrase. Verbs that have only one argument are traditionally called **intransitive**. The verb *devour* requires two arguments, its subject and object noun phrases. Two-argument verbs are **transitive**. And the verb *put* requires a subject, an object, and another phrase that expresses location. If a verb requires three arguments, it is traditionally called **ditransitive**.

The arguments of a verb are often, but not always, obligatory. For example, the verb *eat* must have a subject, and it can have an object, but the object is not necessary.

(2) a. My goat eats tin cans.
    b. My goat eats.

Although it is optional we still consider the object *tin cans* to be an argument of the verb because the verb *eat* implies something eaten, even if that something is not overtly stated; notice that in (2b), we assume that the goat eats something (more specifically, we assume that the goat eats something foodlike, if we don't explicitly say otherwise, as we do in (2a).

Of course, in English it is always possible to add prepositional phrases to a sentence that express the time or location of an action, the instrument with which it is done, or the manner in which it is done (*Fenster put the wombat in the bathtub with great care on Thursday* ...). These extra phrases are not necessary to the meaning of the verb, however, and are not arguments. Instead, they are called **adjuncts**. We will not need to talk about adjuncts here.

Valency-changing morphology alters the number of arguments that occur with a verb, either adding or subtracting an argument, making an intransitive verb transitive or a transitive verb intransitive, for example. English has some morphology that changes argument structure, but other languages, as we will see, have far more morphology of this sort.

8.2.1 Passive and anti-passive

The most obvious example of valency-changing morphology in English is the passive voice. Example (3) shows a pair of active and passive sentences in English:

(3) a. Fenster bathed the wombat.
    b. The wombat was bathed (by Fenster).

In the active sentence, the verb has two arguments, its **agent** (the one who does the action) and the **patient** or **theme** (what gets affected or moved by the action); the agent functions as the subject of the action, and the patient as the object. In the passive sentence, an agent is unnecessary. If it occurs, it appears in a prepositional phrase with the preposition *by*. The patient is the subject of the passive sentence. In effect there is no longer any object, and the passive form of the verb therefore has one fewer argument than the active form.

Part of what signals the passive voice in English is passive morphology on the verb. English passives are formed with the auxiliary verb *be* and a past participle, which is signaled for regular verbs by adding *-ed* to the verb base. Irregular verbs can form the past participle in a number of ways: by adding *-en* (*write* ~ *written*), by internal vowel change (*sing* ~ *sung*), or by internal vowel change and addition of *-t* (*keep* ~ *kept*).

Other languages also have morphological means to signal the change in argument structure in passive sentences. Example (4) shows an active and a passive sentence from West Greenlandic, and (5) an active–passive pair from Maori:

(4) *West Greenlandic (Fortescue 1984: 265)*

a. inuit nanuq taku-aat
people.REL[2] bear see-3PL.3SG.INDIC.
'The people saw the polar bear'

b. nanuq (inun-nit) taku-**niqar**-puq
polar bear (people-ABL) see-PASSIVE-3SG.INDIC.
'The polar bear was seen (by the people)'

(5) *Maori (Bauer 1993: 396)*

a. E koohete ana a Huia i a Pani
T/A scold T/A pers Huia DO pers Pani[3]
'Huia is scolding Pani'

b. I koohete-**tia** a Pani e Huia
T/A scold-pass pers Pani by Huia
'Pani was scolded by Huia'

In (4b), you can see that the morpheme *niqar* makes a verb passive in West Greenlandic, and (5b) shows that a verb in Maori can be made passive by adding the suffix *-tia*.[4] As was the case in English, the addition of these morphemes goes along with passive syntax, that is, making the patient/theme into the subject of the sentence, and making the agent optional. If the agent appears, it is marked with the ablative case in West Greenlandic, and by the preposition *e* in Maori.

Passive sentences are relatively familiar to speakers of English, but English has nothing like what is called the **anti-passive**. Like the passive, the anti-passive takes a transitive verb and makes it intransitive by reducing the number of its arguments. What's different, though, is which argu-

2. The relative case is the case of the transitive subject in West Greenlandic.

3. T/A means 'tense/aspect'; DO means 'direct object'.

4. Bauer (1993: 396–7) actually shows that there are several suffixes that make verbs passive in Maori.

ment gets eliminated. For the passive, it's the transitive subject that disappears (or is relegated to a prepositional phrase or a case form other than that typical for subject), whereas for the anti-passive, it's the transitive object that disappears, as the example in (6) from Yidiɲ shows:

(6) *Yidiɲ (Dixon 1977: 279)*
yiŋu buɲa buga-:ḍiŋ
this.ABSOLUTIVE woman.ABSOLUTIVE eat-ANTIPASSIVE
'This woman is eating.'

In Yidiɲ, the anti-passive is marked on the verb by adding the suffix *-:ḍiŋ*. Since Yidiɲ is an ergative case-marking language (see section 6.2), the subject of a transitive verb is in the ergative case. The subject of an intransitive verb is in the absolutive case, as you see in example (6). So while *'eat'* is normally transitive in Yidiɲ, you can see that it has become intransitive here.

As with the passive, it is also possible to express the 'missing' argument overtly, but in a case form other than that usually used for the direct object. Whereas in an active sentence, the direct object of a transitive verb is marked with the absolutive case, in an anti-passive sentence, the subject is absolutive and the object, if it appears, is either in the dative or the locative case:

(7) *Dixon (1977: 277)*
wagu:ḍa wawa-:ḍiɲu gudaga-nda
man.ABSOLUTIVE saw-ANTIPASSIVE dog-DATIVE
'The man saw the dog.'

While the translation of (7) makes it look like this sentence means exactly the same thing as an active sentence, this is only because there is no real way of capturing the nuance of this sentence in English, a language that lacks the anti-passive.

8.2.2 Causative and applicative

Passive and anti-passive morphology signal a reduction in the number of arguments that a verb has. There are other sorts of morphology that signal that arguments have been *added* to a verb.

Causatives signal the addition of a new subject argument, which semantically is the causer of the action. If the verb has only one argument to begin with, the causative sentence has two, and if it has two to begin with, the causative sentence has three arguments. Compare the Swahili sentences in (8) and (9):

(8) *Vitale (1981: 158)*
a. maji ya-me-chemka
water it-PER-boil
'The water boiled'

b. Badru a-li-chem-sh-a maji
Badru he-PST-boil-CAUSE water
'Badru boiled the water' (lit. 'caused the water to boil')

(9) *Vitale (1981: 156)*

a. Halima a-li-ki-pika chakula
Halima she-PST-it-cook food
'Halima cooked the food'

b. Juma a-li-m-pik-ish-a Halima chakula
Juma he-PST-her-cook-CAUSE Halima food
'Juma caused Halima to cook food'

In (8a), the verb 'boil' has only one argument, its patient/theme. In (8b), along with the causative morpheme *-(i)sh* , an external causer argument is added as the subject of the sentence. Similarly, in (9a), the verb 'cook' has two arguments, an agent (*Halima*) and a patient ('food'); the agent is the subject of the sentence. When the causative suffix *-(i)sh* is added, a third argument (*Juma*) is added and it becomes the subject.

Applicative morphology, like causative morphology, signals the addition of an argument to the valency of a verb. But the added argument is an object, rather than a subject. We can again use Swahili for our example:

(10) *Vitale (1981: 44); Baker (1988: 393)*

a. ni-li-pika chakula
I-PST-cook food
'I cooked some food'

b. ni-li-m-pik-i-a chakula Juma
I-PST-for him-cook-APPL food Juma
'I cooked some food for Juma'

The suffix *-i* signals that a second object (*Juma*) has been added to the verb.

Challenge

Aside from the passive, English is usually said to have little in the way of valency-changing morphology. Consider the following data, though:

i. Fenster ate pickles.
ii. Fenster over-ate.
iii. *Fenster over-ate pickles.

What is the effect of the prefix *over-* on the valency of the verb *eat*? Now consider sentences (iv–vi):

iv. The plane flew.
v. *The plane flew the field.
vi. The plane over-flew the field.

Think about these examples, and try to think of other verbs formed with the prefix *over-* in English. Does *over-* work like any of the valency-changing morphemes we have looked at in this chapter?

8.2.3 Noun incorporation

There is one more way in which morphology interacts with the argument structure of verbs. Consider the data in (11) from the Araucanian language Mapudungun:

(11) *Baker and Fasola (2009: 595)*

a. Ñi chao kintu-le-y ta chi pu waka
my father seek-PROG-IND.3SG.SBJ the COLL cow
'My father is looking for the cows'

b. Ñi chao kintu-waka-le-y.
my father seek- cow-PROG-IND.3SG.SBJ
'My father is looking for the cows'

Sentences (11a) and (11b) mean precisely the same thing in Mapudungun. In (11a), the direct object 'cow' is an independent noun phrase in the sentence, but in (11b), it forms a single compound-like word with the verb root 'seek'. This sort of structure – where the object or another argument of the verb forms a single complex word with the verb – is called **noun incorporation**. Noun incorporation tends to occur in languages with polysynthetic morphology (see section 7.4). In Mapudungun, the object noun follows the verb root in both the incorporated and the unincorporated forms. But this need not be the case, as the example in (12) from the Iroquoian language Mohawk shows:

(12) *Baker (1988: 20)*

a. Ka-rakv ne sawatis hrao-nuhs-aʔ
3N- be.white DET John 3M-house-SUF
'John's house is white'

b. Hrao-nuhs- rakv ne sawatis
3M- house-be.white DET John
'John's house is white'

As (12a) shows, the direct object follows the verb when it occurs independently in Mohawk, but it precedes the verb when it is incorporated.

There is much discussion among morphologists and syntacticians whether noun incorporation should be explained as a result of morphological rules or syntactic rules. We will return to this question in chapter 10.

8.3 On the borders

As we saw in the last section, one point of tangency between morphology and syntax occurs where morphology has an effect on the argument structure of verbs. There, it was clear that affixes – clearly morphological elements – can reduce or increase the number of arguments that a verb takes – clearly a matter of syntax. What we will look at in this section, however, are cases where it is not so clear what belongs to morphology and what belongs to syntax – cases, in other words, that inhabit a sort of borderland between the two levels of organization.

8.3.1 Clitics

One of these borderland creatures is something that linguists call a clitic. Clitics are small grammatical elements that cannot occur independently and therefore cannot really be called free morphemes. But they are not exactly like affixes either. In terms of their phonology, they do not bear stress, and they form a single phonological word with a neighboring word, which we will call the host of the clitic. However, they are not as closely bound to their host as inflectional affixes are; frequently they are not very selective about the category of their hosts. Those clitics that come before their hosts are called **proclitics**, those that come after their hosts **enclitics**.

Two types of clitics are often distinguished: **simple clitics** and **special clitics**. Anderson (2005: 10) defines **simple clitics** as "unaccented variants of free morphemes, which may be phonologically reduced and subordinated to a neighboring word. In terms of their syntax, though, they appear in the same position as one that can be occupied by the corresponding free word." In English, forms like *-ll* or *-d*, as in the sentences in (13), are simple clitics:

(13) a. I'll take the pastrami, please.
b. I'd like the pastrami, please.

In these sentences, *-ll* and *-d* are contracted forms of the auxiliaries *will* and *would*, and they occur just where the independent words would occur – following the subject *I* and before the main verb. Like affixes, they are pronounced as part of the preceding word. Unlike affixes, they do not select a specific category of base and change its category or add grammatical information to it. Contracted forms like *-ll* or *-d* in English will attach to any sort of word that precedes them, regardless of category:

(14) a. The kid over there'll take a pastrami sandwich.
b. No one I know'd want a pastrami sandwich.

In (14a) *-ll* is cliticized to the adverb *there*, and in (14b) *-d* is cliticized to the verb *know*.

Special clitics are phonologically dependent on a host, as simple clitics are, but they are not reduced forms of independent words. Compare the example in (15) from French:

(15) a. Je vois Pierre.
I see Pierre.

b. Je le vois.
I him see.

c. *Je vois le.
I see him.

Although the object pronoun *le* in French is written as a separate word, it is phonologically dependent on the verb to its right; in other words, the object pronoun and the verb are pronounced together as a single phonological word. There is no independent word that means 'him' in French. So *le* and the other object pronoun forms in French are special clitics.

Clitics are of interest both to syntacticians and to morphologists precisely because they have characteristics both of bound morphemes and of syntactic units. Like bound morphemes, they cannot stand on their own. But unlike morphemes, they are typically unselective of their hosts and have their own independent functions in syntactic phrases.

8.3.2 Phrasal verbs and verbs with separable prefixes

Also inhabiting the borderland between morphology and syntax are phrasal verbs in English and verbs with separable prefixes in German and Dutch. **Phrasal verbs** are verbs like those in (16) that consist of a verb and a preposition or particle:

(16) call up 'telephone'
chew out 'scold'
put down 'insult'
run up 'accumulate'

Frequently, phrasal verbs have idiomatic meanings, as the glosses in (16) show, and in that sense they are like words. In terms of structure, the combination of verb and particle/preposition might seem like another sort of compound in English. Remember, however, that one of the criteria for distinguishing a compound from a phrase in English (see section 3.4) was that the two elements making up compounds could not be separated from one another. We cannot take a compound like *dog bed* and insert a word to modify *bed* (for example, **dog comfortable bed*). In contrast, however, the two parts of the phrasal verb can be, and sometimes must be, separated:

(17) a. I called up a friend.
b. I called a friend up.
c. I called her up.
d. *I called up her.

When the object of the verb is a full noun phrase, the particle can precede or follow it. In the former case it is adjacent to its verb, but in the latter case it is separated from the verb. And when the object is a pronoun, the particle must be separated from the verb. So do we consider phrasal verbs to be a matter of study for morphologists, or do we leave them to syntacticians? There is no set answer to this question.

A similar issue arises with what are called **separable prefix verbs** in Dutch. Consider the examples in (18):

(18) *Booij (2002: 205)*

a. ...dat Hans zijn moeder opbelde ~ Hans belde zijn moeder op
that Hans his mother up.called ~ Hans called his mother up

b. ...dat Jan het huis schoonmaakte ~ Jan maakte het huis schoon
that Jan the house clean.made ~ Jan made the house clean

c. ...dat Rebecca pianospeelde ~ Rebecca speelde piano
that Rebecca piano.played ~ Rebecca played piano

Like phrasal verbs in English, separable prefix verbs in Dutch often have idiomatic meanings. For example, *opbellen*, like English 'call up' means 'to telephone'. Each separable prefix verb in Dutch consists of a verb preceded by a word of another category; in (18), *op* is a preposition, *schoon* is an adjective, and *piano* is a noun. These words therefore look a bit like prefixed words or perhaps compounds. But there's a difference.

To understand the examples in (18) you need to know that Dutch exhibits different word orders in main clauses than in subordinate clauses. In main clauses the main verb is always the second constituent in the clause. If the subject is first, the main verb comes right after it. But in subordinate clauses, the main verb always comes last. The examples in (18) show that when the verbs *opbellen* 'call up', *schoonmaken* 'make clean', and *pianospelen* 'play piano' occur in a subordinate clause, those complex verbs come at the end of the clause. The first elements *op, schoon,* and *piano* occur attached to the verb, almost like prefixes. However, when the verb is used in a main clause, the verb itself occurs after the subject, but its first element appears separated from it at the end of the sentence. So unlike normal prefixes, these elements sometimes are not attached to the verbs with which they normally form a unit. Are separable prefix verbs a matter for morphologists or for syntacticians? Again, there is no easy answer to this question, as they lie on the border between the two.

8.3.3 Phrasal compounds

Our final example of a phenomenon that is neither clearly syntactic nor clearly morphological is called a **phrasal compound**. A **phrasal compound** is a word that is made up of a phrase as its first element, and a noun as its second element. Phrasal compounds can be found in many of the Germanic languages, including English, Dutch, and German:

(19) a. *English (Harley 2009)*
stuff-blowing-up effects
bikini-girls-in-trouble genre
comic-book-and-science-fiction fans

b. *Dutch (Hoeksema 1988)*
lach of ik schiet humor
'laugh or I shoot humor'

c. *German (Toman 1983: 47)*
die Wer war das Frage
'the who was that question'

On the one hand, phrasal compounds pass one of the acid tests for compounding: it is impossible to insert a modifying word in-between the phrase and the head of the compound:

(20) a. *stuff-blowing-up exciting effects
b. exciting stuff-blowing-up effects

On the other hand, the first elements are clearly phrases, or even whole sentences, as the example in (21) shows:

(21) God-is-dead theology

And phrases and sentences are the subject matter of syntax. Again, it is no easy question to decide whether phrasal compounds are the subject of morphology or of syntax. Indeed, it would be reasonable to conclude that they should be of interest to both morphologists and syntacticians.

Challenge

Although phrasal compounds may seem somewhat exotic to you, they appear not infrequently in journalistic writing, especially in headlines, and in more informal writing, for example, on the sports pages or in feature-writing. Choose your favorite newspaper and try to find two examples of phrasal compounds. Share your examples with classmates and try to analyze what sorts of phrases can occur as the first elements of your compounds.

Summary

In this chapter we have investigated the relationship between morphology and syntax. We have seen that there are ways in which morphology affects the syntax of sentences, by either reducing or increasing the number of arguments a verb may appear with. We have also looked at cases where it is not entirely clear whether a phenomenon is a matter of morphology or of syntax or of both. Among these phenomena, we find clitics, phrasal verbs, separable prefix verbs, and phrasal compounds. What such phenomena really show us is that morphology and syntax are often intimately intertwined, and often morphologists must investigate both levels of syntactic organization to really understand how a language works. We will see in chapter 10 that phenomena like the ones we've looked at in this chapter raise serious questions for theorists, and have been the matter of much discussion.

Exercises

1. Consider the sentences below and discuss how the passive is formed in Swahili. Use sentences (8)–(10) to help you gloss these sentences. Vitale (1981: 23, 31)
   a. Juma a-li-fungua mlango
      'Juma opened the door'
   b. mlango u-li-fungu-liwa.
      'The door was opened'
2. Consider the prefix *out-* in English:
   a. Fenster ran.
   b. *Fenster ran Letitia.
   c. Fenster outran Letitia.
   d. *Fenster outran.

   Describe the effect that the prefix *out-* has in sentences (a)–(d). Now, think of other verbs formed with *out-* in English. Does *out-* have a consistent effect on the argument structure of verbs it attaches to?
3. Consider the bracketed words in the sentences below and discuss what sorts of issues they raise about the relationship between syntax and morphology:

   We arranged a [five o'clock-ish] meeting.
   Her [old maid-ish] behavior surprised us.
   Those two look very [Mutt and Jeff-ish].
   Since that fight, I consider her an [ex-old friend].
   None of my friends are [pro-Bush and Cheney].
   I need a [post-90 degree day] shower.

4. Discuss the difference in argument structure and in verbal morphology between the pairs of sentences below:
   a. *Malagasy (Keenan and Polinsky 1999: 604)*
      i. mijaly Rabe
         suffers Rabe
         'Rabe suffers.'
      ii. mampijaly an-dRabe Rasoa
         makes-suffer acc-Rabe Rasoa
         'Rasoa makes Rabe suffer.'
   b. *Chichewa (Mchombo 1999: 506)*
      i. Kalúlú akuphíká maûngu
         Hare is cooking pumpkins
         'The hare is cooking pumpkins.'
      ii. Kalúlú akuphíkíra mkángó maûngo
         Hare is cooking lion pumpkins
         'The hare is cooking pumpkins for the lion.'
5. Consider the English sentences below:
   a. The water boiled.
   b. Fenster boiled the water.

   a. The tomatoes grew.
   b. Letitia grew the tomatoes.

   a. The door opened.
   b. Roddy opened the door.

First discuss the difference in argument structure between the (a) sentences and the (b) sentences. Then compare these sentences to the Swahili sentences in (8) (see p. 147). Discuss the differences between the Swahili sentences and the ones here.

6. Musqueam exhibits an interesting set of morphologically related verbs that differ in valency. Analyze the following forms and describe both the affixes used and their effects on argument structure (Suttles 2004: 235) (note that the first two examples are a bit different from the second two):

háy	'finish'	shá·y̓	'finished'	shá·y̓stəx^{w}	'have it finished'
ɬə́lqt	'dip it'	sɬélq	'in the water'	sɬélqstəx^{w}	'keep it in the water'
x̌é·t̓^{θ}t	'measure it'	sx̌eʔét̓^{θ}	'measured, marked'	sx̌eʔét̓^{θ}stəx^{w}	'blaze (as a trail), designate (as a time)'
θə́yt	'fix it'	sθəθəy̓	'right'	sθəθə́y̓stəx^{w}	'keep it on course'

CHAPTER

9 Sounds and shapes: the interface between morphology and phonology

CHAPTER OUTLINE

KEY TERMS

allomorph
assimilation
dissimilation
vowel harmony
intervocalic voicing
palatalization
lexical strata

In this chapter we will learn about the intersection between morphology and phonology, which is the study of the sound structure of languages.

- We will learn that some morphemes exhibit allomorphs, that is, phonologically distinct variants.
- We will learn how to analyze both phonologically predictable and unpredictable allomorphy.
- And we will consider the nature of lexical stratification, where different types of phonological behavior characterize different parts of the morphology of a language.

9.1 Introduction

Phonology is the area of linguistics that is concerned with sound regularities in languages: what sounds exist in a language, how those sounds combine with each other into syllables and words, and how the prosody (stress, accent, tone, and so on) of a language works. Phonology interacts with morphology in a number of ways: morphemes may have two or more different phonological forms whose appearance may be completely or at least partly predictable. Some phonological rules apply when two or more morphemes are joined together. In some languages morphemes display different phonological behavior depending on whether they are native to the language or borrowed into it from some other language. In this chapter we will explore the various ways in which phonology interacts with morphology.

In this chapter we will frequently make use of phonetic transcriptions, so you may want to review the IPA before you begin reading it. We will also make use of terminology which classifies sounds by their point of articulation (labial, dental, alveolar, and so on) and by their manner of articulation (voiced *vs.* voiceless, stop, fricative, liquid, and so on). You can find summaries of this terminology in the charts at the beginning of the book.

9.2 Allomorphs

Allomorphs are phonologically distinct variants of the same morpheme. By phonologically distinct, we mean that they have similar but not identical sounds. And when we say that they are variants of the same morpheme, we mean that these slightly different-sounding sets of forms share the same meaning or function. For example, the negative prefix *in-* in English is often pronounced *in-* (as in *intolerable*), but it is also sometimes pronounced *im-* or *il-* (*impossible, illegal*), as English spelling shows. Since all of these forms still mean 'negative', and they all attach to adjectives in the same way, we say that they are allomorphs of the negative prefix. Another example you've already seen is the regular past tense in English. Although the regular past tense in English is always spelled *-ed*, it is sometimes pronounced [t] (*packed*), sometimes [d] (*bagged*), sometimes [əd] (*waited*).[1] Still all three phonological variants still designate the past tense. Similarly, the plural morpheme in Turkish sometimes appears as *-lar* and sometimes as *-ler*, so Turkish has two allomorphs of the plural morpheme.

As we will see below, in many cases, it is phonologically predictable which allomorph appears where; sometimes, however, which allomorph appears with a particular base is unpredictable. For example, we will see that it is usually possible to predict the form of the regular allomorphs of the English past tense morpheme, but there are quite a few verbs whose past tenses are irregular (for example, *sang, flew, bought*).

1. Or [ɪd] in some dialects.

9.2.1 Predictable allomorphy

Let's look more closely at the prefix *in-* in English. As the examples in (1a) show, it frequently has the form *in-*. However, sometimes it appears as *im-*, *il-*, or *ir-*, as the examples in (b) and (c) show. And if you think about sound rather than spelling, it can also be pronounced [ɪŋ-], as the examples in (1d) show:

(1) a. inalienable
intolerable
indecent

b. impossible

c. illegal
irregular

d. incongruous [ɪŋkɑŋgɹuəs]
incoherent [ɪŋkohiɹənt]

The various allomorphs of the negative prefix *in-* in English are quite regular, in the sense that we can predict exactly where each variant will occur. Which allomorph occurs depends on the initial sound of the base word. For vowel-initial words, like *alienable*, the [ɪn-] variant appears. It appears as well on words that begin with the alveolar consonants [t, d, s, z, n]. On words that begin with a labial consonant like [p], we find [ɪm-]. Words that begin with [l] or [r] are prefixed with the [ɪl-] or [ɪr-] allomorphs respectively, and words that begin with a velar consonant [k], are prefixed with the [ɪŋ-] variant. What you should notice is that this makes perfect sense phonetically: the nasal consonant of the prefix matches at least the point of articulation of the consonant beginning its base, and if that consonant is a liquid [l,r] it matches that consonant exactly. This allomorphy is the result of a process called **assimilation**. Generally speaking, assimilation occurs when sounds come to be more like each other in terms of some aspect of their pronunciation.

If you have studied a bit of phonology, you know that regularities in the phonology of a language can be stated in terms of phonological rules. Phonologists assume that native speakers of a language have a single basic mental representation for each morpheme. Regular allomorphs are derived from the underlying representation using phonological rules. For example, since the English negative prefix *in-* is pronounded [ɪn] both before alveolar-initial bases (*tolerable, decent*) and before vowel-initial bases (*alienable*), whereas the other allomoprhs are only pronounced before specific consonant-initial bases, phonologists assume that our mental representation of *in-* is [ɪn] rather than [ɪr], [ɪl], or [ɪŋ]; often (but not always, as we will see below) the underlying form of a morpheme is the form that has the widest surface distribution.[2] When the underlying form is prefixed to a base beginning with anything other than a vowel or alveolar consonant, the following phonological rule derives the correct allomorph:

2. If you study phonology further, you will find that this is somewhat of a simplification, but for our purposes, it is good enough.

(2) *Nasal assimilation*: a nasal consonant assimilates to the point of articulation of a following consonant, and to the point and manner of articulation of the consonant if it is a liquid.

Phonologists use different forms of notation to express the above rule in a more succinct fashion, but we'll restrict ourselves to informal statements of rules here.

This sort of assimilation – called **nasal assimilation** – is not unusual in the languages of the world. We find something similar in the language Zoque (Nida 1946/1976: 21):

(3) | | | | |
|---|---|---|---|
| pama | 'clothes' | ʔəs mpama | 'my clothes' |
| kayu | 'horse' | ʔəs ŋkayu | 'my horse' |
| tuwi | 'dog' | ʔəs ntuwi | 'my dog' |

As the examples in (3) show, the possessive prefix is a nasal consonant that has three different allomorphs. Which allomorph is prefixed depends on the point of articulation of the noun it attaches to. In Zoque, we might say that part of forming the possessive of a noun involves prefixing an underlying nasal consonant which undergoes a phonological rule that assimilates it to a following consonant.

Another example of a predictable form of allomorphy is the formation of the regular past tense in English. In chapter 2, we looked at the past tense in English in the context of figuring out what the mental lexicon looks like. We can now go into its formation in somewhat more detail. Consider the data in (4), which shows two of the three allomorphs of the regular past tense:

(4) a. *Verbs whose past tense is pronounced [t]*
slap, laugh, unearth, kiss, wish, watch, walk

b. *Verbs whose past tense is pronounced [d]*
rub, weave, bathe, buzz, judge, snag, frame, can, bang, lasso, shimmy

The regular past tense in English illustrates a different sort of assimilation, called **voicing assimilation** where sounds become voiced or voiceless depending on the voicing of neighboring sounds. The verbs that take the past tense allomorph [t] all end in voiceless consonants: [p, f, θ, s, ʃ, ʧ, k]. Those that take the [d] allomorph, all end either in a voiced consonant [b, v, ð, z, ʤ, g, m, n, ŋ] or in a vowel (and all vowels are voiced, of course). Why just this distribution? Clearly, the past tense morpheme has come to match the voicing of the final segment of the verb base: verbs whose last segment is voiceless take the voiceless variant.

There is one allomorph of the past tense we haven't covered yet. Consider what happens if the verb base ends in either [t] or [d]:

(5) *Verbs whose past tense is pronounced [əd]*
defeat, bond

Here, a process of **dissimilation** is at work. Dissimilation is a phonological process which makes sounds less like each other. A schwa separates the [t] or [d] of the past tense from the matching consonant at the end of the verb. Again, this makes perfect sense phonetically; if the [t] or [d] allomorph were used, it would be indistinguishable from the final consonant of the verb root.

What is the underlying form of the past tense morpheme in English? As I indicated before, it is often a good strategy to assume that the allomorph with the widest distribution is the underlying form. But there is something else to consider as well. Phonologists typically assume that the underlying form of a morpheme must be something from which all of the other allomorphs can be derived using the simplest possible set of rules. In this case, the allomorph [d] has the widest distribution, because it occurs with all voiced consonants except [d], and with all vowel-final verb stems. And if we assume that the underlying form of the regular past tense is [d], we need only two simple rules to derive the other allomorphs:

(6) *The Past Tense Rule*

a. If the verb stem ends in [t] or [d] (the alveolar stops), insert [ə] before the past tense morpheme (e.g. defeated [dəfit + d] → [dəfit + əd]).

b. Assimilate [d] to the voicing of an immediately preceding consonant (e.g., licked [lɪk + d] → [lɪk + t]).

Challenge

Rather than take my word for it that choosing the allomorph [d] as the underlying representation of the past morpheme yields the simplest set of rules, construct an argument that the set of rules in (6) really is simpler than alternatives. To do so, first suppose that we had chosen [t] instead of [d] as the underlying morpheme. Try to state informally what the rule(s) would have to be to derive the other allomorphs of the past tense. Then suppose that we'd chosen [əd] as the underlying representation. What would the rules have looked like then? Now compare the rules to each other and discuss which set is simplest.

A third example of regular and predictable allomorphy comes from Turkish. As we've seen, in Turkish, virtually every morpheme, derivational and inflectional alike, has more than one allomorph. For example, the plural morpheme has the allomorphs *-ler* and *-lar*, and the genitive suffix has the allomorphs *-in, -un, -ɯn,* and *-ün*. The reason for this is that Turkish displays a process of **vowel harmony** whereby all non-high vowels in a word have to agree in backness, and all high vowels in both backness and roundness. When suffixes are added to a base, they must agree in the relevant vowel characteristics with the preceding vowels of the base:

(7) *From Lewis (1967: 29ff)*

	'hand'	'measure'	'evening'	'fear'
Abs. pl.	el-ler	ölçü-ler	akşam-lar	korku-lar
Gen. sg.	el-in	ölçü-n-ün	akşam-ın	korku-n-un

Since the roots of the nouns *el* 'hand' and *ölçü* 'measure' have front vowels, the plural suffix must agree with them in frontness, so the *-ler* allomorph appears. On the other hand, *akşam* 'evening' and *korku* 'fear' have back vowels, and the *-lar* allomorph appears. Since the genitive ending has a high vowel, the vowel harmony is more complicated. If the noun root consists of vowels that are front and non-round, we find the genitive allomorph with a front, non-round vowel, that is, *-in*. Similarly, if the root contains front, round vowels, so does the suffix; so *ölçü* gets the front round allomorph *-ün*. Roots with back non-round vowels like *akşam* take the *-ın* allomorph, and roots with back round vowels like *korku* take the *-un* allomorph.

We might ask in this case what the underlying form of these affixes is, and here it's a bit difficult to pick one of the existing allomorphs as our choice. For example, neither plural allomorph *-ler* nor *-lar* has a wider distribution than the other. One possibility that we might consider, then, is that the mental representation of the plural morpheme in Turkish is something like what we find in (8):

(8) Turkish plural morpheme = $\text{-l}\begin{bmatrix}\text{V}\\ \text{non-high}\\ \text{non-round}\end{bmatrix}\text{r}$

Part of the rule of vowel harmony in Turkish might then say that a non-high vowel in a suffix comes to match the backness of the vowels in a root that precedes it.

Challenge

We have proposed an underlying form for the plural morpheme in Turkish. Now propose one for the genitive suffix and try to give an informal statement of the rule of vowel harmony that gives rise to the different allomorphs.

Our final example of predictable allomorphy also comes from Turkish, but this time it concerns consonants, rather than vowels. Let's look at a bit more data from Turkish, in Lewis (1967: 10):

(9)

	Abs. sg.	*Abs. pl.*	*Acc. sg.*
'bread'	ekmek	ekmekler	ekmeği
'book'	kitap	kitapler	kitabı
'son-in-law'	damat	damatlar	damadı

You already know that the plural morpheme in Turkish is *-ler/-lar* (or in its underlying form in (8)). This of course suggests that the roots of the nouns 'bread', 'book', and 'son-in-law' are *ekmek, kitap,* and *damat* respectively. When we look at the third column of examples, it appears that the accusative singular ending is *-i/-ı* but we find that the roots now end in *ğ, b,* and *d*. In other words, where the roots normally end in voiceless consonants, in the accusative singular they appear to have allomorphs that end in voiced consonants.[3] In the absolute case, the voiceless consonants are at the end of the word, and in the absolute plural they occur before another consonant, but in the accusative singular forms, the root-final consonant is now between vowels. What occurs is a process that is called **intervocalic voicing**. In other words, a consonant is voiced when it occurs between two vowels.

9.2.2 Unpredictable or partially predictable allomorphy

As we've seen above, some allomorphy is regular enough to be captured by phonological rules. But not all allomorphy is regular. Take, for example, past tenses of verbs in English. We have already looked at the regular past tense. Every native speaker or student of English knows that there are also quite a few verbs that don't form the past tense by adding *-ed*. Consider table 9.1, which gives a selection of examples.

Table 9.1. (based on classes in Huddleston and Pullum 2002)

	Infinitive	*Irregular past*	*Pattern*
1	burn	burnt	devoicing of suffix
2	keep	kept	vowel shortening
3	hit	hit	no change
4	feel	felt	vowel shortening with devoicing of suffix
5	bleed	bled	vowel shortening and no suffix
6	leave	left	devoicing of stem consonant
7	sing	sang	vowel ablaut (ɪ ~ æ)
8	win	won	vowel ablaut (ɪ ~ ʌ)
9	fight	fought	vowel ablaut (ai ~ ɔ)
10	come	came	vowel ablaut (ʌ ~ e)

If you think back to chapter 2, when we discussed the mental lexicon, we suggested that irregular past tense allomorphs are simply stored in the mental lexicon, and not derived by rules. So speakers of English have a lexical entry for the verb root *sing*, and along with it an associated entry for past tense *sang*. It is possible, though, that things are a bit more complicated. Think back to the experiment in section 6.3 where you asked a number of friends to make the past tense of the hypothetical verb *gling*. Probably a significant number of them offered either *glang* or *glung*. Since

3. The symbol ğ is used in Turkish orthography for the sound [ɣ], which is a voiced velar fricative. In the case of roots that end in [k], then, the voiceless stop not only voices but also becomes a fricative.

this is not a real verb, clearly they didn't have a past tense stored for it. Rather, they must have been making use of some sort of pattern to create these forms. In English there happen to be quite a few verbs whose present and past tenses show the same ɪ ~ æ alternation as *sing* or the ɪ ~ ʌ alternation of *win*. There appears to be an abstract pattern that speakers are tapping into here that relates a present tense with [ɪ] to a past tense with [æ] or [ʌ] if the verb ends in a nasal or a nasal plus some other consonant (for example, like *swim, ring, sting, win, stink*). Psycholinguists continue to work towards figuring out the exact nature of such patterns.

The example of unpredictable allomorphy we looked at above concerns English inflection. Let's look at another example that has to do with derivation. Consider the forms in (10):

(10)				
a.	designate	[**dɛ**zɪgneɪt]	designation	[dɛzɪg**neɪ**ʃ+ʌn]
b.	unionize	[**jun**jənɑɪz]	unionization	[junjənɑɪ**z+e**ɪʃʌn]
c.	prosecute	[**pɹɑ**səkjut]	prosecution	[pɹɑsə**kju**ʃ+ʌn]
d.	resolve	[ɹə**zɑlv**]	resolution	[ɹɛzə**l+u** ʃʌn]
e.	expedite	[**ɛk**spədɑɪt]	expedition	[ɛkspə**dɪ**+ʃʌn]
f.	define	[dəf**ɑɪn**]	definition	[dɛfə**n+**ɪʃʌn]
g.	absorb	[əb**zɔrb**]	absorption	[æb**zɔrp**+ʃʌn]
h.	circumcise	[**səɹ**kʌmsɑɪz]	circumcision	[səɹkəm**sɪ**ʒ+ʌn]
i.	decide	[dəs**ɑɪd**]	decision	[də**sɪ**ʒ+ʌn]

All of the verbs in the lefthand column have noun forms with the suffix *-tion*. But if you compare the transcriptions of the verbs and nouns carefully, you will see that both the verb bases and the derivational affix have various allomorphs. For example, the suffix seems to be *-ʌn* in (10a and c) but *-eɪʃʌn* in (10b). It looks like *-uʃʌn* in (10d), but *-ɪʃʌn* in (10f), and *-ʃʌn* in (10g). In (10a, c, and e) the [t] at the end of *designate, prosecute,* and *expedite* seem to have changed to [ʃ], the [v] at the end of *resolve* seems to have disappeared, and the [b] at the end of *absorb* has changed to [p]. And if you look carefully at many of these forms, the stress pattern on the derived noun is different from that of its verb base (the stressed syllable is shown in boldface). In other words, there is quite a complicated pattern of allomorphy associated with this suffix.

Is it predictable? Parts of it are. For example, if a verb ends in [v] and has a derived noun with the *-tion* suffix, it will always lose its [v] and the suffix will be pronounced *-ution* (think about the derived nouns for *dissolve, absolve, revolve*, etc.). Similarly, if a verb ends in [t] and takes the *-ion* suffix, the [t] will become [ʃ]. And if a verb ends in [z] or [d] and takes the *-tion* suffix, those consonants will become [ʒ]. Since the sounds [ʃ] and [ʒ] are palatal sounds, this process is called **palatalization**.

But the choice of allomorphs is not entirely predictable. For example, it's not clear if we can predict when we will get *-ation*, say, as opposed to *-ion* on a particular verb base: we find *-ation* on the verbs *unionize* and *refute*, but not in *circumcise* and *prosecute*; those have the *-ion* allomorph. The derived noun form from *combust* is *combustion*, but that of *infest* is *infestation*. Why not *combustation* and *infestion* instead? The verb base *propose* yields *proposition*, but *accuse* yields *accusation*. Why not *proposation*, or *accu-*

sition? To some extent the choice of allomorphs seems to be quite arbitrary. We will leave this affix here, but return to it in section 9.4, where we will consider why this affix (and a number of others) display such pervasive and unpredictable allomorphy.

9.3 How to: analyzing allomorphy

So far we've looked at allomorphy in English and a couple of other languages. In this section, we'll take a close look at another language and see how morphologists go about analyzing allomorphy in a language that's unfamiliar. Take a look at the data in (11) from the Philippine language Tagalog (Schachter and Otanes 1972: 290–1):

(11)	*Verb root*	*Actor focus or derived verb form*[4]	
	anak	manganak	'give birth (to)'
	bakya	mambakya	'hit with a wooden shoe'
	dukot	mandukot	'steal'
	gulo	manggulo	'create disorder'
	hiwa	manghiwa	'cut (sthg. intentionally)'
	kailangan	mangailangan	'need'
	ligaw	manligaw	'pay court to'
	manhid	mamanhid	'get numb'
	nood	manood	'watch'
	pili	mamili	'choose (several things)'
	sakit	manakit	'cause pain'
	takot	manakot	'frighten (several people)'
	walis	mangwalis	'hit with a broom'

The first thing that should leap out at you when you see these data is that the forms in the right-hand column (let's refer to them as the derived forms) seem to have some sort of prefix. But it's not always exactly the same prefix. The prefix looks like *mang-* in the first form, *mam-* in the second, and *man-* in the third. There's clearly some allomorphy displayed in this set of data. To see better what's going on, it is often a good strategy to rearrange the data so that similar forms are put together. This allows you to begin to see patterns. There are a number of ways of doing this, but in (12), I've rearranged them into four groups. In the first, we can clearly segment off the prefix *mang-*. In the second group, it's still possible to segment off a prefix and leave behind something that looks exactly like the verb root. What's left over is either *mam-* or *man-*. The examples in (12c) look like something is missing, though. If we were just putting together a prefix with the stem, we might expect *mammanhid* and *mannood*, rather than the forms we actually find. And finally in (12d), we have forms in which the initial consonant of the verb root clearly seems to be absent.

4. The data in (11) represent two different types of verbs in Tagalog that are formed with the same prefix. The 'actor focus' verbs are roughly like active (as opposed to passive) verb forms in English, and what Schacter and Otanes call "derived" verb forms are ones that denote destructive activity or activity directed at several objects or people. For the purposes of this problem, it doesn't matter that the prefix has several different uses.

(12) a.

Verb root	*Actor focus verb*	
anak[5]	manganak	'give birth (to)'
gulo	manggulo	'create disorder'
hiwa	manghiwa	'cut (sthg. intentionally)'
walis	mangwalis	'hit with a broom'

b.

bakya	mambakya	'hit with a wooden shoe'
dukot	mandukot	'steal'
ligaw	manligaw	'pay court to'

c.

manhid	mamanhid	'get numb'
nood	manood	'watch'

d.

pili	mamili	'choose (several things)'
takot	manakot	'frighten (several people)'
sakit	manakit	'cause pain'
kailangan	mangailangan	'need'

Let's start with the forms in (12a) and (12b) that are easily segmentable. Segmenting the derived verbs, we find the allomorphs *mam-*, *man-* and *mang-*. The first occurs on a root beginning with [b], the second with roots beginning with [d] and [l], and the third with roots beginning with [ʔ], [g], [h], or [w]. This far, the data should not surprise you: Tagalog seems to have a process of nasal assimilation, just as English and Zoque do. The labial-final allomorph *mam-* occurs with a labial consonant, the alveolar-final allomorph *man-* occurs with alveolar initial roots, and the velar-final allomorph *mang-* occurs with roots that begin with either velar or glottal consonants. So far, things seem fairly neat.

When we turn our attention to the data set in (12c), however, we will see that there's more to be said about the derived forms of the verb. It's not so clear how to segment the forms in this set. Suppose we assume that the prefix is *mam-* or *man-*, as it was in (12a, b); we are then left with *anhid* or *ood* as allomorphs of the roots. Alternatively, we might assume that the prefix in these cases is just *ma-*. If we do so, then the bases would be exactly the same as the roots, namely *manhid* and *nood*. This might seem like the best solution at the moment – just adding another allomorph to the set we already have of *mang-*, *man-*, and *mam-*, but let's keep our minds open to both solutions until we've finished looking at all the data.

The data in (12d) present us with a new problem. If we assume that Tagalog has nasal assimilation, we would expect that we would put together *mam-* with *pili* to get *mampili* and *man-* with *takot* to form *mantakot*, and so on. But instead we get *mamili* and *manakot*. The initial consonant of the stem seems to disappear when the prefix is attached. Now, if we look back and compare the verb roots that we find in (12b) and compare them to those we find in (12d), we will see that the former begin with voiced labial or alveolar consonants, whereas those in (12d) begin with voiceless consonants. It looks like when the prefix attaches to a base that begins with a voiceless conso-

5. Although the spelling suggests that this form begins with a vowel, it is pronounced with a glottal stop before the vowel, so phonetically it is actually [ʔanak].

nant, the prefix first assimilates to the point of articulation of the following voiceless consonant, and then that consonant disappears.

Here, we need to stop and think more about the nasal assimilation rule. In section 9.2 I suggested that each set of allomorphs has a single underlying form, from which the others are derived by phonological rule. Since nasal assimilation in Tagalog seems to be a predictable process, we would assume this to be the case here as well. So we need to decide at this point what the underlying form should be. Remember that it's often a good strategy to pick as the underlying form the allomorph that has the widest distribution, in other words the one that occurs with the most classes of sounds. Here, as the data in (12) show, the allomorph *mang-* occurs with glottal initial roots ([h] and [ʔ]), as well as with velars ([g], [k], [w]). The allomorph *mam-* occurs only with labial-initial roots ([p],[b]), and the *man-* allomorph only with alveolar-initial roots ([d], [t], [l]). We can reasonably make the hypothesis then that the underlying form of the prefix is *mang-*, since it occurs with two different classes of sounds. If so, then the forms in (12) have the following underlying representations:

(13) a. mang + anak
mang + gulo
mang + hiwa
mang + walis

b. mang + bakya
mang + dukot
mang + ligaw

c. mang + manhid
mang + nood

d. mang + pili
mang + takot
mang + sakit
mang + kailangan

Now we can give an informal statement of two phonological rules that will derive the allomorphs from the underlying forms:

(14) The nasal of *mang-* assimilates to the point of articulation of a following consonant.
A voiceless consonant is deleted when preceded by a nasal consonant.

For the forms in (12a), neither rule applies. For those in (12b), only the first applies, since the verb roots don't begin with voiceless consonants. But in (12d) both rules apply.

(15)		
	No rules:	mang + gulo → mang + gulo
	Rule (14a) only:	mang + bakya → mam + bakya
	Both rules:	mang + pili → mam + pili → mam + ili

What about the examples in (12c), however? Remember that we were undecided as to whether the allomorph of the prefix should end in a nasal at all, and we were leaning towards the solution in which the allomorph was *ma-*, as it would allow us to say that the verb roots always had the same form. We can see now, however, that that might not be the right solution. Suppose that we were to assume that the correct allomorph is *ma-*; since we have postulated that the underlying version of the prefix is *mang-*, we would have to derive *ma-* from underlying *mang-*. This in turn would require us to add a third rule that would delete *-ng* before a nasal-initial verb root:

(16) mang + manhid → ma + manhid

Before we add this third rule, however, let's see what happens if we assume that for these bases the allomorphs for the prefix are *mam-* or *man-*. Note that we already have an assimilation rule that accounts for which of the allomorphs shows up – we get *mam-* before an *m-* initial root, and *man-* before an *n-* initial root. And we already have a rule that deletes consonants after a suffix that ends in a nasal. If we tweak that rule slightly, we can derive the forms in (12c) without adding a third rule:

(17) A nasal or voiceless consonant is deleted when preceded by a nasal consonant.

The forms in (12c) can then be derived as follows:

(18) mang + manhid → mam + manhid → man + anhid
mang + nood → man + nood → man + ood

So although it seemed at first that assuming the allomorph of the prefix in (12c) to be *ma-* made more sense, looking at the bigger picture, making the other choice allows us to derive all the allomorphs using a simpler set of rules. We assume then that this is the right solution. We must keep in mind, though, that we've only looked at a tiny set of data. If we were to continue looking at the morphology and phonology of Tagalog, we might decide that the analysis we've decided upon here needs to be revised again.

9.4 Lexical strata

What we have seen in this chapter is that building complex words is frequently accompanied by phonological effects such as assimilation or vowel harmony. In this section we will see that in some languages such phonological effects do not apply uniformly across the entire lexicon of the language, but instead are confined to a subset of the lexicon. Indeed some languages have two or more different layers to their lexicons which behave differently in terms of phonological effects. In this section we will look at three such languages, English, Dutch, and French.

9.4.1 English

As we saw in section 9.2, the suffix *-tion* is associated with complex and partially unpredictable allomorphy, both of the suffix itself and of the bases it attaches to. It turns out that it's not the only suffix in English that acts that way. Consider the examples in table 9.2.

Table 9.2. Some non-native suffixes in Engish

Affix	*Rule*	*Stem change*	*Stress change*	*Attaches to bound bases*	*Attaches to words*	*Attaches to non-native bases*	*Attaches to native bases*
-al	N→A	sacrificial	architectural	minimal	architectural	yes	(tidal)
-ian	N→N,A	Christian	contrarian	pedestrian	Bostonian	yes	(earthian)
-ic	N→A	dialogic	Germanic	geographic	problematic	yes	no
-ive	V→A	allusive	alternative	nutritive	impressive	yes	(talkative)
-ity	A→ N	historicity	historicity	atrocity	similarity	yes	(oddity)
-ory	V→A	delusory	excretory	perfunctory	contradictory	yes	no
-tion	V→N	decision	revelation	perception	restoration	yes	(starvation)

All seven of the suffixes in table 9.2 are non-native to English. Specifically, they were borrowed from Latin either directly or by way of French. All of them are like *-tion* in showing complex patterns of allomorphy. When they are added to bases, the final consonants of those bases sometimes change:

(19)	sacrifice	[s]	sacrific-ial	[ʃ]
	Christ	[t]	Christ-ian	[tʃ]
	dialogue	[g]	dialog-ic	[ʤ]
	allude	[d]	allus-ive	[s]
	historic	[k]	historic-ity	[s]
	delude	[d]	delus-ory	[s]
	decide	[d]	decis-ion	[ʒ]

The stress pattern on the base often changes as well:

(20)	**archi**tecture	archi**tec**tural
	contrary	con**trar**ian
	German	Ger**man**ic
	alternate	al**ter**native
	his**to**ric	histo**ri**city
	ex**crete**	**ex**cretory[6]

Furthermore, all of these suffixes can attach either to bound bases or to full words. And all of them prefer to attach to bases that are themselves

6. Note that the stressing in the last pair in (20) is American English. Speakers of other dialects of English might stress these words differently.

non-native to English. The items in the last column in the table are in parentheses because they are among the few native bases (sometimes the only one) on which these affixes can be found.

If we now look at suffixes that are native to English – that is, suffixes that were present in Old English, rather than borrowed from some other language – we find quite a different pattern: consider table 9.3.

Table 9.3. Some suffixes native to English

Affix	*Rule*	*Stem change*	*Stress change*	*Attaches to bound bases*	*Attaches to words*	*Attaches to non-native bases*	*Attaches to native bases*
-dom	N→N	none	none	no	kingdom	yes	yes
-er	V→N	none	none	no	writer	yes	yes
-ful	N→A	none	none	(vengeful?)	sorrowful	yes	yes
-hood	N→N	none	none	no	knighthood	yes	yes
-ish	N,A→A	none	none	no	mulish	yes	yes
-less	N→A	none	none	no	shoeless	yes	yes
-ness	A→N	none	none	no	happiness	yes	yes

When these suffixes attach to bases, they change neither the sounds of those bases nor their stress pattern:

(21) **poo**dle — **poo**dledom
systematize — **sys**tematizer
sorrow — **sor**rowful
neighbor — **neigh**borhood
hermit — **her**mitish
bottom — **bot**tomless
happy — **hap**piness

Typically they attach freely to either native or non-native bases, but they do not attach to bound bases; the word *vengeful* is in parentheses because it seems to be the only example where one of these suffixes might be said to be attached to a bound base, but it's a questionable example, since *venge*, according to the OED, is an obsolete word in English.

In fact, the different behavior of the two sets of affixes can be nicely illustrated by comparing the suffixes *-ic* and *-ish*, both of which can take nouns and make adjectives from them. Compare the adjectives they form from the non-native base *dialogue*:

(22) dialogue — dialogic — dialoguish
[**daɪ**əlɑg] — [daɪə**lɑ**ʤɪk] — [**daɪ**əlɑgɪʃ]

The suffixes themselves differ only in their final sound, but *-ic* both changes the final consonant of its base and causes its stress pattern to change, whereas *-ish* has neither effect. What this illustrates is that English derivational morphology exhibits two different lexical strata, layers of lexeme formation that display different phonological behavior.

We can make one more interesting observation about the lexical strata of English. Consider the derived words in (23):

(23) a. *Two non-native suffixes:*

-al + -ity	sequentiality
-ian + -ity	Christianity
-tion + -al	organizational
-ive + -ity	productivity

b. *Two native suffixes:*

-ful + -ness	sorrowfulness
-less + -ness	hopelessness
-er + -hood	riderhood
-er + -less	printerless

c. *Native outside non-native*

-al + -ness	sequentialness
-ian + -ness	Christianness
-tion + -less	organizationless
-ive + -ness	productiveness

d. *Non-native outside native*

-hood + -al	*knighthoodal
-ish + -ity	*mulishity
-less + -ity	*shoelessity
-ness + -ic	*happinessic

Not every suffix can attach to other suffixed words in English, but sometimes we can get complex words with two or more layers of suffixes. As (23) shows, we can often affix a non-native suffix to a base that already has a non-native suffix, and similarly put a native suffix on a base that already has a native suffix. Further, we can often stack up two suffixes if the first (the innermost in terms of structure) is non-native and the second native. What's much more difficult – although not absolutely impossible, as we will see in chapter 10 – is to first affix a native suffix and then put a non-native suffix outside it. This makes perfect sense: non-native suffixes prefer to attach to non-native bases. Once a native suffix has been added to a base, regardless of whether that base was native or non-native to begin with, the derived word counts as a native word as far as further affixation is concerned.

The affixes we've looked at here show very clear and very different behavior, which justifies our saying that English derivational morphology displays two different lexical strata. To be honest, not all suffixes in English are as easily classified as the ones we've looked at in this section. While the other affixes that are native to English behave much as those discussed here, this is not the case with all non-native affixes. Some affixes that are borrowed, and therefore should be part of the non-native stratum of English, behave more like native affixes in that they have no phonological effects on their bases and attach indiscriminately to both native and non-native bases. We will not go further into the intricacies of

English derivation here, but merely point out that while the outlines of the two strata are quite clear, there is some blurring between them.

9.4.2 Dutch and French

Dutch and English are closely related languages, and they share a history of contact with French and Latin. It is therefore not surprising that the morphology of Dutch exhibits two lexical strata, just as English does. We'll give just a brief illustration here. In Dutch, the suffix *-heid* '-ness' is of native origin, and *-iteit* '-ity' is non-native. As we saw in English, the native suffix attaches easily either to native or non-native bases, but the non-native one can only occur on non-native bases (Booij 2002: 95):

(24)	*-heid*	blindheid 'blindness'	(native base)
		diversheid 'diverness'	(non-native base)
	-iteit	*blinditeit	(native base)
		diversiteit 'diversity'	(non-native base)

As in English, non-native affixes can occur on either bound bases or free words, whereas native affixes only occur on free words. And as in English, if a word contains both native and non-native affixes, the native ones must occur outside the non-native ones.

What may be somewhat more surprising is that French, a language itself descended directly from Latin, also shows signs of lexical strata (Huot 2005). French suffixes can be divided into those that are called 'popular' (in French 'populaire') and those that are called 'learned' (in French 'savant'). The former have descended from Latin undergoing all the sound changes that the vocabulary of French has been subject to. The latter come from scholarly Latin by borrowing later in the history of French. Popular suffixes typically attach to popular roots, and learned suffixes to learned roots (Huot 2005: 65):

(25) *Popular suffixes that prefer popular roots*

-age	doublage 'doubling', grattage 'scratching'
-ier	jardinière 'gardener', pétrolier 'oil-tanker'
-eux	chanceux 'lucky', venteux 'windy'

Learned suffixes that prefer learned roots

-ion	inscription 'inscription', punition 'punishment'
-if	actif 'active', duratif 'durative'
-aire	articulaire 'articular', réfractaire 'refractory'

Popular suffixes sometimes do attach to learned roots, but learned suffixes do not attach to popular roots:

(26) *Popular suffix on learned root*
infectieux 'infectious', torrentueux 'torrential'

Popular suffixes tend not to attach to already suffixed words, but learned suffixes can sometimes attach to other learned suffixes:

(27) démiss + ion + aire   démissionnaire 'one who has resigned'

And finally, popular roots sometimes have corresponding learned allomorphs:

(28)

Popular		*Learned*	
angle	'angle'	angul + aire	'angular'
cercle	'circle'	circul + aire	'circular'
peuple	'people'	popul + aire	'popular'

So what we see here is that there are two sets of affixes that display somewhat different patterns of behavior. The lexicon of French thus gives us another example where morphology is not neat and homogeneous, but instead seems to be organized into two relatively discrete layers.

Summary

In this chapter we have looked at the connection between phonology and morphology. Morphemes frequently have allomorphs, phonologically distinct variants that occur in different environments. Sometimes, as we saw, those environments are predictable, and we can postulate phonological rules that explain the distribution of the allomorphs. Indeed, we can often postulate a single underlying phonological form from which all the allomorphs can be derived. We have looked at a number of typical kinds of phonological rules that explain allomorphy in various languages: assimilation of various sorts, dissimilation, vowel harmony, and intervocalic voicing. We have also seen that not all allomorphy is entirely predictable; as the morphology of English shows, it can be quite unpredictable where one allomorph or another shows up. Finally, we have looked at three cases in which different segments of the lexicon constitute different lexical strata displaying different phonological behavior or different patterns of allomorphy.

Exercises

1. The following forms are from the now-extinct language Wappo, until recently spoken in California (Thompson, Park, and Li 2006: 125–7). The first set of examples is glossed for you. Using them as a model, first analyze the next two sets of data and then answer the questions below.

   a. olol - asaʔ   'is making X dance'
      dance - CAUS:DUR

      olol – is - taʔ   'made X dance'
      dance – CAUS – PST

      olol – is - ya:miʔ   'will make X dance'
      dance - CAUS - FUT1

olol – asiʔ dance - CAUS : IMP	'make X dance!'
olol - asa - lahkhiʔ dance - CAUS : DUR - NEG	'isn't making X dance'
olol - isn - ta – lahkhiʔ dance - CAUS : PST – NEG	'wasn't making X dance'
olol - is – lahkhiʔ dance - CAUS : IMP – NEG	'don't make X dance!'

b.

hicasaʔ	'is making X pound Y'
hicistaʔ	'made X pound Y'
hicisya:miʔ	'will make X pound Y'
hicasiʔ	'make X pound Y!'
hicasalahkhiʔ	'isn't making X pound Y'
hicistalahkhiʔ	'wasn't making X pound Y'
hicislahkhiʔ	'don't make X pound Y'

c.

hintoʔasaʔ	'is making X sleep'
hintoʔistaʔ	'made X sleep'
hintoʔisya:miʔ	'will make X sleep'
hintoʔasiʔ	'make X sleep!'
hintoʔistalahkhiʔ	'wasn't making X sleep'
hintoʔislahkhiʔ	'don't make X sleep!'

Once you have segmented and glossed the (b) and (c) sets of data, list all the allomorphs of all morphemes. Is all of the allomorphy predictable? Where you can, explain informally what seems to determine the distribution of the allomorphs.

2. In Tagalog, the circumfix *ka … an* creates nouns designating the class or group of whatever the base denotes. Identify all allomorphs in the forms below and explain their distribution using informal phonological rules (Schachter and Otanes 1972: 101):

banal	'devout'	kabanalan	'devoutness'
bukid	'field'	kabukiran	'fields'
bundok	'mountain'	kabundukan	'mountains'
lungkot	'sadness'	kalungkutan	'sadness'
pangit	'ugly'	kapangitan	'ugliness'
pulo	'island'	kapuluan	'archipelago'
dagat	'sea'	karagatan	'seas'
dalita	'poverty'	karalitaan	'poverty'
Tagalog	'a Tagalog'	katagalugan	'the Tagalogs'

3. The Dutch diminutive has several allomorphs. Determine what they are, and explain their distribution (De Haas and Trommelen 1993: 279):

a.	gum	'eraser'	gumetje
b.	roman	'novel'	romanetje
c.	parasol	'parasol'	parasoletje
d.	kar	'cart'	karetje
e.	lichaam	'body'	lichaampje

f.	pruim	'plum'	pruimpje
g.	bezem	'broom'	bezempje
h.	koning	'king'	koningkje
i.	haring	'herring'	haringkje
j.	streep	'stripe'	streepje
k.	kabinet	'cabinet'	kabinetje
l.	almanak	'almanac'	almanakje
m.	wereld	'world'	wereldje
n.	banaan	'banana'	banaantje
o.	tuin	'garden'	tuintje
p.	kuil	'hole'	kuiltje
q.	altaar	'altar'	altaartje

HINT: Examples a–d have short vowels in their final syllables. Examples n–q have long vowels or diphthongs in their last syllables.

4. Form the plurals of the following words in English, and transcribe them in the IPA:

lip	lathe
pot	kiss
tack	buzz
club	church
thud	garage
thug	judge
cliff	arena
path	hero
stove	

   a. How many allomorphs are there for the plural morpheme in English?
   b. Which of the allomorphs makes the best candidate for the underlying form of the plural morpheme?
   c. Formulate a phonological rule that derives the various allomorphs of the plural morpheme from the underlying form.

5. Thinking about the pattern you discovered in exercise 4, now consider the plurals of the following words:

wolf
calf
house
mouth
elf
knife

How do these differ from the plurals you discussed above?

6. In exercise 1 of chapter 5 you looked at a process of infixation in the Austronesian language Leti. Some of the data you looked at there are given again in (i) (Blevins 1999):

(i)	kakri	'cry'	kniakri	'the act of crying'
	pali	'float'	pniali	'the act of floating'
	sai	'climb'	sniai	'the act of climbing'
	teti	'chop'	tnieti	'the act of chopping'
	vaka	'ask'	vniaka	'the act of asking'
	vanunsu	'knead'	vnianunsu	'massage' = 'the act of kneading'

Now compare those data to the ones in (ii):

(ii)	kili	'look'	knili	'the act of looking'
	kini	'kiss'	knini	'the act of kissing, kiss'
	surta	'write'	snurta	'the act of writing, memory'
	tutu	'support'	tnutu	'the act of supporting, support'
	virna	'peel'	vnirna	'the act of peeling'

What are the two allomorphs of the nominalizing affix in Leti? What determines which allomorph goes with which bases?

7. Consider the data below from the Mayan language Tzutujil (Dayley 1985: 206–7):

k'uluuj	'to meet, encounter'	k'ulaani	'married'
jaqooj	'to open'	jaqali	'open'
d'eb'ooj	'to stain with thick liquid'	d'eb'eli	'thick (of liquid)'
b'olooj	'to twine, boil meat'	b'olaani	'cylindrical'
d'oyooj	'to cut with an axe'	d'oyoli	'cuttable'
wonooj	'to push with the head'	wonoli	'bent over'
ketooj	'to cut with a very sharp machete'	keteli	'discoid, wheel-shaped'
ch'ikooj	'to clean land for tilling'	ch'ikili	'stuck in'
jotooj	'to raise'	jotoli	'be above'
ch'anooj	'to spank a naked person'	ch'anali	'naked'

Identify all allomorphs and try to state the conditions under which each occurs. What morpho-phonological process is illustrated by the data in the second column?

CHAPTER

10 Theoretical challenges

CHAPTER OUTLINE

KEY TERMS

Item and Arrangement
Item and Process
Word and Paradigm
realizational model
multiple exponence
Lexical Integrity Hypothesis
blocking
bracketing paradoxes

In this chapter you will get your first taste of the theoretical challenges that morphologists face.

- We will consider what the best way is to characterize morphological rules.
- And we will examine several theoretical controversies that have occupied morphologists in recent years: the extent to which rules of morphology and rules of syntax can interact, the nature of blocking, the best way to analzye so-called bracketing paradoxes, and the characterization of affixal polysemy.

10.1 Introduction

Up to this point, we've spent a lot of time looking at the way morphology works in languages – what kinds of morphemes there are, what to call them, how to analyze data, and so on. This is an important and necessary first step to becoming a morphologist, but there's more to morphology than just being able to analyze data. When we study morphology, or indeed any of the other subfields of linguistics, we have a much larger goal in mind, which is to characterize and understand the human language faculty. Put a bit differently, our ultimate goal as linguists is to figure out the way in which language is encoded in the human mind. For morphologists, our specific goal is to figure out how the mental lexicon is encoded in the mind. Doing so requires us to model the mental representation of language, to make claims about exactly what morphological rules look like, and to propose hypotheses about what is possible in human languages and what is impossible.

A good hypothesis about language is one which is empirically testable: it should be clear what sort of data to look for that would disprove the hypothesis. To illustrate this, let's look first at two examples of theoretical hypotheses that have been proposed by morphologists. I start with these two precisely because they make clear claims about what sorts of morphology we should expect to find in languages and because these claims have subsequently been disproven.

The first hypothesis we'll look at is called **the Righthand Head** Rule:

(1) *The Righthand Head Rule (Williams 1981: 248)*
"In morphology, we define the head of a morphologically complex word to be the righthand member of that word."

You'll recall from chapter 3 that the **head** of a compound was the morpheme that determined the syntactic and semantic category of the compound. Clearly, in English, it's the righthand element in the compound that's the head (so *sky blue* is syntactically an adjective like *blue* and semantically a type of blue as well). More broadly, the **head** of a word is that morpheme that determines the category of the word, and in languages that have gender in nouns, or inflectional classes in nouns and verbs, the head determines the gender or class of the word as well. For example, in German, the suffix *-heit* attaches to adjectives to form nouns, specifically feminine nouns. Since *-heit* determines the category and gender of the derived noun, it is the head of the word. The Righthand Head Rule is a theoretical hypothesis that basically says that all compounds should be right-headed, and only suffixes (and not prefixes) can be the heads of words.

At first glance, this hypothesis is plausible enough when we look at English. Compounds are indeed right-headed, and for the most part in English it's the suffix that determines the category of a complex word. However, the Righthand Head Rule can easily be disproven by looking at data from other languages. For example, in chapter 3 we saw that both Vietnamese and French have left-headed compounds:

(2) *French* timbre poste 'stamp-post' = 'postage stamp'
Vietnamese nhá thuong 'establishment be-wounded' = 'hospital'

And it is not hard to find languages in which prefixes change the category of words and determine their gender or class. Even English has at least one prefix that changes category, and therefore would have to be recognized as the head of the derived word:

(3) *de-* debug
delouse
de-ice

The prefix *de-* attaches to nouns and makes verbs. Similarly, Swahili has a prefix *ku-* that forms nouns from verbs:

(4) *From Vitale (1981: 10)*
ku-tafutwa kwa Juma
-ing-search for Juma
'the searching for Juma'

Since this prefix determines the category of the derived word, we would have to consider it to be the head of the word. These examples show, then, that the Righthand Head Rule cannot be correct.

A second theoretical proposal that turns out not to be correct is the **Unitary Base Hypothesis**:

(5) *The Unitary Base Hypothesis (Aronoff 1976: 48)*
"We will assume that the syntacticosemantic specification of the base, though it may be more or less complex, is always unique. A WFR [word formation rule] will never operate on either this or that."

The Unitary Base Hypothesis in effect says that we should never expect to find in a language a morpheme that attaches to bases of two different categories, say adjective and noun, or noun and verb. We have seen, however, that there are many affixes that can attach to more than one base: *-ize* in English attaches to both adjectives (*legalize*) and nouns (*unionize*) to form verbs, and *-er* attaches to both verbs (*writer*) and nouns (*villager*) to form nouns.[1] It seems that affixes sometimes (in fact frequently!) do attach to "either this or that." The Unitary Base Hypothesis makes a clear claim about what we should expect to find in the languages of the world, but that is not in fact what we find.

Why start out a chapter on theory with two incorrect hypotheses? What is important is that these hypotheses are testable: we know what sort of data to look for, and having looked for those data can determine that

1. Aronoff is aware of examples like these, and is forced to argue that there are two different *-ize* suffixes and two different *-er* suffixes that are homophonous, that is, that sound identical. It is generally accepted, though, that this is not a strong defense of the Unitary Base Hypothesis, and that the hypothesis is therefore almost certainly incorrect.

these hypotheses cannot correctly characterize our theoretical model of the mental lexicon. Notice that I haven't talked about proving hypotheses to be true. In fact, it is never possible to prove a scientific hypothesis to be true: since there will always be some linguistic data we have not yet looked at, there is always some chance that further study will prove a hypothesis to be false. We take a theoretical hypothesis to be sound, just as long as we have not yet found evidence against it.

Good hypotheses must therefore be testable, and we would like them to explain a wide range of data. But there is one more thing we would want of a good theoretical hypothesis: it must also be simple. Since generative linguists are ultimately concerned with the mental representation of language, part of their concern is to explain how children acquire knowledge of those mental representations so quickly and with such ease. We assume that the simpler our proposed mental representations, the easier it would be for children to acquire them, and therefore the more plausible they should be.

With this in mind, we can now go on to look at a number of other theoretical proposals for characterizing our mental representation of morphology that are less easy to dismiss. Keep in mind that we can look at only a few interesting points of morphological theory here; in the last three decades there has been a great deal written about morphological theory that we will not be able to cover. So what I hope to do here is to give you a taste of theory and to whet your appetite for further study.

10.2 The nature of morphological rules

Up to this point we've talked about morphological rules for affixation, compounding, internal stem change and other means of creating new words, but we have only characterized those rules informally. One of the important parts of modeling the mental lexicon is to characterize morphological rules formally. In this section we will look at different formal systems for characterizing morphological rules and try to see how they make different claims about the sorts of morphology we ought to find in the languages of the world.

10.2.1 Morphemes as lexical items: Item and arrangement morphology

Let's take another look at one of the informal rules of word formation that we proposed in chapter 2:

(6) *-ize* attaches to adjectives or nouns of two or more syllables where the final syllable does not bear primary stress. For a base 'X' it produces verbs that mean 'make/put into X'.

One way of making this sort of rule formal is to assume that in our mental lexicons the morpheme *-ize* has a lexical entry, just as free morphemes do, and that part of its lexical entry is the following:

(7) *The -ize rule (more formal version)*

-ize	structural information:	$[[\ ]_{A,N} —]_V$
	semantic information:	'make A; make/put into N'
	phonological information:	$[\ldots\sigma\sigma_W$ aɪz]

The first line of this rule gives structural information: it says that *-ize* is a suffix that attaches to nouns or adjectives, and produces verbs. In fact, it says somewhat more than this, as the brackets indicate that when the suffix is added, a bit of hierarchical structure is formed:

(8)

The second line of the rule tells us what the resulting word means; this part of the rule can be formalized as well, using special notation, but we will not do so here. We'll merely say that when the piece *-ize* is added to a base, it also adds the meaning 'make A or make/put into N'. Finally, the third line uses the Greek letter sigma (σ) to stand for 'syllable', and the subscript W to stand for a 'weak' or unstressed syllable. This, then, encodes the information that *-ize* requires a base that has at least two syllables, the last of which must not bear stress.

This kind of theory in effect makes a claim that affixes are just like free morphemes in that they have lexical entries that include various types of information. The only difference between the entry for an affix and for a base is that the affix is a bound morpheme, and therefore as part of its structural information requires another category to attach to. Theories that propose rules of this sort are traditionally referred to as **Item and Arrangement** (IA) theories, because they claim that morphemes have independent existence in the mental lexicon with their own structural, semantic, and phonological information, and that they can be arranged hierarchically into words.

10.2.2 Morphemes as processes and realizational morphology

This is, of course, not the only way of formalizing morphological rules. Indeed, many morphologists believe that it is a mistake to count morphemes as 'things' that have their own independent existence in our mental lexicons. The alternative, they argue, is to allow only free morphemes to have lexical entries of their own, and to introduce bound morphemes using rules that contain the phonological form and the semantic content of the bound morpheme. The *-ize* rule might look like (9) in such a theoretical framework:

(9) *The -ize rule*
X → Xize, where X = N,A and Xize = V meaning 'make, put into X'[2]

In the case of the *-ize* rule, this may not look terribly different than the lexical entry we proposed above. But consider the sort of rule we would have to propose for an irregular past tense form like *sang* in English. Since the past tense in this form is created by a process of ablaut, we can propose a rule that changes the vowel [ɪ] to [æ] to produce *sang*.

(10) *Irregular past rule for the* sing, swim, ring *class of verbs*

CɪN	→	CæN
[−past]		[+past]

If C stands for any consonant, and N for any nasal consonant, we can express the vowel change that takes place in the past tense very simply with such a rule. It is not so easy to see how to express an internal vowel change using the 'morpheme as thing' model; it doesn't seem to make sense to say that the past tense in such verbs is a morpheme that consists of only the vowel [æ]. The sort of theoretical framework that treats morphemes as parts of rules is sometimes called an **Item and Process (IP)** theory, because morphological rules are conceived as operations or processes that act on free morphemes.

Related to the Item and Process model is the **Word and Paradigm (WP)** model. WP models are also sometimes known as a **realizational models.** They are often proposed to account for inflectional word formation in languages that have complex paradigms, especially the sort of paradigm which exhibits a characteristic called **multiple exponence. Multiple exponence** occurs when particular inflectional characteristics – say past tense, or third person – are signaled by more than one morpheme in a word. For example, in the Latin second person singular past tense verb form *amāvisti* 'you-sg loved' we might say that the root is *am* and the stem with theme vowel *amā*. The past tense is signaled by the morpheme *-v*, and the second person singular morpheme is *-isti*. But this is not quite correct, because the morpheme *-isti* is a person/number ending that is only used in the past tense; in some sense, *-isti* bears the meaning of past tense along with its person/number meaning. The past tense meaning is signaled twice in the word *āmāvisti*. This is what we mean by multiple exponence. In an IA theory of morphology, multiple exponence is problematic. IA models work best when there is a one-to-one correspondence between morphemes and meanings. In other words, each morpheme expresses one and only one inflectional or derivational meaning. **WP** or **realizational models**, on the other hand, do not separate out morphemes into discrete pieces, but rather state rules that associate meanings (single or multiple) with complex forms. For example, a realizational rule for the second person singular past tense form of the verb in Latin might be (11):

2. For the moment, we can set aside how the phonological information is stated in this sort of theory.

(11) $\begin{bmatrix} \text{X} \\ \text{+past} \\ \text{2nd person} \\ \text{sg.} \end{bmatrix}$ → [Xvisti]

The realizational model does not recognize *-v* and *-isti* as separate morphemes. Instead, the form *amāvisti* is conceived as a unit that expresses past tense, second person, and singular number conjointly. The existence of multiple exponence causes no problems in a realizational model, because inflected words need not be segmented into discrete pieces.

10.2.3 Can we decide between them?

You might at this point be wondering if it really makes a difference whether we conceive of morphemes as things with discrete meanings and their own lexical entries, or as parts of morphological rules that realize unanalyzable words with complex meanings. Our conception of what morphological rules look like really does matter, because it makes predictions about what sorts of morphology we should expect to find in the languages of the world. On the one hand, Item and Arrangement theories predict that morphology ideally should be agglutinative, with words segmentable into several pieces, each of which has a distinct meaning. In some languages this is the case – recall our sketch of Turkish in chapter 7. On the other hand, Word and Paradigm theories, although they do not strictly preclude agglutinative morphology, lead us to expect that morphology typically ought not to be agglutinative; rather, it should contain lots of multiple exponence, as is the case in Latin, but not in Turkish. The problem, of course, is that neither of these predictions is quite right. Some languages are more agglutinative than others. Some languages have lots of multiple exponence, and others have little or none.

So it does make a difference which kind of theory we choose. But the choice is made difficult by the complexity and variety of morphology we actually do find in the languages of the world. It is made even more difficult by the fact that each of these models is not really just a single theory, but a kind of umbrella that encompasses a number of different theories. For example, in their simplest form IA models say that the correspondence between meanings and 'pieces' ought to be one-to-one, but they need not say this. It is possible to propose an IA model in which the relationship between pieces and meanings is ideally, but not strictly, one-to-one. Similarly, there are a number of different versions of WP or realizational models that are plausible. We will not be able to go into the various theoretical possibilities here, but you will no doubt encounter them in a more advanced course in morphology. It seems safe to say, though, that each theory must be tested against a wide variety of languages with all different sorts of word formation, and a wide variety of inflectional and derivational word formation processes including not only affixation, but also compounding, conversion, reduplication, and templatic morphology. We will end this section by simply saying that the jury is still out on whether IA, IP, or realizational models of morphology constitute better models of how morphology is organized in the human mind.

Challenge

Review the examples of reduplication that we discussed in chapter 5. Which of the three models discussed above (IA, IP, or WP) is best suited to modeling rules of reduplication?

10.3 Lexical integrity

In chapter 8 we considered the relationship between morphology and syntax and saw several ways in which these two segments of the grammar are closely intertwined. The relationship between morphology and syntax indeed has given rise to one of the most interesting and longest-standing theoretical controversies among morphologists. Early in the history of generative morphology, several theorists proposed what has come to be called the **Lexical Integrity Hypothesis**. One version of this hypothesis is (12):

(12) *Lexical Integrity Hypothesis*
"No syntactic rule can refer to elements of morphological structure." (Lapointe 1980: 8)

What this means is that syntactic rules – phrase structure or movement rules, for example – cannot look into words and manipulate their internal structures. The Lexical Integrity Hypothesis requires that morphological and syntactic rules be fundamentally different. Morphological rules are concerned with affixes and bases, with rules of reduplication and ablaut, and so on, that affect the internal structure of words. Rules of syntax take words as unanalyzable wholes and form them into phrases and sentences. One way of ensuring this separation between morphology and syntax that was proposed early in the history of generative morphology was to order morphological rules before syntactic rules, as if there were something like a linguistic assembly line that started with the smallest units of structure and proceeded to larger and larger units:

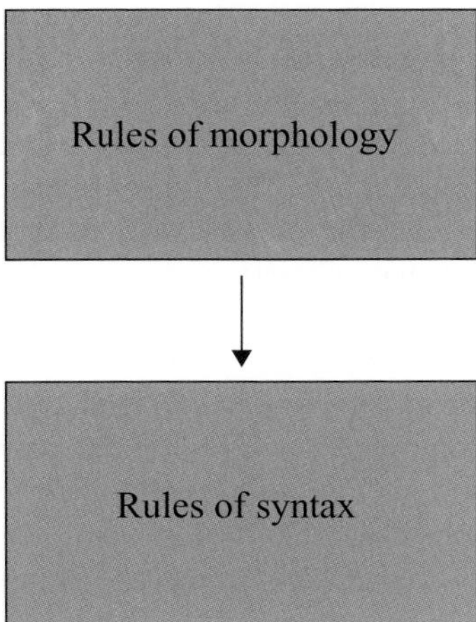

FIGURE 10.1
One way of organizing the grammar

The model in figure 10.1 ensures the separation of morphology and syntax because syntax only gets to look at already-formed words. Many linguists no longer believe that rules operate in a strict 'assembly-line' fashion, but nevertheless continue to maintain that morphological and syntactic rules must be kept separate from one another.

The Lexical Integrity Hypothesis is both plausible and testable: indeed it makes a clear prediction that we should never find fully formed phrases or sentences inside words. If phrases are formed by syntactic rules and syntactic rules are separate from morphological rules, words should not contain phrases or sentences. However, as we saw in chapter 8, there are some sorts of words that do seem to contain phrases and even sentences. Among these are phrasal compounds like those in (13):

(13) stuff-blowing-up effects
bikini-girls-in-trouble genre
comic-book-and-science-fiction fans
God-is-dead theology

It is also possible in some languages – including English – to conjoin two prefixes or two bases:

(14) a. *English*
mouse- and rat-like
pre- and post-war

b. *Turkish (Lewis 1967: 41)*
tebrik ve teşekkür-ler-im-i
congratulation and thank-PL-MY-ACC
'my congratulations and thanks'

In English a few suffixes (*-like, -ish*) can take conjoined bases, and a few prefixes (*pre-, post-, hyper-, hypo-*) can themselves be conjoined and attached to a base. Turkish allows some of its inflectional endings to apply equally to two conjoined bases. If conjunction is a syntactic operation, and conjoined forms can occur inside words, then the strict separation of morphological and syntactic rules required by the Lexical Integrity Hypothesis cannot be correct.

Linguists have therefore proposed alternatives to the Lexical Integrity Hypothesis. Some linguists have proposed models in which limited interaction between morphology and syntax is possible. Others, however, have taken a more radical approach, arguing that there should be no separation between morphology and syntax, and that syntactic rules should be responsible for at least some sorts of word formation.

One sort of word formation that has been used to argue for this hypothesis is noun incorporation, which you looked at briefly in chapter 8. To refresh your memory, consider the Mohawk examples in (15) (Baker 1988: 20):

(15) a. Ka-rakv ne sawatis hrao-nuhs-a?
3N- be.white DET John 3M-house-SUF
'John's house is white'

b. Hrao-nuhs- rakv ne sawatis
3M- house-be.white DET John
'John's house is white'

In (15a) the noun 'house' is part of an independent noun phrase (NP). In (15b), however, it has been incorporated into the verb 'be white' so that together they form a single word. In a syntactic analysis of noun incorporation (15b) starts out with the noun 'house' part of an NP with 'John's'. However, a syntactic movement rule plucks 'house' from its NP and attaches it to the verb 'be white', as (16) illustrates:[3]

(16) *From Baker (1988: 20)*

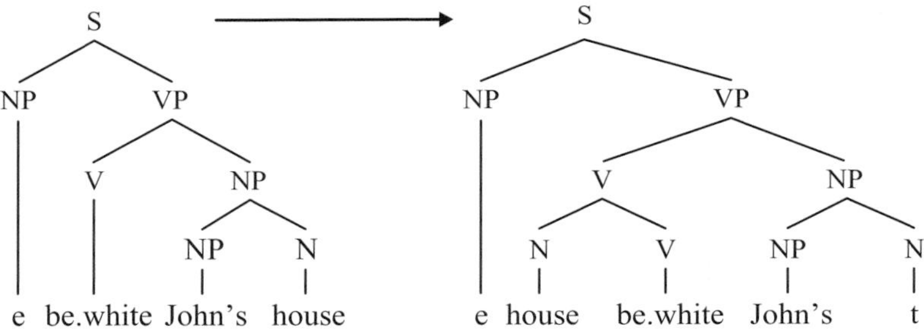

There is a great deal that might be said about the pros and cons of this analysis, although we cannot do so here. I should point out, though, that while some linguists find the evidence for this analysis convincing, others are less convinced and prefer to work within theoretical models that treat noun incorporation as the result of morphological rules, and allow less interaction between morphology and syntax. As with many other theoretical issues in morphology, the jury is still out on the best way to treat the relationship between morphology and syntax.

10.4 Blocking

Consider the data in (17):

(17) a. curious curiosity
generous generosity
impetuous impetuosity

b. glorious *gloriosity
furious *furiosity
gracious *graciosity

Generally, as the examples in (17a) suggest, it seems possible in English to derive an *-ity* noun from an adjective that ends in the suffix *-ous*. But in

3. In (16) 'e' indicates that the subject NP is empty, and 't' stands for 'trace', which marks the place from which a constituent has been moved.

some cases – for example, those in (17b) – the *-ity* form just does not seem possible. Why should this be? The examples in (17) illustrate a phenomenon called **blocking. Blocking** occurs when there is another word that bears the same meaning or fulfills the same function as the non-existent word. In the case of the examples in (17b), but not (17a), there are simple, underived nouns from which the *-ous* adjectives are formed: *glory, fury,* and *grace*. Since those words exist in English, they block or preclude the formation of the *-ity* nouns. The *-ous* adjectives in (17a) do not derive from free morphemes (they are built on bound bases), and therefore can form nouns by affixation of *-ity*.

Blocking can also be seen in nominalized verbs in English:

(18)	*occuration	occurrence	*occurment
	reservation	*reservance	*reservment
	*amusation	*amusance	amusement

As the examples in (18) show there are a number of different suffixes that form nouns from verbs, among them *-tion, -ance,* and *-ment*. Each verb seems to choose one affix with which its nominalization is derived. Other nominalizing affixes cannot attach. It appears that the existence of one nominalization blocks the existence of others.

Blocking can be seen in inflectional paradigms as well as in cases of derivation. For example, in English the suppletive past tense form *went* blocks the formation of a regular past tense form **goed*, and the existence of the irregular plural form *children* blocks the formation of the irregular plural **childs*.

The obvious question that a theorist might ask is why blocking occurs. One possible answer is that languages tend to avoid synonymy. Once we have a word that means 'more than one child' or 'the process or result of reserving', why would we need another? Evidence that supports this hypothesis in fact comes from the relatively rare examples where we do find 'doublets' – bases that do take more than one plural or nominalizing affix. Consider the examples in (19):

(19)	a. brothers	brethren	
	b. commission	commital	commitment

Superficially, these examples seem to provide evidence against blocking. In (19a) we have two plurals of the word *brother*, one the regular plural *brothers* and the other an archaic plural *brethren*. In (19b) we can see that the verb *commit* has three different nominalizations, not just one. But these examples do not really argue against blocking, because we don't in fact have cases of synonymous forms. Although *brethren* was at one time just a plural of *brother*, it has specialized in meaning and is used in religious contexts to refer to members of the same church. In the case of the different nominalizations of the verb *commit*, each one has a specific lexicalized meaning. *Commission*, for example, is the act of committing, and a *commission* an order to create a piece of art. A *commital* is an order to send someone to prison or to the hospital. And a *commitment* is a pledge of certain sorts. Blocking doesn't occur in these cases because we do not have words that are synonymous.

Challenge

Is it really true that languages avoid synonymy? Try to think of examples of words that you might consider to be perfectly synonymous. You may consider simplex as well as complex words.

Our hypothesis that blocking is the result of the tendency to avoid synonymy would therefore seem to be a strong one. Nevertheless, there are other data that call it into question. Consider the examples in (20):

(20)	curiosity	curiousness
	generosity	generousness
	impetuosity	impetuousness

As the examples in (20) show, alongside a noun formed with *-ity* it is always possible to form a noun with *-ness*. Although occasionally the two words have distinct meanings (for example *monstrosity* and *monstrousness* mean different things), much of the time the *-ity* and *-ness* words do appear to be synonymous, contrary to our hypothesis. It is therefore not possible to say that blocking always occurs to avoid synonymy, although we can say that this is a clear tendency in languages. One reason for the ability of *-ness* to form nouns alongside *-ity* is that *-ness* is so very productive in English. We might therefore say that blocking can only be overridden by the most productive of affixes.

10.5 Constraints on affix ordering

At various points in this book we have talked about how affixes are ordered with respect to each other. For example, in chapter 6 we noted that inflectional affixes generally come outside of derivational affixes in the languages of the world. We also mentioned in chapter 7 (Bybee 1985) that among inflectional affixes, tense and aspect inflection tends to come closer to the stem than person and number inflection, the reason being that tense and aspect are more closely relevant to the meaning of the verb than person and number.

In this section, we will look more closely at the issue of how English derivational affixes are ordered with respect to each other, as this has been a matter of theoretical dispute for some time. The problem is this: if the only thing that constrained the ordering of affixes in English were the categorial restrictions on their attachment (for example, that *-ness* only attaches to adjectives, or that *-ize* attaches to both nouns and adjectives), we would expect to find many more combinations of affixes than we do find. In fact, we find very few of the potential combinations of affixes. The theoretical issue, then, is what restricts the combination of affixes, and how we explain those restrictions.

We have already touched upon this problem. In chapter 9 we noted that native derivational affixes in English typically come outside of non-native ones. One explanation that has been proposed for this generalization is that the two strata of English derivational morphology are ordered with respect to each other such that non-native affixation precedes native affixation. If the two strata are strictly ordered with respect to each other, then non-native affixes will never be able to attach outside of native ones. We might call this the **Stratal Ordering Hypothesis.**[4]

There are two problems with this hypothesis, however. One is that it's not quite accurate. There are non-native affixes that do not cause stress or phonological changes, like other non-native affixes, and that are perfectly happy attaching to native bases, for example *-ee* (*standee*), *-ize* (*winterize*), *-able* (*singable*). Occasionally it is even possible to attach a non-native affix to a word formed with a native suffix; the words *softenable* or *whitenable*, for example, have native *-en* followed by non-native *-able*. This has led theorists to lump *-ee, -ize* and *-able* in with native affixes, thus blurring the lines between the strata.

More seriously, if the only thing which constrained the ordering of derivational affixes in English were the ordering of the two strata, we would still expect to find many more combinations of affixes than we do. For example, the suffixes *-age* and *-ize* are both non-native. The suffix *-age* forms nouns, and *-ize* attaches to nouns, so *-ize* should attach to *-age* words. But we never find words with the combination *-ageize*, and words we might coin on the spot sound quite odd (*orphanageize?, baggageize?*). Similarly, *-ify* forms verbs, and non-native *-ance* forms nouns from verbs, but we never get nouns like *purifiance*. So another problem for the theory of stratal ordering is that the combinations of affixes within strata are more limited than the Stratal Ordering Hypothesis would lead us to expect.

How else might we constrain the ordering of affixes? One possibility that has been proposed (Plag 1999; Giegerich 1999) is that affixes cannot only select what they attach to (native or non-native bases of particular categories), but also what attaches to them. For example, according to this hypothesis, the reason that we don't find words like *purifiance* is that the suffix *-ify* selects the suffix *-ation* as its nominalizer. So we find *purification*, and we predict that any new verb in *-ify* that we create (say, *Bushify*), will allow *-ation* to attach to form its nominalization (therefore *Bushification*). Similarly, any verb formed with the prefix *en-* in English (e.g. *entomb*), will form its nominalization with *-ment*, because *en-* selects *-ment* as its nominalizer (so *entombment*, rather than *entombal* or *entombation*). This sort of selection is called **base-driven selection.**[5]

4. In the literature on morphology, the term Level Ordering Hypothesis has frequently been used, for reasons we do not need to go into here.

5. Note that the term *base* in this context is used in a broader sense than I have used it in this book. For Plag and Giegerich the base of a word is whatever simple or complex form an affix attaches to.

Another proposal is called **Complexity Based Ordering**. According to Hay and Plag (2004: 571), the gist of this proposal is that "the less phonologically segmentable, the less transparent, the less frequent, and the less productive an affix is, the more resistant it will be to attaching to already affixed words." For example, the suffix *-ness* is extremely productive, its meaning is always transparent, and it's easily segmentable from its bases. According to this hypothesis, it should not be resistant at all to attaching to other affixes, and this is indeed what we find, as the examples in (21a) show. By contrast, the verb-forming suffix *-en* (as in *shorten, deepen*), is not terribly productive or frequent, and because it is vowel-initial, is less easily segmentable from its base than is *-ness*, which is consonant-initial. As the hypothetical examples in (21b) show, it is difficult to find any suffixes that *-en* can attach to:

(21) a. courtliness, amateurishness, aimlessness, carefulness
b. *hopefulen, *happinessen, *shoelessen

Indeed the only affix that *-en* can attach to is *-th* (*lengthen, strengthen*), which is completely unproductive in English, and even less segmentable from its bases than *-en* itself is.

What we can see is that there are a number of hypotheses that partially explain how derivational affixes are ordered with respect to each other in English, but that this question is by no means settled. Theorists will continue to work on this problem for some time to come.

10.6 Bracketing paradoxes

Bracketing paradoxes are cases in which either the semantic interpretation or the phonological organization of a word seems to conflict with its internal structure. Consider the words in (22):

(22) ungrammaticality
blue-eyed
unhappier

At first glance, these are unremarkable words. But if we look more closely at them, you'll see that they raise some problems. The word *ungrammaticality* needs to have the structure in (23):

(23)

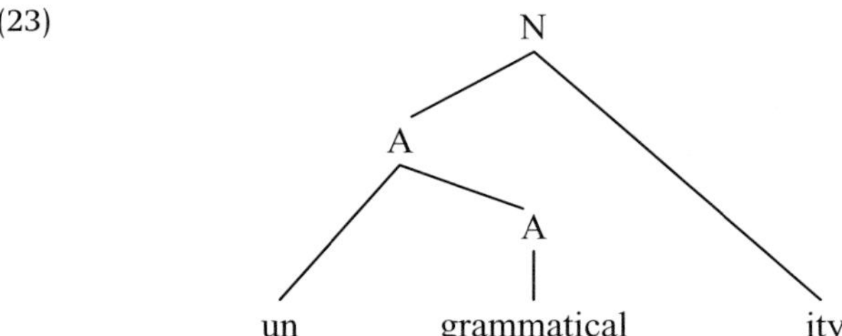

Since the prefix *un-* attaches to adjectives and does not change category, it must attach first to the base *grammatical*.[6] The suffix *-ity* attaches to adjectives and forms nouns. So the structure in (23) would be justified according to the structural requirements of the affixes. But *un-* is a native prefix, and *-ity* a non-native suffix. The structure in (21) therefore requires that a native prefix go inside a non-native suffix, contrary to the generalization we saw in section 10.5. In other words, if there really is some sort of constraint against non-native suffixes appearing outside native suffixes, the word *ungrammaticality* is paradoxical.

Of course, this example may not be such a problem after all, since – as we saw above – there are other cases in which a non-native affix appears outside of a native one. The word *blue-eyed*, however, is paradoxical in a way that cannot be attributed to stratal ordering. It appears to be a compound of the adjectives *blue* and *eyed*, the second of which is itself a complex word consisting of the noun *eye* and an adjective-forming suffix *-ed*:

(24)

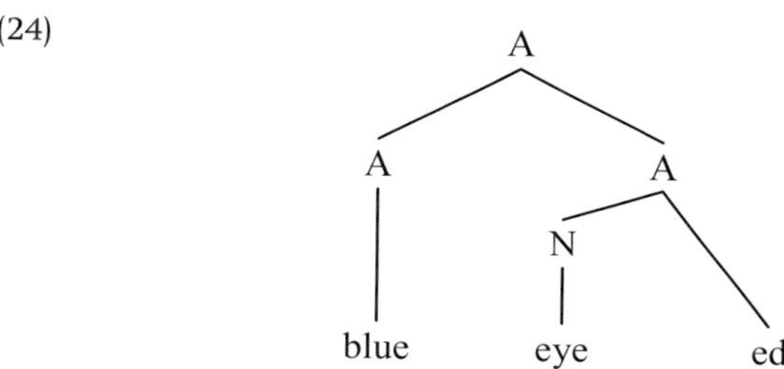

But the structure in (24) implies that there is an independent adjective *eyed* and that seems not to be the case. Besides, the word *blue-eyed* seems to mean 'having blue eyes', which would suggest the structure in (25), rather than the one in (24):

(25) [[blue eye] ed]

How do we explain this paradox? In fact, a number of solutions to this paradox have been suggested. The most plausible is that the structure in (24) is in fact correct, and that there is a pragmatic reason why we don't find an independent word *eyed*. We don't find such a word because it's usually not a useful concept. People assume that living organisms have eyes, so we'd never have a reason to point out the 'eyed one' as opposed to the one without eyes. But given a context in which such a contrast is plausible – say, comparing two space aliens – it no longer seems so absurd to think of an independent word *eyed*.

Our final example of a bracketing paradox is the word *unhappier*, which is paradoxical for yet a different reason. Here, the semantic interpretation of the word would suggest the structure in (26):

6. This is of course itself a complex word, but as its internal structure is not relevant to the issue we're discussing here, we will ignore that internal structure.

(26)

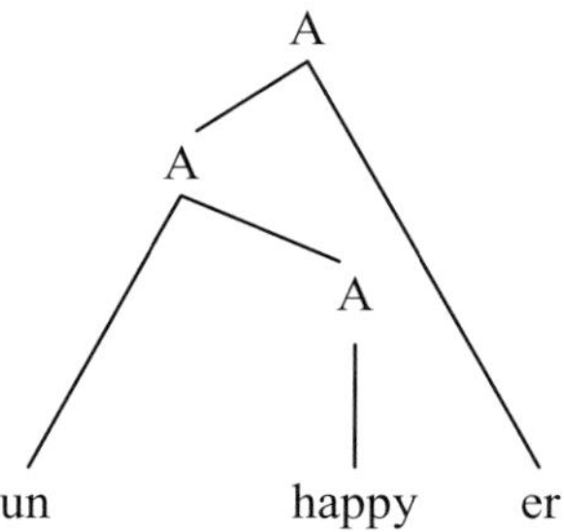

The word *unhappier* seems to mean 'more unhappy', with the comparative suffix *-er* applying to the negated adjective, so the semantic interpretation of the word corresponds to this structure. However, the comparative suffix *-er* has a phonological restriction on its attachment that calls the structure in (26) into question. Consider the forms in (27):

(27)	pure	purer	
	red	redder	
	happy	happier	
	comfy	comfier	
	aghast	*aghaster	(more aghast)
	upset	*upsetter	(more upset)
	intelligent	*intelligenter	(more intelligent)
	terrible	*terribler	(more terrible)

The comparative suffix attaches to one-syllable adjectives, and to two-syllable adjectives whose second syllable is unstressed. Two-syllable adjectives whose stress falls on the second syllable (for example *aghast* or *upset*) cannot take the comaparative *-er* suffix, but have only the periphrastic comparative (*more aghast, more upset*). And three-syllable adjectives never form their comparatives with *-er*. The problem with the structure in (26), then, is that *-er* looks like it has attached to the complex adjective *unhappy*, which consists of three syllables. Of course, if the *-er* were first attached to *happy* and then *un-* attached outside that, as in (28), there would be no problem:

(28) [un [[happy]er]]

But this does not accurately reflect the meaning of the word. The structure in (28) suggests that the word means 'not happier' rather than 'more unhappy'.

Here too, there is a potential solution to the paradox. Many morphologists believe that words have two separate structures, one which reflects the syntax and semantics of the word, and a separate structure which reflects the prosodic organization of the word into syllables, feet, and higher levels of phonological organization. We will not go into the details of different levels of phonological organization here, but I can give you just a suggestion of what I mean. Suppose that the word *unhappier* has two simultaneous structures:

(29)

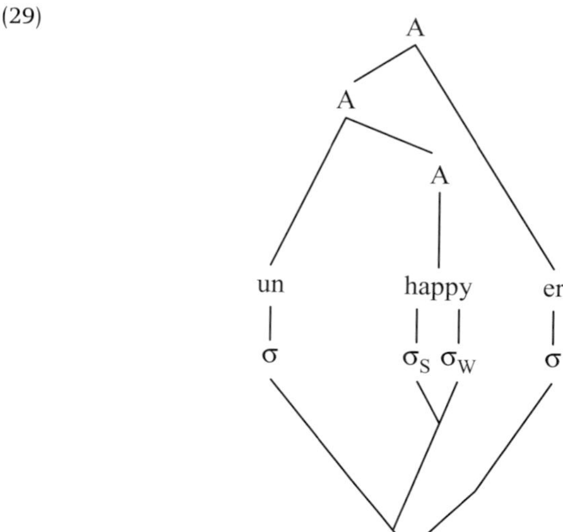

The top structure is identical to the one in (26) and reflects the semantic organization of the word. The one on the bottom reflects the phonological organization of the word, where σ stands for 'syllable', σ_S for 'stressed syllable' and σ_W for 'unstressed syllable'. If words are allowed to have two separate and simultaneous representations, one for their syntactic and semantic structure, and another for their phonological structure, the word *unhappier* is no longer paradoxical.

10.7 The nature of affixal polysemy

Unlike the problems of affix order and bracketing paradoxes, which have received a great deal of attention from morphologists, the problem we will take on in this section has received little attention, but it is no less interesting. In chapter 3 we briefly touched upon the issue of affixal polysemy. To refresh your memory, affixal polysemy is the tendency for affixes to have several closely related meanings. For example, we pointed out in chapter 3 that it is a curious fact that the affix that is used for making agent nouns in languages is frequently also used for making instrument nouns. As I pointed out, this is the case in English, and Dutch – not surprising, as they are closely related languages – but also in Yoruba, a Niger-Congo language, Turkish (Lewis 1967: 225), Kannada (Sridhar 1990: 273), and many other languages. It cannot be an accident that agent nouns and instrument nouns are so often created by the same affixes. So the theoretical question that arises is why this should be. To answer this question, let's again look a bit more closely at English.

(30)			
	-er	agent	writer, driver, thinker, walker
		instrument	opener, printer, pager
		experiencer	hearer
		patient/theme	fryer, sinker
	-ant/-ent	agent	accountant, claimant, servant
		instrument	adulterant, irritant
		experiencer	discernant
		patient/theme	descendant

It appears that in English the suffix *-er* forms not only agent and instrument nouns, but also nouns that denote the experiencer of an action, or even the patient or theme of an action. Even more curious, the suffix *-ant* covers the same range of meanings. The theoretical question we must raise in light of these data is why *-er* and *-ant* nouns cover just this range of meanings and not some others.

The first step in explaining this affixal polysemy is to figure out just what *-er* and *-ant* mean. One suggestion that has been made (Lieber 2004) is that these affixes don't actually mean 'agent' or 'instrument', but something much more abstract – something like 'concrete noun concerned with a process or event'. In this, they are semantically analogous to simple nouns like *poet* or *awl* that denote people or things defined by what they do. One piece of evidence for this claim is that *-er* can attach to nouns as well as to verbs, and when it does, it always adds an active or eventive element of meaning to its noun base. So, for example, a *villager* is someone who lives in a village, and a *freighter* is something that carries freight. No verb is necessary for the active part of the meaning – this comes directly from the suffix.

The second part of the answer to our question has to do with understanding the argument structures of verbs. You'll recall from chapter 8 that the argument structure of a verb consists of those arguments that are semantically necessary to the verb (see section 8.2). What is most interesting for our purposes is that in English there is a range of semantic roles that the subject of a verb can play:

(31)			
	a.	Fenster ate the pizza.	(agent)
	b.	The key opened the door.	(instrument)
	c.	We heard the neighbors fighting.	(experiencer)
	d.	The boat sank rapidly.	(theme)

In (31a), the subject of the sentence is the **agent** or 'doer' of the action. In (31b), the subject is called an **instrument** rather than an agent, because it is an inanimate noun that does something. In (31c), we call the semantic role that the subject plays the **experiencer** rather than agent, because one can hear something without doing anything at all – to be an agent, one must act intentionally. Finally, the subject in (31d) is not the agent, but the **theme**, in other words, the noun that undergoes or is moved by the action.

What is interesting is that *-er* and *-ant* nouns denote exactly the semantic role conveyed by the subject of their base verb. So an *eater* is an agent, just as the subject of the verb *eat* is an agent, an *opener* is an instrument,just as the subject of *open* is an instrument, a *hearer* is an experiencer, just as the subject of *hear* is an experiencer, and a *sinker* is a theme, just as the subject of *sink* (intransitive) is a theme. The reason that *-er* and *-ant* display exactly the range of meanings that they do is that they are linked to the subject argument of the verb. They can mean whatever the subject of a verb can mean.

10.8 Reprise: what's theory?

The few topics I've touched upon here just barely scratch the surface of theoretical questions that linguists can raise about morphology. Most of the issues we've looked at in this chapter concern English, although if we had time to delve further into them, we'd see that they concern many other languages as well. What is important to keep in mind, though, is that there are many theoretical issues that come up only when we look beyond English to the analysis of other languages. You have also barely gotten the chance to see how one argues for or against theoretical proposals. In this book, you have learned to find, analyze, and think about morphological data. You are now ready to embark on further theoretical challenges, both looking at issues raised by word formation in the languages of the world, and learning how to make theoretical proposals and support them. We leave these challenges to your next course in morphology.

Summary

In this chapter we have first considered what we mean by morphological theory, and then explored a number of theoretical topics that have been important to generative morphologists over the years. We have looked at the nature of morphological rules and the predictions specific models of morphology make about the sorts of morphology we ought to find in the languages of the world. We have explored the issue of the relation between morphology and syntax and the extent to which these two levels of linguistic organization can be kept separate from one another. We have looked at how the patterns of ordering in derivational affixes can be explained, how bracketing paradoxes can be resolved and how affixal polysemy can be explained.

Exercises

1. Consider the sort of templatic morphology that we looked at in section 5.5. Do you think that templatic morphology presents any problems for Item and Arrangement theories of morphology?
2. Consider the words *mice* and *mouses.* Do they offer evidence for or against blocking?

3. Consider the words *pomp, pompous,* and *pomposity.* Do they offer evidence for or against blocking?
4. Why might the following words be considered bracketing paradoxes?

   three-wheeler
   whitewashed
   transformational grammarian
   nuclear physicist

5. In section 10.7 I suggested that the suffix *-er* can have whatever semantic role is carried by the subject of its base verb. Consider the words *loaner* and *keeper* in the sentences below:

   i. My car was in the garage so they gave me a loaner.
   ii. This book is a keeper.

   What challenge do these forms present for the hypothesis in 10.7?
6. The suffix *-ee* is usually said to form 'patient nouns', that is, nouns that denote the person who undergoes or is subject to the action denoted by the base verb. Consider the following examples, and discuss the extent to which *-ee* exhibits affixal polysemy:

   employee
   nominee
   standee
   escapee
   addressee
   amputee

Glossary

ablative: The case typically assigned to objects of prepositions denoting instruments or sources.

ablaut: Internal vowel change. Also known as ***apophony***.

absolutive: In an ergative-absolutive case system, the case that is assigned to the subject of an intransitive clause and the object of a transitive clause.

accusative: In a nominative-accusative case system, the case assigned to the direct object of the clause, and in some languages to objects of prepositions.

acronym: A word made up of the initial letter or letters of a phrase and pronounced as a word. For example, from *self-contained underwater breathing apparatus* we get the acronym *scuba,* pronounced [skubə].

active: A voice in which the subject of the clause is (typically) the agent, instrument, or experiencer and the direct object the theme or patient. In English an active clause would be *Fenster ate the pizza*, as opposed to a passive *The pizza was eaten*.

adjuncts: Non-argumental phrases that are not necessary to the meaning of a verb.

affix: A bound morpheme that consists of one or more segments that typically appear before, after, or within, a base morpheme.

affixal polysemy: Multiple related meanings of an affix.

agent: The argument of the verb that performs or does the action. Agents typically are sentient and have intentional or volitional control of actions.

agglutinative: One of the four traditional classifications of morphological systems. Agglutinative systems are characterized by sequences of affixes each of which is easily segmentable from the base and associated with a single meaning or grammatical function.

agrammatism: A form of aphasia in which comprehension is good, production is labored, and grammatical or function words largely absent.

agreement: Contextual inflection of elements of a phrase or sentence to match another element of that phrase or sentence. For example, in the Romance languages the inflection of adjectives in a noun phrase must match the gender and number of the head noun. In Latin the verb must be inflected to match the person and number of its subject.

allomorph: A phonologically distinct variant of a morpheme.

analytic: One of the traditional four classifications of morphological systems. In analytic systems words consist of only one morpheme. Also known as **isolating**.

anti-passive: Morphology that decreases the valency of verbs by eliminating the object argument.

apophony: Internal vowel change. Also known as ***ablaut***.

applicative: Morphology that increases the valency of a verb by adding an object argument.

argument: A noun phrase that is semantically and often syntactically necessary to the meaning of a verb. The arguments of a verb consist of its subject and complement(s).

aspect: A type of inflection that conveys information about the internal composition of an event.

assimilation: A phonological process in which segments come to be more like each other in some phonological feature such as voicing or nasality.

attenuative affixes: Affixes that denote 'sort of X' or 'a little X'.

attributive compound: A compound in which the two elements bear a modifier-modified relationship to one another.

augmentative: A kind of expressive morphology which conveys notions of larger size and sometimes pejorative tone.

backformation: A morphological process in which a word is formed by subtracting a piece, usually an affix, from a word which is or appears to be complex. In English, for example, the verb *peddle* was created by back formation from *peddler* (originally spelled *peddlar*).

base-driven selection: Choice of an affix by its base, whether a simple or complex word. For example, in English, words prefixed by *en-* always form nouns by suffixation of *-ment*. The complex base *enX* therefore selects its affix.

binyan: A templatic pattern associated with a specific meaning or function.

blend: A type of word formation in which parts of words that are not themselves morphemes are combined to form a new word. For example, the word *smog* is a blend of *smoke* and *fog.*

blocking: The tendency of an already existent word to preclude the derivation of another word that would have the same meaning. For example, the existence of the word *glory* precludes the derivation of *gloriosity* and the existence of *went* precludes the formation of the regular past tense *goed.*

bound base: A morpheme which is not an affix but which nevertheless cannot stand on its own. In English, bound bases are items like *endo, derm,* and *ology,* from which neo-classical compounds like *endoderm* and *dermatology* are formed.

bracketing paradoxes: Complex words in which there is a mismatch between syntactic structure and phonological form or between syntactic structure and semantic interpretation. Within theories that admit stratal ordering, bracketing paradoxes can also involve mismatches between the structure required on the basis of word formation rules and the structure consistent with stratal ordering.

case: Inflectional marking which signals the function of noun phrases in sentences.

causative: Valency-changing morphology that adds an external causer to a verb.

circumfix: A morpheme that consists of the simultaneous attachment of a prefix and a suffix which convey meaning or function only when they appear together.

clipping: A word formed by subtraction of part of a larger word. For example, in English *math* is a clipping from *mathematics* and *ad* is a clipping from *advertisement.*

clitic: Small grammatical elements that cannot occur independently but are not as closely bound to their hosts as inflectional affixes are.

closed class: A fixed list from which particular forms can be lost, but to which no new forms can be added.

coinage: A word that is made up from whole cloth rather than by affixation, compounding, conversion, blending, reduplication, or other processes.

completive: An aspectual distinction that focuses on the end of an event.

complex word: A word made up of more than one morpheme.

Complexity Based Ordering: The hypothesis that suffixes which are more transparent, more productive, and more easily segmented from their bases will occur outside those that are less transparent, less productive, and less easily segmented from their bases.

compositional: The semantic interpretation of a word is compositional to the extent that it can be computed as the sum of the meanings of each of its morphemes.

compound: A word made up of two or more separate lexemes.

conjugation: The traditional name for the inflectional paradigm of a verb.

consonant mutation: A form of internal stem change in which consonants of a base differ systematically in different morphological contexts.

contextual inflection: Inflection which is determined by the syntactic construction in which a word finds itself.

continuative: An aspectual distinction that focuses on the middle of an event as it progresses.

conversion: A type of word formation in which the category of a base is changed with no corresponding change in its form. For example, in English the verb *to chair* is formed by conversion from the noun *chair*. Also called ***functional shift***.

coordinative compound: A type of compound in which the two elements have equal semantic weight. Examples in English are *producer-director* or *blue-green*.

corpus: A database comprised of spoken language and/or written texts that can be mined for various forms of linguistic study.

cran morph: A bound morpheme that occurs in only one word. An example in English is *cran* in *cranberry*.

creativity: The conscious use of unproductive word formation processes to form new words that are often perceived as humorous, annoying, or otherwise worthy of note.

dative: In languages which mark case, the case assigned to the indirect object and frequently to objects of prepositions.

declarative: The mood/modality of ordinary statements (as opposed to questions or imperatives, for example).

declension: The traditional name for the inflectional paradigm of a noun, especially in languages that display case marking.

default endings: Inflectional markings that are used when no more specific marking is applicable.

dependent-marking: Morphological marking of the dependents of a phrase rather than its head. For example, in noun phrases marking occurs on determiners and adjectives rather than the noun.

derivation: Lexeme formation processes that either change syntactic category or add substantial meaning or both.

diminutive: Evaluative morphology that expresses smallness, youth, and/or affection.

dissimilation: A phonological process in which sounds come to be less alike in terms of some phonological characteristic.

double marking: Morphological marking of both the head of a phrase and its dependents. For example, in a noun phrase marking would occur on both the head noun and on adjectives and/or determiners that modify it.

dual: Number-marking that denotes exactly two objects.

enclitic: A clitic that is positioned after its host.

endocentric: Having a head. In endocentric compounds the compound as a whole is the same category and semantic type as its head.

ergative: In an ergative/absolutive case system, the marking of the subject of a transitive verb.

ergative/absolutive case system: A case-marking system in which the subject of an intransitive verb is marked with the same case as the object of a transitive verb, and the subject of a transitive verb receives a different marking.

etymology: The study of the origins and development of words.

evaluative affixes: Affixes, including diminutives and augmentatives, that denote size and/or negative or positive associations.

evaluative morphology: Morphology that conveys information about size and frequently also about positive or negative valuation.

exclusive: Person-marking in which the hearer is not included.

exocentric: Lacking a head. In exocentric compounds the compound as a whole is not of the category or semantic type of either of its elements.

fast mapping: The ability of language-learners to rapidly create lexical entries for new words that they hear.

free base: A base that can occur as an independent word.

frequency of base type: The number of different bases that are available for an affix to attach to, thus resulting in new words.

frequentative: Aspectual marking that signals repetition of an action. See also ***iterative***.

full reduplication: A word formation process in which whole words are repeated to denote some inflectional or derivational meaning.

functional shift: See ***conversion***.

fusional: One of the four traditional classifications of morphological systems. In fusional systems words are complex but not easily segmentable into distinct morphemes. Morphological markings may bear more than one function or meaning.

Gavagai problem: A philosophical problem concerning how children come to associate the meaning of a word with the action or entity the word denotes.

gender: Inflectional classes of noun that may be either arbitrary (***grammatical gender***) or semantically based (***natural gender***). See also ***noun classes***.

genitive: The case assigned to the possessor of a noun.

habilitative: A verb form meaning 'can V'.

habitual aspect: Aspectual marking that designates that an action is usually or characteristically done.

hapax legomenon: A word that occurs only once in a corpus.

head: The morpheme that determines the category and semantic type of the word or phrase.

head-marking: Morphological marking of the head of a phrase rather than its dependents. For example, in noun phrases marking occurs on the noun itself, rather than on determiners and adjectives that modify the noun.

imperative: The mood/modality used for commands.

imperfective: Aspectual distinction in which the event is viewed from inside as on-going.

implicational universal: In linguistic typology a generalization that if one linguistic characteristic is found in a language, another characteristic is expected to occur as well.

inceptive: Aspectual distinction that focuses on the beginning of an event.

inclusive: Person-marking that includes the hearer as well as the speaker.

index of fusion: Typological measure of how many meanings may be packed into a single inflectional morpheme in a language.

index of synthesis: Typological measure of how many morphemes there are per word in a language.

infix: An affix which is inserted into a base morpheme, rather than occurring at the beginning or the end.

inflection: Word formation process that expresses a grammatical distinction.

inflectional class: Different inflectional subpatterns displayed by a category. See also ***noun classes, gender***.

inherent inflection: Inflection that does not depend on context. For example, the inflectional category of aspect is inherent in verbs. The inflectional category of number is inherent in nouns.

initialism: A word created from the first letters of a phrase, and pronounced as a sequence of letters. For example, FBI is an initialism created from Federal Bureau of Investigation, and pronounced [ɛf bi ɑɪ].

interfix: See ***linking element***.

internal stem change: Morphological process which changes a vowel or consonant in the stem. Also sometimes called ***simulfixation***. Internal vowel change is called ***ablaut*** and internal consonant change is called ***consonant mutation***.

interrogative: The mood/modality of questions.

intervocalic voicing: A phonological process which voices consonants when they occur between two vowels.

intransitive: The valency of a verb that takes only one argument.

irrealis: A mood/modality signaling that an event is imagined or thought of but not verifiable.

isolating: See ***analytic***.

Item and Arrangement Model (IA): A theoretical model of word formation in which affixes have lexical entries just as bases do, and words are built by rules which combine bases and affixes hierarchically.

Item and Process Model (IP): A theoretical model of word formation in which derivation and inflection are accomplished by rules that add affixes, or perform reduplication, internal stem change, and other processes of word formation.

iterative: Aspectual distinction that signals that an action is done repeatedly. See also ***frequentative***.

jargon aphasia: A form of language impairment in which the subject produces fluent sentences in which function words are evident but content words are often replaced by nonsense words.

lexeme: Families of words that differ only in their grammatical endings or grammatical forms. For example, the words *walk, walking, walked,* and *walks* all belong to the same lexeme.

Lexical Contrast Principle: The principle that the language learner will always assume that a new word refers to something that does not already have a name.

Lexical Integrity Hypothesis: The hypothesis that syntactic rules may not create or affect the internal structure of words.

lexical strata: Layers of word formation within a single language that display different phonological properties and different patterns of attachment.

lexicalization: The process by which complex words come to have meanings that are not compositional.

lexicalized: The property of having a meaning that is not the sum of the meanings of its parts.

lexicography: The art and science of making dictionaries. ***Lexicographer:*** One who writes dictionaries.

linking element: A meaningless vowel or consonant that occurs between the two elements that make up a compound.

logographic writing: A writing system in which each symbol stands for one word.

mental lexicon: The sum total of all the information a native speaker of a language has about the words, morphemes, and morphological rules of her/his language.

mood/modality: Inflectional distinctions that signal the kind of speech act in which a verb is deployed.

morpheme: The smallest meaningful part of a word.

multiple exponence: The property of having an inflectional distinction marked in a single word by more than one morpheme.

Mutual Exclusivity Principle: The tendency of language learners to assume that each object has one and only one name.

nasal assimilation: A phonological process in which a nasal assimilates to the point of articulation of a preceding or following consonant.

negative affix: An affix that means 'not-X'.

neo-classical compound: In English, a compound that consists of bound bases that are derived from Greek or Latin.

nominative: In a nominative/accusative case system, the case assigned to the subject of the sentence.

nominative/accusative case system: A case system in which the subject of a transitive sentence receives the same marking a the subject of an intransitive sentence, and the object of a transitive sentence receives a different case.

nonce word: A word that occurs only once.

noun classes: Groupings of nouns that share the particular inflectional forms that they select for. Noun classes can be based roughly on gender, shape, animacy or some combination of these semantic properties, but frequently the membership in noun classes is largely arbitrary.

noun incorporation: A form of word formation in which a single compound-like word consists of a verb or verb stem and a noun or noun stem that functions as one of its arguments, typically its object.

number: An inflectional distinction that marks how many entities there are.

orthography: The spelling system of a language.

palatalization: A phonological process by which one segment takes on a palatal point of articulation, frequently in the environment of a front vowel.

paradigm: A grid or table consisting of all of the different inflectional forms of a particular lexeme or class of lexemes.

parasynthesis: A type of word formation in which a particular morphological category is signaled by the simultaneous presence of two morphemes.

partial reduplication: A type of word formation in which part of a base morpheme is repeated.

passive: A voice in which the theme/patient of the verb serves as the subject and the agent is either absent or marked by a preposition or oblique case marking.

past: Tense that signals that an action has occurred before the time of the speaker's utterance.

patient: The noun phrase in a sentence that undergoes the action.

perfect: An aspectual distinction that expresses something that happened in the past but still has relevance to the present.

perfective: An aspect in which an event is viewed as completed. The event is viewed from the outside, and its internal structure is not relevant.

periphrastic marking: Marking by means of separate words, as opposed to morphological processes. For example, in English one- or two-syllable adjectives form the comparative by affixation of *-er* (*redder, happier*) but three-syllable adjectives form their comparatives periphrastically (*more intelligent*).

person: Inflectional distinction that expresses the involvement of the speaker, the hearer, or a person other than the speaker or hearer.

personal affix: Derivational affixes that produce either agent nouns (*writer, accountant*) or patient nouns referring to humans (*employee*).

PET (positron emission tomography) scan: An imaging technique that measures the level of blood flow to different parts of the brain, which in turn shows us areas of activation in those parts.

phrasal compound: A compound that consists of a phrase or sentence as its first element and a noun as its second element. For example, *stuff-blowing-up effects*.

phrasal verb: A combination of a verb plus a preposition, frequently having an idiomatic meaning. Phrasal verbs have the characteristic that the preposition can and sometimes must occur separated from its verb. For example, *call up*.

polysynthetic: One of the four traditional typological classifications of morphological systems. In polysynthetic languages words are frequently extremely complex, consisting of many morphemes, some of which have meanings that are typically expressed by separate lexemes in other languages.

progressive: Aspectual distinction that expresses on-going action.

prepositional/ relational affix: Affixes that convey notions of space and time. For example, *over-, pre-*.

present: Tense relating the speaker's utterance to the moment of speaking.

privative affixes: Affixes that denote 'without X' (for example *-less* in English) or 'remove X' (for example *de-* in English).

proclitic: A clitic that is positioned before its host.

productivity: The extent to which a morphological process can be used to create new words.

quantificational aspect: An aspect denoting the number of times or the frequency with which an action is done.

quantitative affixes: Affixes that express something relating to amount (for example, *multi-* or *-ful* in English).

realis: A mood/modality in which the speaker means to signal that the event is actual, that it has happened or is happening, or is directly verifiable by perception.

realizational model: A theoretical model of word formation that does not separate out morphemes into discrete pieces, but rather states rules that associate meanings (single or multiple) with complex forms.

reduplication: A morphological process whereby words are formed by repeating all or part of their base.

Righthand Head Rule: A theoretical hypothesis that defines the head of a morphologically complex word to be the righthand member of that word.

root: The part of a word that is left after all affixes have been removed. Roots may be free bases, as is frequently the case in English, or bound morphemes, as is the case in Latin.

root and pattern morphology: See ***templatic morphology.***

root compound: A compound in which the head element is not derived from a verb (cf. ***synthetic compound***). *Dog bed, windmill, blue-green*, and *stir-fry* are root compounds.

semelfactive: An aspectual distinction that expresses that an action is done just once.

separable prefix verb: A kind of verb found in Dutch and German which consists of two parts which frequently together have an idiomatic meaning and which occur as one word in some syntactic contexts but separated from each other in other syntactic contexts.

simple clitic: A clitic that appears in the same position as the independent word of which it is a variant. In English, the contractions *'ll* and *'d* are simple clitics.

simplex: Consisting of one morpheme.

simulfix: See ***internal stem change***.

special clitic: A clitic that is not a reduced form of an independent word. The object pronouns in Romance languages are examples of special clitics.

Specific Language Impairment (SLI): A genetic disorder in which individuals display normal intelligence and have no hearing impairment but are slow to produce and understand language, and display speech characterized by the omission of various inflectional morphemes.

speech act: Ways in which we can use words to perform actions, for example, asking a question or giving a command.

stem: The part of a word that is left when all inflectional endings are removed.

Stratal Ordering: Hypothesis: The hypothesis that English morphology is divided into levels, each of which is comprised of a set of affixes and phonological rules. Strata are strictly ordered with respect to each other such that the rules of an earlier stratum cannot apply to the output of a later stratum.

strong verb: In Germanic languages, verbs whose past tenses and past participles are formed by internal stem change.

subjunctive: A mood/modality that is used to express counterfactual situations or situations expressing desire.

subordinative compound: A compound in which one element bears an argumental relation to the other. Compounds like *truck driver* or *dog attack* in English are subordinative.

suppletion: An instance in which one or more of the inflected forms of a lexeme are built on a base that bears no relationship to the base of other members of the paradigm.

syncretism: An instance in which two or more cells in a paradigm are filled with the same form

synthetic compound: A compound in which the head is derived from a verb and the non-head bears an argumental relationship to the head. Examples of synthetic compounds in English are *truck driver* and *hand washing*.

template: In a root and pattern system of morphology, a pattern of consonants and vowels that is associated with some meaning.

templatic morphology: A kind of morphological process in which words are derived by means of arranging morphemes according to meaningful patterns of consonants and vowels or ***templates***. Also called ***root and pattern morphology***, ***simulfixation*** or ***transfixation***.

tense: Inflectional morphology that gives information about the time of an action.

theme: The noun phrase in a sentence that gets moved by the action.

theme vowel: In languages like Latin and the Romance languages, the vowel that attaches to the root before inflectional and derivational affixes are added.

token: In counting words in a text or corpus, each instance of a word counts as a token of that word. This gives the raw number of words that occur with a particular affix.

transfix: See ***templatic morphology.***

transitive: A valency in which a verb takes two arguments, generally a subject and object.

transparent process: A morphological process resulting in words that can be easily segmented such that there is a one-to-one correspondence between form and meaning.

transpositional affixes: Affixes that change syntactic category without adding meaning.

triliteral root: A root consisting of three consonants. These typically occur in the templatic morphology of the Semitic languages.

type: In counting words in a text or corpus, only the first instance of each word is counted. This gives the number of types with a particular affix.

typology: Linguistic subfield that attempts to classify languages according to kinds of structures, and to find correlations between structures and genetic or areal characteristics.

umlaut: Phonological process in which the vowel of the base is fronted or raised under the influence of a high vowel in the following syllable.

Unitary Base Hypothesis: The theoretical hypothesis that affixes will not select bases of more than one category.

usefulness: The extent to which a morphological process produces words that are needed by speakers.

valency: The number of arguments selected by a verb.

voice: A category of inflection that allows different arguments to be focused in sentences. In active voice sentences, the agent is typically focused because it is the subject, and is passive sentences, the patient is focused because it is the subject.

voicing assimilation: A phonological process whereby segments come to be voiced in the environment of voiced segments or voiceless in the environment of voiceless segments.

vowel harmony: A phonological process whereby all the vowels of a word come to agree in some phonological feature, for example in backness or rounding.

weak verb: In the Germanic languages, verbs that form their past tenses and participles by suffixation.

Whole Object Principle: The principle that word learners will not assume that a new word refers to a part of the object or its color or shape if they do not already have a word for the object as a whole.

Williams Syndrome: A genetic disorder in which individuals (in addition to certain physical traits and some developmental delay) speak fluently and produce sentences with correct regular past tenses, but have more trouble with irregular ones.

word:	A linguistic unit made up of one or more morphemes that can stand alone in a language.
Word and Paradigm Model (WP):	See ***realizational model***.
word forms:	Differently inflected forms that belong to the same lexeme. For example, *walks, walking, walk*, and *walked* are all word forms that belong to the same lexeme.
zero affixation:	An analysis of conversion in which a change of part of speech or semantic category is effected by a phonologically null affix.

References

Anderson, Stephen. 2005. *Aspects of the Theory of Clitics*. Oxford: Oxford University Press.

Arnott, D.W. 1970. *The Nominal and Verbal Systems of Fula*. Oxford: Oxford University Press.

Aronoff, Mark. 1976. *Word Formation in Generative Grammar*. Cambridge, MA: MIT Press.

Baayen, Harald. 1989. A Corpus-based Approach to Morphological Productivity: Statistical Analysis and Psycholinguistic Interpretation. Free University, Amsterdam, dissertation.

Baayen, Harald and Rochelle Lieber. 1991. "Productivity and English derivation: a corpus based study." *Linguistics* 29: 801–43.

Badecker, William and Alfonso Caramazza. 1999. "Morphology and aphasia." In Andrew Spencer and Arnold Zwicky (eds.), *The Handbook of Morphology*, 390–405. Oxford: Blackwell.

Baerman, Matthew. 2007. "Syncretism." *Language and Linguistics Compass* 1, 4: 539–51.

Baker, Mark. 1988. *Incorporation*. Chicago: University of Chicago Press.

Baker, Mark and Carlos Fasola. 2009. "Araucanian: Mapudungun." In R. Lieber and P. Stekauer (eds.), *The Oxford Handbook of Compounding*. Oxford: Oxford University Press.

Bauer, Laurie. 2001. *Morphological Productivity*. Cambridge: Cambridge University Press.

Bauer, Winifred. 1993. *Maori*. London: Routledge.

Baugh, Albert and Thomas Cable. 1993. *A History of the English Language*. 3rd edition. New York: Prentice Hall.

Bhat, D.N.S. 1999. *The Prominence of Tense, Aspect and Mood*. Amsterdam: John Benjamins.

Bisetto, Antonietta and Sergio Scalise. 2005. "The classification of compounds." *Lingue e Linguaggio* 4, 2: 319–32.

Blevins, Juliette. 1999. "Untangling Leti infixation." *Oceanic Linguistics* 38, 2: 383–403.

Bloom, Paul. 2000. *How Children Learn the Meanings of Words*. Cambridge, MA: MIT Press.

Booij, Geert. 2002. *The Morphology of Dutch*. Oxford: Oxford University Press.

Booij, Geert and Rochelle Lieber. 2004. "On the paradigmatic nature of affixal semantics in English and Dutch." *Linguistics* 42: 327–57.

Bybee, Joan. 1985. *Morphology: A Study of the Relation Between Meaning and Form*. Amsterdam: John Benjamins.

Carey, Susan. 1978. "The child as word learner." In Morris Halle, Joan Bresnan, and George Miller (eds.), *Linguistic Theory and Psychological Reality*. Cambridge, MA: MIT Press.

Ceccagno, Antonella. Undated ms. An Analysis of Chinese Neologisms: Compound Headedness and Classification Issues. University of Bologna.

Clahsen, Harald, Melanie Ring, and Christine Temple. 2004. "Lexical and morphological skills in English-speaking children with Williams Syndrome." In Susanne, Bartke and Julia Siegmuller (eds.), *Williams Syndrome Across Languages*, 221–44. Amsterdam: John Benjamins.

Comrie, Bernard. 1981/1989. *Language Universals and Linguistic Typology*. 2nd edition. Chicago: University of Chicago Press.

Corbett, Greville. 1991. *Gender*. Cambridge: Cambridge University Press.

Cowell. Mark. 1964. *A Reference Grammar of Syrian Arabic*. Washington, DC: Georgetown University Institute of Language and Linguistics.

Dayley, Jon. 1985. *Tzutujil Grammar*. Berkeley: University of California Press.

De Haas, Wim and MiekeTrommelen. 1993. *Morfologisch Handboek van het Nederlands*. The Hague: SDU Uitgeverij.

Demuth, Katherine. 2000. "Bantu noun class systems: loanword and acquisition evidence of semantic productivity." In Gunter Senft (ed.), *Systems of Nominal Classification*, 270–92. Cambridge: Cambridge University Press.

Dixon, R.M.W. 1972. *The Dyirbal Language of North Queensland*. Cambridge: Cambridge University Press.

__________ 1977. *A Grammar of Yidiɲ*. Cambridge: Cambridge University Press.

Fennell, Barbara. 2001. *A History of English: A Sociolinguistic Approach*. Oxford: Blackwell.

Foley, William. 1991. *The Yimas Language of New Guinea*. Stanford, CA: Stanford University Press.

Fortescue, Michael. 1984. *West Greenlandic*. Dover, NH: Croom Helm.

Fukushima, Kazuhiko. 2005. "Lexical V-V compounds in Japanese: Lexicon vs. syntax." *Language* 81, 3: 568–612.

Garrett, Andrew. 2001. Reduplication and infixation in Yurok: morphology, semantics, and diachrony. *International Journal of American Linguistics* 67, 3: 264–312.

Giegerich, Heinz. 1999. *Lexical Strata in English*. Cambridge: Cambridge University Press.

Greenberg, Joseph. (ed.) 1963. *Universals of Language*. Cambridge, MA: MIT Press.

Haas, Mary. 1940. "Ablaut and its function in Muskogee." *Language* 16, 2: 141–50.

Haenisch, Erich. 1961. *Manschu-Grammatik*. (Lehrbücher für das Studium der Orientalischen Sprachen 6) Leipzig: VEB Verlag Enzyklopädie.

Haiman, John. 1980. *Hua: A Papuan Language of the Eastern Highlands of New Guinea*. Amsterdam: John Benjamins.

Hardy, Heather and Timothy Montler. 1988. "Alabama radical morphology: h-infixation and disfixation." In William Shipley (ed.), *In Honor of Mary Haas*, 377–410. Berlin: Mouton de Gruyter.

Harley, Heidi. 2009. "Compounding in Distributed Morphology." In R. Lieber and P. Stekauer (eds.), *The Oxford Handbook of Compounding*. Oxford: Oxford University Press.

Hay, Jennifer and Ingo Plag. 2004. "What constrains possible suffix combinations? On the interaction of grammatical and processing restrictions in derivational morphology." *Natural Language and Linguistic Theory* 22, 3: 565–96.

Hewitt, B.G. 1979. *Abkhaz*. Amsterdam: North-Holland.

Hitchings, Henry. 2005. *Defining the World*. New York: Farrar Straus and Giroux.

Hoeksema, Jack. 1988. "Head-types in morpho-syntax." In G. Booij and J. van Marle (eds.), *Yearbook of Morphology* 1: 123–138.

Hohenhaus, Peter. 2006. "Bouncebackability: A web-as-corpus-based case study of a new formation, its interpretation, generalization/spread and subsequent decline." *SKASE* 3, 2: 17–27.

Horn, Laurence. 2002. "Uncovering the un-word: a study in lexical pragmatics." *Sophia Linguistica* 49: 1–64.

Huddleston, Rodney and Geoffrey Pullum. 2002. *The Cambridge Grammar of the English Language*. Cambridge: Cambridge University Press.

Humboldt, Wilhelm von. 1836. *Über die Vershiedenheit des menschlichen Sprachbaues und ihren Einfluss auf die geistige Entwicklung des Menschengeschlechts*. Berlin: Königliche Akademie der Wissenschaften.

Huot, Hélène. 2005. *La Morphologie*. Paris: Armand Colin.

Inkelas, Sharon and C. Orhan Orgun. 1998. "Level (non)ordering in recursive morphology: evidence from Turkish. In Steven Lapointe, Diane Brentari, and Patrick Farrell (eds.), *Morphology and its Relation to Phonology and Syntax*, 360–410. Stanford: CSLI.

Jaeger, Jeri, Alan Lockwood, David Kemmerer, Robert Van Valin, Brian Murphy, and Hanif Khalak. 1996. "A positron tomographic study of regular and irregular verb morphology in English." *Language* 72, 3: 451–97.

Keenan, Edward and Maria Polinsky. 1999. "Malagasy (Austronesian)." In A. Spencer and A. Zwicky (eds.), *The Handbook of Morphology*, 563–623. Oxford: Blackwell.

Kimball, Geoffrey. 1991. *Koasati Grammar*. Lincoln: University of Nebraska Press.

Kornfilt, Jaklin. 1997. *Turkish*. London: Routledge.

Landau, Sidney. 2001. *Dictionaries, The Art and Craft of Lexicography*. 2nd edition. Cambridge: Cambridge University Press.

Langdon, Margaret. 1970. *A Grammar of Diegueño*. Berkeley: University of California Press.

Lapointe, Steven. 1980. A Theory of Grammatical Agreement. Amherst: University of Massachusetts doctoral dissertation.

Lederer, Herbert. 1969. *Reference Grammar of the German Language*. New York: Charles Scribner's Sons.

Lehnert, Martin. 1971. *Rückläufiges Wörterbuch der englischen Gegenwartssprache*. Leipzig: VEB Verlag Enzyklopädie.

Lewis, G.L. 1967. *Turkish Grammar*. Oxford: The Clarendon Press.

Li, Charles and Sandra Thompson. 1971. *Mandarin Chinese. A Functional Reference Grammar*. Berkeley: University of California Press.

Li, Ya Fei. 1995. The thematic hierarchy and causativity. *Natural Language and Linguistic Theory* 13: 255–82.

Lieber, Rochelle. 1987. *An Integrated Theory of Autosegmental Processes*. Albany: SUNY Press.

__________ 2004. *Morphology and Lexical Semantics*. Cambridge: Cambridge University Press.

Macauley, Monica. 1996. *A Grammar of Chalcatongo Mixtec*. Berkeley: University of California Press.

Marchand, Hans. 1969. *The Categories and Types of Present-Day English Word Formation. A Synchronic-Diachronic Approach*. Munich: Beck.

McCarthy, John. 1979. Formal Problems in Semitic Phonology and Morphology. Cambridge, MA: MIT doctoral dissertation.

__________ 1981. "A prosodic theory of nonconcatenative morphology." *Linguistic Inquiry* 12: 373–418.

__________ 1983. "Phonological features and morphological structure." *Papers from the Parasessions*, 153–61. Chicago: Chicago Linguistic Society.

__________ 1984. "Prosodic structure in morphology." In Mark Aronoff and Richard Oehrle (eds.), *Language Sound Structure*. Cambridge, MA: MIT Press.

Mchombo, Sam. 1999. "Chichewa (Bantu)." In A. Spencer and A. Zwicky (eds.), *The Handbook of Morphology*, 500–20. Oxford: Blackwell.

McLaughlin, Fiona. 2000. "Consonant mutation and reduplication in Seereer-Siin." *Phonology* 17: 333–63.

Mithun, Marianne. 1999. *The Languages of Native North America*. Cambridge: Cambridge University Press.

Mosel, Ulrike and Even Hovdhaugen. 1992. *Samoan Reference Grammar*. Oslo: Scandinavian University Press.

Newman, Paul. 2000. *The Hausa Language*. New Haven: Yale University Press.

Nguyen, Hy-Quang and Eleanor Jorden. 1969. *Vietnamese Familiarization Course*. Washington, DC: Foreign Service Institute.

Nichols, Johanna. 1986. "Head-marking and dependent-marking grammar." *Language* 62,1: 56–119.

Nida, Eugene. 1946/1976. *Morphology: the Descriptive Analysis of Words*. 2nd edition. Ann Arbor: University of Michigan Press.

O'Neil, Wayne. 1980. "The evolution of the Germanic inflectional systems: a study in the causes of language change." *Orbis* 27: 248–86.

Pinker, Steven. 1999. *Words and Rules*. New York: Perennial.

Plag, Ingo. 1999. *Morphological Productivity: Structural Constraints in English Derivation*. Berlin: Mouton de Gruyter.

Press, Margaret. 1979. *Chemehuevi: A Grammar and Lexicon*. University of California Publications in Linguistics, vol. 92. Berkeley: University of California Press.

Pulleyblank, Douglas. 1987. "Yoruba." In Bernard Comrie (ed.), *The World's Major Languages*. New York: Oxford University Press.

Redmond, Sean and Mabel Rice. 2001. "Detection of irregular verb violations by children with and without SLI." *Journal of Speech, Language and Hearing Research* 44: 655–69.

Sapir, Edward. 1921. *Language*. New York: Harcourt, Brace, Jovanovich.

Schachter, Paul and Fe Otanes. 1972. *Tagalog Reference Grammar*. Berkeley: University of California Press.

Shaw, Patricia. 1980. *Dakota Phonology and Morphology*. New York: Garland.

Smith, Norval. 1985. "Spreading, reduplication and the default option in Miwok nonconcatenative morphology." In Harry van der Hulst and Norval Smith (eds.), *Advances in Nonlinear Phonology*, 363–80. Dordrecht: Foris.

Sridhar, S.N. 1990. *Kannada*. London: Routledge.

Suttles, Wayne. 2004. *Musqueam Reference Grammar*. Vancouver: UBC Press.

Thompson, Sandra, Joseph Sunh-Yul Park, and Charles Li. 2006. *A Reference Grammar of Wappo*. Berkeley: University of California Press.

Toman, Jindrich. 1983. *Wortsyntax*. Tübingen: Max Niemeyer Verlag.

Valentine, J. Randolph. 2001. *Nishnaabemwin Reference Grammar*. Toronto: University of Toronto Press.

Vitale, Anthony. 1981. *Swahili Syntax*. Dordrecht: Foris.

Wentworth, Harold. 1941. "The allegedly dead suffix -dom in modern English." *PMLA* 56, 1: 280–306.

Whaley, Lindsay. 1997. *Introduction to Typology*. Thousand Oaks: Sage Publications.

Williams, Edwin. 1981. "On the notions 'lexically related' and 'head of a word'." *Linguistic Inquiry* 12: 245–74.

Williams, Marianne Mithun. 1976. *A Grammar of Tuscarora*. New York: Garland.

Yu, Alan. 2004. "Reduplication in English Homeric infixation. In Keir Moulton and Matthew Wolf (eds.), *Proceedings of NELS 34*, 619–33. Amherst, MA: GLSA.

Index